ISRAELI
ECSTASIES/JEWISH AGONIES

ISRAELI ECSTASIES/ JEWISH AGONIES

IRVING LOUIS HOROWITZ

New York
OXFORD UNIVERSITY PRESS
1974

"The Jewish Community of Buenos Aires," *International Review of Community Development and Planning*. Whole No. 9, Summer 1962. pp. 187-213.

"The Jewish Community of Buenos Aires," *Jewish Social Studies*. Vol. XXIV, No. 4, Oct. 1962.

"Israeli Imperatives and Jewish Agonies," *Judaism: A Quarterly Journal*. Vol. 16, No. 4, Fall 1967.

"Liquidation or Liberation: The Jewish Question as Liberal Catharsis," *Judaism: A Quarterly Journal*. Vol. 18, No. 3, Summer 1969.

"The Student as Jew," *The Antioch Review*. Vol. XXIX, No. 4, Winter 1969-70.

"Political Systems of the Middle East," in *People and Politics in the Middle East*, edited by Michael Curtis. New Brunswick: Transaction Books—E. P. Dutton, 1971.

"Israel—Remembering it is Foreign," *Sh'ma: A Journal of Jewish Responsibility*. Vol. 2, Whole No. 30, April 1972.

"Israel Developing," *Worldview*. Vol. 15, No. 9, Sept. 1972.

"Shouldn't Jews Transcend Their Class?" *Sh'ma: A Journal of Jewish Responsibility*. Vol. 2, Whole No. 39. Oct. 1972.

"The Jewish Vote," *Commonweal*. Vol. XCVII, No. 2, Oct. 13, 1972.

"Jewish Ethnicism and Latin American Nationalism," *Midstream: A Monthly Jewish Review*. Vol. XVIII, No. 9, Nov. 1972.

"Coalition for a Democratic Majority: The Operators Make Their Play," *The Nation*. Vol. 216, No. 3, Jan. 15, 1973.

"The Holocaust: Sharing in the Ultimate Act," *Commonweal*. Vol. XCVIII, No. 6, April 13, 1973.

"Forced Coexistence: The Soviet State and its Russian Jews," *Present Tense: A Magazine of Jewish World Affairs*. Vol. I, No. 2, Winter 1973.

"Political Terrorism," *Journal of Political and Military Sociology*. Vol. I, No. 1, Spring 1973.

PRINTED IN THE UNITED STATES OF AMERICA

To my dear, departed friend from a Harlem childhood,
Arthur Grumberger (1929-1969),
who in his piety never lost his humanity
and who in the process of growing up
taught me daily lessons in courage.

PREFACE
AND ACKNOWLEDGEMENTS

This volume is built on the belief that plural identities are possible, even necessary, as a survival mechanism for any ethnic or racial group in American life. To be sure, the orchestration of such plural concerns and considerations to the dominant culture is more difficult in practice than in theory. American Judaism under economic affluence and Israeli society under military threat are both at the crossroads. This dialectical relationship is summed up in the title *Israeli Ecstasies/Jewish Agonies*. What appears on the scene of history as paradox, reappears in the mind of the person as anguish. It is the purpose of this work to lay bare the sources of both the objective paradoxes and the subjective anxieties of contemporary Judaism, and in so doing, provide a social scientific framework for living with and working out the problems confronting Jews within and without a State of their own. The volume establishes three broad contexts: first, Israelis and Arabs interacting in the Middle East; second, Jews and their host countries in the three largest centers in which they now congregate: the United States, the Soviet Union, and Argentina; and third, the Jewish condition as a confrontation with problems of economic participation, political ideology, social status, and military terror. My effort represents a basic encounter of contemporary Judaism with the sociological experience, and beyond that, Judaism as an expression of that experience.

This work, comprised of papers largely written over a recent time span, is an attempt to fuse several strains in my thinking: to utilize the sense and substance of social science findings on the themes of contemporary Judaism with a special aim at addressing those problems of deepest concern to those of the younger generation possessing a radical persuasion. By no means can any set of papers compress, much less comprehend all three of these major themes into a systematic entity. Yet, I do believe that my experiences are shared by many, but so far, articulated by few. Growing up in a world in which the rationalism of social science took unprecedented priority over any form of inherited belief system and in a nation where the demonstrable exploitation of racial minorities took priority over any forms of religious discrimination, the results at this point in the tunnel have proven less than satisfactory.

Social science has not failed, nor has the condition of racial oppression been exaggerated. Neither of these oft-repeated canards would be correct. The vision of my generation was sound, but simply far too restricted. Cosmopolitanism in scientific and political judgments became a mechanism of evasion, a way to systematically avoid coming to terms with the dilemmas in the special distinct heritages that make up the American dream. My concern in things Jewish is neither to celebrate nor to condemn, but to understand. That is why the basic theme of the book is juxtaposed in terms of the dialectic of Israeli achievements in contrast to Jewish agonies. In this, my understanding derives from, and owes much to, the thinking of my friend and Israeli counterpart, J. L. Talmon.

I examine the same problems he has posed, but from the American shores. I speak not as an exile in Diaspora, but as an American Jew, of Russian ancestry, sensing multiple obligations and marginal affiliation to nation, ethnicity, and religion. And it is my fervent opinion that all authentic scientific generalizations have to remain multiple and marginal in the above stated sense.

It will be clear to the reader, even at first glance, that my volume was assembled prior to the outbreak of the fourth round of hostilities in the Arab-Israeli conflict. It would be both gratuitous and foolish to try to capture the sense of the immediate moment in a volume which is addressed to long standing issues. Little *structural* alteration has occurred as a result of the 1973 clashes between the Egyptian and Syrian armies and Israel. Indeed, this most recent round of Middle East warfare completes a paradigm: the 1956 "second round" consecrated the 1948 geographic boundaries; while the 1973 "fourth round" similarly legitimated and gave, with some modifications, something more than *de facto* status to the boundaries established by the cease fire of 1967. In short, the 1973 fighting led to an *operational* alteration: the round of warfare in 1956 and 1973 served to guarantee the sovereignty and hegemony gained in 1948 and 1967, respectively. This may be of supreme importance to the politics and policies of the Middle East, but it scarcely changes fundamental issues dealt with in *Israeli Ecstasies/Jewish Agonies*. It would be more to the point to say that events have confirmed the basic propositions presented in this work. For the growing intensity, bitterness, and cost of the Middle East struggles have not only increased the sense of anguish for the Jewish communities throughout the world, but also brought into sharper focus for the Israelis themselves their dual relationship to other nations (largely indifferent, if not downright hostile), in contrast to their ethnic-religious compatriots the world over (largely sympathetic, if not uniformly supportive). And so the subjective dialectic of joy and anguish continues to inform the objective tenuousness of victory and defeat.

I gratefully acknowledge permissions granted by the following publications to use materials from articles originally published by them. The citations here are to the original articles only, with the chapters of the book containing material from these articles given in parentheses. These articles have been revised, either slightly or substantially, depnding on their age and their applicability to the overall design of the book.

For the most part, each original article represents only a fraction of the chapter as it herein appears. Unlike my previous efforts at collections, I felt that the relative brief range of time covered by these essays, my own strong and continuing interest in the subjects covered, and the need to carry out from first chapter to final chapter the dialectical theme of the book, permitted and even required a substantial overhaul—where this was deemed necessary.

The only chapter left unaltered is "Israeli Imperatives and Jewish Agonies." Since this piece was done jointly with my colleague Maurice Zeitlin in the summer of 1967, it would clearly be unfair at this late date to make unilateral changes. Beyond that, this chapter somehow strikes me as the least in need of any sort of face lift. The chapter, "The Organization and Ideology of the Jewish Community in Argentina" has been left largely intact since the data on which it is based remain the most up to date yet available. I chose rather to add a postscript to that chapter to bring the political and sociological aspects of Jewish life in Argentina up to the present. Beyond that, the other ten chapters have been stripped, augmented, and amplified to meet the practical needs of the time and to take account of the intellectual gains registered in the past several years.

I must register my sincere thanks to the people who in one or more of these chapters, provided their time and energy in commentary and criticism of my work. Specifically, I would like to thank Michael Curtis of Rutgers University, Kalman H. Silvert of New York University, Maurice Zeitlin of the University of Wisconsin, Abdul A. Said of American University, and Alejandro Dehollain of the University of Buenos Aires. To the many other people who encouraged me to organize in systematic form my writings on the sociological condition of modern Jewry goes this final expression of gratitude.

IRVING LOUIS HOROWITZ

Rutgers University
October 12, 1973

CONTENTS

ISRAELI
ECSTASIES/JEWISH AGONIES

1 ISRAELI IMPERATIVES AND JEWISH AGONIES

The thoroughness of the Israeli military success over the combined efforts of the Arab states raises more problems than it resolves. Indeed, before the month of victory, June 1967, let out, the defeated were making all sorts of demands, and the winners were making all sorts of concessions. As Israeli Foreign Minister Abba Eban wryly remarked, "This is the only war in history where the victors sued for peace and the vanquished demanded unconditional surrender."

The David-and-Goliath imagery is weakened by the extraordinary thoroughness of the defeat of the Arab armies. Numbers do not add up to power. The many were beaten by a technologically sophisticated army. Arab states without a sense of nationhood were beaten by the Israeli nation they had not accorded the legitimization of statehood. These are not simply scholastic paradigms but a set of results that illustrate the continued ambiguity of Israel's political position, however decisive its military success. This ambiguity extends the political reaction of world Jewry to the Israeli victory. This could hardly have been otherwise, since the Jewish people have been marginal members, with multiple loyalties, of all states throughout recent history; whereas in Israeli society, this

* This chapter was written jointly with Maurice Zeitlin.

situation has been entirely reversed: not only is Israel a Jewish state, but the Israelis have come to behave as marginal members of the international Jewish community, despite Israel's constant protestations of concern for that community.

AMBIGUITIES IN THE ISRAELI VICTORY

The victory of the Israeli army in June 1967 may be the great historical watershed separating the Jew and the Israeli. In place of the Jew as victim stands the Jew as victor. Paradoxically, it is this very victory on the battlefield, the vision of the Jew as military strategist and citizen-soldier, that has caused widespread reactions not of joy but of hostility among statesmen, intellectuals, men of the left, right, and center. The Jew as aggressor, as Realpolitician, as "imperialist," has both replaced and fused with the usual stereotypes in the lexicon of hostile images of the Jews. Tragically, this new lexicon is restricted not to the big-power statesmen, whether British, American, or Soviet, but finds its most vociferous voices in representatives of the newly independent ex-colonial and even revolutionary regimes.

Anti-Semitism was once, as August Bebel called it, the "socialism of fools." Now anti-Zionism performs the same role. Zionists once dreamed that the territorial concentration of the Jewish people in Palestine, their historic homeland, would abolish the conditions of insecurity and hostile surroundings in which they were compelled to live while in the *Galut*. But the concrete reality is that of a small nation caught in the conflicts of the Cold War and trapped into becoming the cement between the legitimate national aspirations of the Arabs and regimes which misrepresent and pervert these aspirations.

The "Jewish Revolution" of our times is the profound distinction between nationalism and cosmopolitanism, or, perhaps Zionism and Judaism. The Israeli authorities have shown the same contempt for those choosing to ignore or minimize the importance of territorial imperatives that the Soviets have displayed for "rootless cosmopolitans"—their special language for Diaspora Jews.

There is a sense in which the radical has reacted to Israeli victory not as a problem in Jewish identity, so much as a problem of identifying with victory itself. For the current behavior of Israel is notably that of a matured nation. On the battlefield, in the United Nations debates, in various policy utterances, Israelis have definitely not behaved like representatives of a "small nation" or an "underdeveloped nation." Like any big power, Israel insists on the geographic spoils of victory. She desires a rationalization of her boundaries: the Jordan River, the Straits of Tiran, the Suez Canal. She insists that the rights of her citizenry take precedence over the rights of Arab refugees. She desires not just *de facto* gains, but *de jure* status, that is, the recognition by the Arab states of Israeli legitimacy. In such insistence, in the act of forging a united national front from within, Israel's military victory has fractured its support abroad. For if radicals, particularly those dedicated to a "thermonuclear pacifist" position, are discomfited by military success, the ruling conservative elements—and here we can include the established positions of ambivalence taken by the United States and the United Kingdom, as well as the anti-Israeli militance pursued by the Soviet Union in the United Nations debates—are self-righteously indignant over a state daring to lay claim to big-power status by the use of classical big-power techniques of armed violence. The United States is markedly ambivalent toward the Israeli military victory—for, while the United States does not suffer any immediate loss of influence in the Near East, it clearly places the Americans on the periphery rather than at the center of policy making in the area.

Both radical and reactionary critics of Israel's military victory have sensed, rather than articulated, that a new nation had been born in 1967. The period between the writing of *The Jewish State* by Herzl and its actual creation was inconclusive, comprised as it was of a patchwork of bribes, land purchases, and hard labor. The Arabs could claim that Israel's existence was guaranteed first by the United Nations in 1947 and then by Great Britain and France in the Suez debacle in 1956. The 1967 conflict, however, was comprised of Israeli military might and Realpolitik. To be sure, not even world Jewry was particularly convinced it was otherwise. Their great fears that the latest round of Arab threats and blockades would result in the decimation of Israel, and their consequent impulsive rallying to the Israel cause, even to the point of demanding United States armed intervention, indicated that the Soviets were not alone in their underestimation of Arab weakness and Jewish might. Now that Israel has become a realized state, a first-rate, albeit small, power in the Middle East, the need for sovereignty rather than support could drive a wedge between Israel and Judaism that might be deeper than any in the past.

Beneath the current euphoria of troubled pride in a military victory gained by Jews, unparalleled since the legendary victory of the Macabees in the pre-Christian era, is the fear that, far from unifying the Jewish people, Israel's recent victory will establish a relationship between Israel and Jews much like that between other nations and their own dispersed national minorities. The victory of Israel, if it endures, compels a re-evaluation by all sectors of world Jewry of its *freedom from* Israel, just as the defeat of Israel would have compelled re-evaluation of Jewish *responsibility to* Israel.

The problem of "dual loyalty" for the individual Jew tied to two nations was far more intimate before the Israeli victory. For the American Jew, a generalized sentiment in favor of kith and kin will now have to yield to the realization that Israel is a prime military force. The Soviet Jew, for his part, is faced with the larger dilemma that any show of support for Israel would even more likely be construed as anti-Soviet behavior. In other words, support for a powerful nation (other than one's own) is not the same as philanthropic underwriting of a poor nation.

It is a tragic fact that today's most vociferous, if not virulent, anti-Israel advocates are to be found (aside from those in the Arab world) in the governments of the Soviet Union, China, and left-of-center Third World nations. Anti-imperialists and revolutionaries seem at last to have found an issue on which they can unite. However, the coexistence of "dual loyalties" to the struggle against imperialism and to the national aspirations of oppressed and exploited people, whether they be Jew or Gentile, Arab or Israeli, African or Vietnamese, cannot allow us to stand by in silence.

It is a fact, to which many radicals are apparently impervious, that the "Arab world" contains within it not only such supposedly "progressive" regimes as the Nasserist Egyptian and the Ba'athist Syrian, but also the Hashemite monarchy of Jordan, ruled by King Hussein, and the feudal backwater of King Faisal in Saudi Arabia. Can revolutionaries legitimately ignore, nay deny, such facts while attacking Israel, a relatively democratic state built by its citizenry in the face of diplomatic, political, economic, and military harassment by its neighbors, as well as by the former colonial power dominant there, Great Britain? How, in the name of revolutionary politics, can a new state, mobilizing its citizenry to defend itself against a foreign aggressor and emerging victorious, be condemned by the very world that ordinarily would applaud such an event? This would be unfathomable were it not that neither the Cold War nor nationalism allow for political rationality.

ISRAEL AND COLONIALISM

Israel's incontrovertible right to a peaceful national existence and her expedient alignment with the Western powers must be clearly distinguished. The ultimate and irreducible issue is whether Israel has the right to exist. The Arab position, in defeat or otherwise, has been clear and unequivocal. As was stated by General Abdul Rahman Arif, Head of State and

Government Chief of Iraq: "The existence of Israel," he said on June 28, 1967, "is in itself an aggression and must therefore be repulsed, and there must be a return to a normal situation." The Arab definition of "normality" is a Palestine without Israel. No matter how many times the Arabs have repeated these sentiments, there is resistance to taking them seriously. Perhaps this stems from the apparent distinctions they make between Israeli and Jew, Zionism and Judaism. This is not the place to argue neat ideological distinctions. The American Council on Judaism has made similar distinctions, and so has the Soviet government. In fact, probably a good many Jews living in the Diaspora would prefer a less strident definition of the complete Jew than provided by David Ben-Gurion—namely, to live in Israel. However strained the continued identification between Jews in exile and Jews in torment, the anti-Zionist view implies an eternal Diaspora without a temporal center. It implies a return to a condition of Jewish life in the interstices of society—monetary maneuvering, intellectual competition, and political dependence. The question is not whether the Jews can survive without an Israel; even granting that they could and would, the question has shifted from the *survival of* to the *quality of* Jewish life. This quality has been profoundly influenced by the Nazi experience of mass murder, the Soviet experience of betrayal, and the American experience of mindless absorption.

Even were the existence of the State of Israel to encourage negative tendencies in Jewish identity, would that mean that Jews have less right to a national state than Arabs do? Would the Moslem peoples be willing to entrust their survival to religious and cultural forms alone, without territorial reinforcements? The frequent Arab proclamations of sovereignty over Palestine indicate that to the Arab leaders Israel represents a national threat and not a religious or cultural threat. Indeed, Arab propaganda has sought to make this distinction central.

That the leaders of states themselves struggling for nationhood should attack another people's right to exist as a nation—
a "people which," in Israeli Foreign Minister Abba Eban's
eloquent words, "had given nationhood its deepest significance
and its most enduring grace"—indicates only that incredible
myths about Israel have been accepted as truth even by otherwise critical and independent minds, or subscribed to for reasons of Realpolitik. They would deny the right of national
existence to a people almost destroyed in the gas chambers and
ovens of Dachau, Buchenwald, and Auschwitz. They attack a
state built by the labor and sacrifice of several generations of
one of the most brutalized peoples history has known. They
attack a state which, even at the termination of the war, when
hundreds of thousands of refugees were homeless, ill, and
spiritually destroyed, could not absorb the remnants of a mur-
dered people without a life-and-death struggle for existence
against the combined maneuvers of imperial England and the
armies of corrupt feudal regimes. How can a nation be defined
as beyond the pale once again, this time by the very movements
and regimes which claim to be leaders of national redemption
and social liberation? There are so many issues intertwined in
the Arab-Israeli conflict that it is necessary to re-examine
fundamentals.

At the center are issues of colonialism and nationalism in all
their manifestations. The truth about Israel is not so simple as
the delegates assembled in Cairo early in July, representing
fifty states, would have it. Is Israel a "treacherous aggressor"
and the "spearhead of imperialism"? The question can be resolved into two parts: first, the connection between Israel and
the struggles of the former colonial world for national sovereignty and, second, the role of colonialism in Israel's establishment. Was Israel, from its inception, an act of "aggression" and
of colonialism? Does Israel constitute a European imperialist
excrescence amidst the indigenous people of the Middle East,
pushing them from their ancestral lands and exploiting those

who remained? The historic facts cannot be reconciled with such a simplistic interpretation of Israel's birth.

The Soviet Union itself was able to put aside in this instance its own formulas and recognize the historic right of the Jewish people to a homeland in Israel and the great obligation of the United Nations to aid in that undertaking. The Soviet Union was the first to give Israel its de jure recognition, and Czechoslovakia, even after the Communist coup, was Israel's major source of arms to defend itself against the invading feudal armies of the Farouks, Sauds, and Husseins. Great Britain not only abstained from voting in favor of Israel's admission to the United Nations, it did all within its power, diplomatically and even militarily, to abort the new state before its birth and then to aid in "strangling it in its cradle." At the time of the Palestinian partition, Bartley C. Crum, a member of the Anglo-American Committee of Inquiry on Palestine, commented in his book, *Behind the Silken Curtain:*

Fully seventy per cent of the British colonial officials whom I met in Palestine were either, at worst, openly anti-Semitic, or, at best, completely unsympathetic and resentful toward Jewish hopes in Palestine. . . . [Britain placed] Palestine under the Colonial Office with administrators taken from the ranks of the Colonial and Indian services, where their experience had been almost totally that of overlords dealing with subservient and illiterate natives.

It was Chamberlain who returned from Munich to announce that there would be "peace in our time"; the same Chamberlain was responsible for imposing limits on Jewish immigration into Palestine, for using British troops to prevent the early refugees from Nazism from entering Palestine, and for disarming and imprisoning members of the Jewish self-defense forces. He did so at the behest and under the pressure of the Grand Mufti and oppressive Arab regimes which were allies of the Nazis. Little wonder, then, that the present pious British attitude toward the "Jerusalem issue" is discounted by Israelis.

ARAB POLICIES

In the 1930's Arab terrorists and "guerrillas" waged a continuous war against Jewish settlements in Palestine: arson, destruction of wells and pipelines, and murder. Then as now, they were part of the apparatus of "Arab liberation." It was with the active propaganda and financial support of the Nazis and Fascists that Haj Amin El Husseini, Mufti of Jerusalem and Nazi propagandist, advocated mass murder of the Jews. Ahmed Shukeiri, present head of the so-called Palestine Liberation Organization, is a large landowner, an unmistakable heir of the revanchist chauvinism of the pro-Nazi Arab, who dares to proclaim himself leader of a national liberation struggle and offer "support" to the Vietnamese Liberation Front. One day the head of the reactionary Syrian delegation to the United Nations, another day leader of the Saudi Arabian delegation, on yet another day he heads "guerrilla war" against Israel, a war against individual citizens, with "guerrillas" who never dare attack a military force, a "guerrilla force" which is, in fact, not a guerrilla force at all but a band of mercenaries in the pay of a foreign power, Egypt. And Nasser? He had a dream of destruction, a dream which in June 1967 took the shape of a "final battle that will bring Israel's defeat. In this battle the dream of the Arabs to exterminate Israel will come true." This "progressive" has spoken of the *Protocols of the Elders of Zion* with favor, and his government has published a series of National Books, one of which bears the title *Talmudic Human Sacrifices,* resurrecting the blood-ritual myth. The rhetoric of anti-imperialism disguises an irrational messianic drive to destroy a neighboring country—a drive which, if successful, would inevitably lead to the murder of its citizenry. What sort of socialism encourages the publication and use of university texts in which such examples of "socialism" as "Hitler's German Socialism" (*Arab Society and Arab Socialism*) or the "Nazi experience in attempting to achieve progress and build the new society" (*On Socialist Society*) are offered and in which Marxism is attacked "because Karl Marx decided to take as his starting point a certain social phenomenon, when the truth was that the problem existed inside man himself . . ." (*Arab Socialism*), and Marxism is "rejected root and branch as a purely materialistic philosophy" (*The July 23 Revolution*), preaching such "evils as equality between man and woman" (*The Arab Ideology*)? Nor is this primarily a matter of ideological disputations. For the "anti-imperialist" leadership of Nasser inflicted poison-gas warfare on his fellow-Arab Yemenis.

We are not concerned here with evaluating the Arab regimes which now claim to be "progressive" and "anti-imperialist." The fact is that they are not led by revolutionaries fighting for social justice. It is a delusion to think so. One would be entitled to such a private illusion were it not for its tragic public consequences. Moreover, even were those regimes engaged in the job of revolutionary construction at home, there would be no excuse for the irrational chauvinism that characterizes their leadership. Even the Israeli Communist Party was, in its electoral campaign for the Sixth Knesset, moved to denounce Nasser's "dangerous chauvinism which threatens the stability of the entire region," and to proclaim, "Let it be known that the Communist Party of Israel . . . will be the shield of Israel's existence. . . ."

Just such anti-imperialists and revolutionaries as King Farouk of Egypt, Abdullah of Jordan, and Nouri Said of Iraq launched an unholy religious war in 1947-48 against Israel with the intention of "pushing her into the sea," an intention which has remained the constant pivot of Arab policy. Precisely this policy gave birth to the mass exodus of Arab refugees from Israel. The Arab Higher Committee ordered the evacuation, the Mufti instilled an ungovernable animus into the Arab masses via radio propaganda, alternately cajoling, threatening, and warning them to leave or suffer the consequences which would be worse than death. The Arab exodus was in part a planned evacuation for the temporary duration of the war, as part of Arab military strategy, and in part, perhaps mainly, a fear-driven flight from unreal horrors. The one genuine horror, the massacre at Deir Yassin of innocent Arab men, women, and children by Israeli right-wing terrorists (whose perpetrators were severely condemned by Israeli public opinion), came *after* the great exodus had begun—though obviously it served by word of mouth as an "example" of what awaited Arabs who tarried. In fact, many Israelis viewed the exodus with dismay and tried to stem it, urging the Arabs to remain, and guaranteeing them protection and security.

JEWS IN PALESTINE

Nor is the Arab attack on Israel understandable as an attempt to recover lands usurped by a foreign conqueror that had imposed his will on the indigenous peoples. Quite the contrary, it bears repetition that the Jewish people had not only maintained their spiritual contact with Palestine throughout the centuries in the *Galut* but also that Jews have been continuously an indigenous, though a minority, population of Palestine. In some areas of the country, such as Peki'in in the Galilee, there are even families (about fifty) which trace their genealogy directly back to the Hebrews; in Jerusalem and Safed they were a majority throughout this century; and they formed substantial communities in Tiberias and Hebron. For centuries after the devastating defeat of the Jews by the Romans, in the last of a series of colonial revolts against the Assyrian and Roman empires, the Jews constituted the major population of Palestine. When the majority of the Jewish people finally became dispersed throughout the world, it was the return to Palestine which acted as a major culturally unifying bond maintaining the national existence. This remote province of the Ottoman Empire remained a center of Jewish nationalism. In fact, the first great nationalist leader of the

Arabs, Prince Feisal, in a famous letter to Justice Frankfurter, had wished "the Jews a most hearty welcome home" in 1919, recognizing their link to Palestine: "We Arabs," he said, "look with the deepest sympathy on the Zionist movement." In this controversial statement, he concluded by saying, "Our two movements complete one another. The Jewish movement is national and not imperialistic. . . . Indeed, I think that neither can be a real success without the other."

Throughout the centuries Jewish inhabitants formed a persistent part of the population in Palestine. As the historian James Parkes points out, "Apart from neolithic survivals and the Copts in Egypt, Jews are the longest settled of the present identifiable inhabitants in some [countries of the Middle East], and have lived longer in all the others, than Arabs have in Palestine or Egypt." The Jewish presence and immigration into Palestine was constant, though it became most significant only in the twentieth century. At the turn of the century, 18 per cent of the Palestinians were Jews; and by World War I the Jewish population of Palestine was already 100,000. If the Jews did not increase their percentage of the Palestinian population, it was because Arab immigration into Palestine considerably outdistanced the Jewish immigration and was stimulated by the economic opportunities opened up in consequence of the one area in the Middle East undergoing rapid economic development. In the portion of Palestine which was to become the Jewish State under the United Nations Partition Plan, the Jews were an even greater part of the population. What is important is that Jews constituted a continuous minority within the area from the fall of the Second Commonwealth to the establishment of Israel. They were hardly strangers in Palestine. Moreover, 65 per cent of Israel's present population are Arab Jews—Jews from Morocco, Tunisia, Syria, Iraq, Yemen, Jordan, and other parts of the Middle East. Of the remaining 35 per cent, a large number are indigenous sabras. This amounts to an exchange of Arab population along religious lines.

Nor did the presence of "European" Jews lead, as colonialism has always done, to the exploitation of the Arab masses. On the contrary, from its inception, immigration inspired by Zionism was imbued with an ethic of return to the soil, of a religion of labor, and, indeed, of socialism. The cardinal principle of the agricultural settlements, the kibbutzim, was the end of exploitation of man by man; they refused to hire workers, Jewish or Arab, preferring to build their communities entirely by their own collective labor. Obviously, Arab workers and peasants were exploited in Palestine, as they were in contemporary Israel, and as they are in any system employing wage labor in private firms producing for the profit of their owners. But the characteristic pattern of Jewish settlement in Palestine, while separatist in form, was anti-colonial and non-exploitative in substance.

The land acquired by Jewish settlers was purchased from Arab landowners with money collected from hundreds of thousands of Jews contributing to the Jewish National Fund. Land became the collective property of the entire Jewish people. Much of it was barren swampland, owned by absentee sheikhs, and usually unpopulated. Where there were tenants, the Jewish National Fund made the extraordinary effort of compensating them with other land or money. That Jewish settlement proceeded in this way can be no more condemned than land acquired by Arab landlords; certainly less so, given the fertilization of once barren soil. The class structure, in which a few sheikhs ruled the agrarian population, exploiting their labor and living comfortable lives in the cities on their "earnings" from lands tilled by subsistence peasantry in the villages of Palestine, was, in fact, increasingly altered as Jewish settlement and agricultural and industrial development impinged on the feudal ruling patterns.

When the State of Israel was established in 1948, Jews owned only 8.6 per cent of the land and Israeli Arabs 3.3 per cent, with another 17 per cent abandoned by Arab owners. Seventy per cent of the land in Israel's part of Palestine, in fact, had been "Crown lands" owned by the British under the Mandate, taken from the crumbling Ottoman Empire, most of it in the Negev, a barren and uninhabited desert.

BRITISH COLONIALISM AND JEWISH ZIONISM

Not only was the pattern of Jewish settlement in Palestine non-colonial, it was, in fact, anti-colonial. The end of British rule in Palestine came largely as the result of the Zionist movement, Jewish settlement, and the Yishuv's (Palestinian Jewry) struggle against the British. Britain, the classic colonial power in the area, resisted the establishment of the Israeli State, abstaining from voting in favor of its admission to the United Nations, and doing all within its power until then to forestall independence. The British consistently opposed and thwarted Arab-Jewish attempts at rapprochement, inflaming Arab chauvinisim to defeat Arab and Jewish nationalism.

When the British Mandate came into effect in 1922, there were numerous meetings between Jews and Arabs at Cairo, Geneva, and London to work out political and economic cooperation between them. Negotiations between representatives of the Zionist Executive (among them Chaim Weizmann, then future President of Israel) and Arab spokesmen were stopped under British compulsion. A year later, similar attempts at direct negotiation with Arab leaders were thwarted by the British. As late as 1943, there were efforts made by important Arab leaders to work out an agreement for a binational state with Zionist representatives. Precisely at this time (November 19, 1943) a number of repressive measures against the Jewish community in Palestine were launched by the British administration. Settlements were cordoned off and besieged by British soldiers, ostensibly to search for deserters from the Polish army (sic!), resulting in many Jewish casualties. In the months that followed, various kibbutz leaders were imprisoned, and there were repeated attempts to deprive the Jews of their defense arms. Intensified search operations were conducted, and "illegal immigrants"—victims of Nazi oppression who had managed to reach Palestinian shores—were arrested and deported. Large-scale arrests took place, designed to smash the Jewish apparatus of defense and regrouping of the exiles.

During the two years following World War II and preceding the establishment of Israel, the British colonial regime encouraged the return to power within the Arab community of the Husseini party, most of whose principal leaders had spent the war years in occupied territories of Europe, collaborating with the Fascists. The Grand Mufti, Haj Amin El Husseini, wanted in Europe as a Nazi collaborator, managed to "elude" British capture, return to Cairo, and resume direction of the Arab forces opposed to conciliation with Jews. When the Arab right organized para-military terrorist formations, the British ignored them. In every way, the most intransigent, chauvinist, reactionary elements in Arab leadership were encouraged by the British. Finally, when the State of Israel was declared, the British made a last desperate effort to provide the Arabs with strategic military strongholds, such as the famous Kastel on the Jerusalem-Tel Aviv Road, and permitted British Centurion tanks mysteriously to fall into Arab hands. It was the Israeli military victory against the Arab regimes, based on the exploitation of Palestine, that set in motion movements within some of these countries to establish genuine nationalist and reform regimes.

Nasser's Egypt, rather than choosing the path of peaceful cooperation with the new Jewish State, chose to re-assert Arab chauvinism and to divert itself from the task of completing an authentic social revolution. Moreover, while attacking "imperialist Israel" as a "monster state" and threatening to "grind [Israel] into the dust," Nasser did not disturb major foreign investments in Egypt itself. Indeed, the increasing penetration of American foreign investment into Egypt was a constant in the

Nasser era. Imports from the United States alone roughly equal those from Europe as a whole and amount to more than twice that of imports from the Soviet Union. Aside from the seizure of the Suez Canal, in itself scarcely a major revolutionary act, though a symbolic significance, Egypt's struggle against imperialism has been largely a war of words. Holding the Tri-Continental Conference in Cairo cost Nasser little but gave him precisely the "nationalist" facade which allows him to compel many on the left and in the Third World to support his formula of "Palestine" against Israel.

GUERRILLA WARFARE IN ISRAEL

The strategy of guerrilla warfare has now been proposed for conducting the "fourth round" against Israel. The model provided for Cuba, Algeria, and Vietnam has become the euphoria of defeat. The Algerians, mistaking their own anti-colonial struggle against France with Arab revanchism in the Middle East, have called for guerrilla warfare against Israel to regain lost national territory. The Cubans, falsely projecting their own nationalist struggles onto the "Arab peoples" and identifying the situation with their own experience with United States occupation of their country, have supported this call. Ricardo Alarcón, speaking in the United Nations on behalf of Cuba, began with the eloquence one might have hoped to hear from a revolutionary government that has had to defend its own people's right to an independent national existence:

With regard to the Near East problem, this delegation wishes to express that the people and the Revolutionary Government of Cuba, as a matter of principle, are opposed to every manifestation of religious, national, or racial prejudice, whatever the source may be. Likewise, they believe that any political proclamation whose aim is the annihilation of any people or state is to be condemned. This principle is equally applicable to the Palestinian people, unjustly and brutally dispossessed of its territory, and the Hebrew people

who, for 2000 years, have suffered under persecution and racial prejudice and—during the not-too-distant era of Nazism—suffered under
one of the most cruel attempts at mass extermination ever recorded.

These words emphatically distinguish the Cuban position
from the Arab position explicated by Nasser on May 28, 1967.
"We intend to open a general assault against Israel. This will
be total war. Our basic aim is the destruction of Israel." Nonetheless, the Cubans, who were clearly aware of the constancy of
such Arab proclamations, were able to take a position which is
neither revolutionary nor just and demonstrably incorrect:

Our position with regard to the State of Israel in the Middle East
crisis is determined by that state's aggressive conduct as an instrument of imperialism turned against the Arab peoples to settle existing problems; it has done so in the most treacherous and indefensible
form: a Nazi-style surprise attack carefully prepared in advance.
. . . The State of Israel enjoyed the full benefit of the agreement to
an unconditional cease fire. But this is not enough for her. She has
also declared that she will maintain possession of the occupied territories. If they do not withdraw without delay, the Arab peoples have
the legitimate right to resume the fighting. . . . The only alternative
left for the Arab peoples facing imperialism in Asia, Africa, and
Latin America: to resist and fight. Patria o Muerte! Venceremos!

That these words are appropriate not to the Arab but to the
Israeli cause—"Homeland or Death! We shall overcome!"—
seems to have escaped the Cuban delegate's notice. That they
should have escaped the Soviet delegate's notice could surprise
no one who is aware of the Soviet's demonstrated willingness to
sacrifice nationalist and revolutionary movements—as in China,
Vietnam, and Greece—for their own perceived national interests. That the Cubans, who have no national interests at stake
in the Middle East and who, despite their precarious and dependent situation, have generally maintained an independent
revolutionary line and international posture, should now accept Arab propaganda is particularly revealing; it underlines

the extent to which the Arab leaders have succeeded in confusing the issues by the select use of anti-imperialist rhetoric.

The "occupied territories"—the Gaza Strip, the west bank of the Jordan, and the "Old City" of Jerusalem—were conquered and annexed in the first place by Egypt and Jordan in open combat against the newly founded State of Israel; these territories were intended by the United Nations Partition Plan to constitute an independent Arab State in Palestine (which was never established because of those regimes); and Jerusalem was to be internationalized. These facts seem to have escaped the notice not only of the Cuban delegation but also of the new breed of nonhistorical "materialists" from the Socialist European bloc.

Of more fundamental importance is the striking misperception of the real significance of Israel's military victory and of popular "resistance" and guerrilla warfare. In Algeria, as in Vietnam, guerrilla warfare has proved an effective weapon in the hands of indigenously based nationalist forces resisting the material military superiority of a foreign and colonial (or would-be colonial) power attempting to subject the population to its will. This is precisely the Israeli situation. Spurred by their consecration to the national cause and in defense of the "homeland," the Israelis have successfully resisted Arab aggression. They won, just as the Algerians won, and as the Vietnamese National Liberation Front persisted against foreign aggression.

Moshe Dayan, Israel's Defense Minister, has drawn the parallel between the Israelis and the Vietcong, and cogently stated the essential meaning of guerrilla warfare:

Guerrilla war is the weapon of the weak—but it is not a weak weapon. Whatever the ultimate outcome of the strife in Vietnam, it will remain a fact that in the previous decade the Vietcong succeeded in defeating the French forces and that now, with a small army, low-grade weapons, and extremely primitive equipment, they are holding out against the strongest army in the West, that of the United States of America. . . . There are, of course, crucial differences between the Vietcong War and the sabotage and terror operations of Ahmed Shukeiri's units. In contrast to the guerrilla fighters in Vietnam, who make use of every opportunity to attack American troops, the Arab gangs avoid all direct contact with Israeli forces. The aim of the Vietcong fighters is to drive the foreigner—the American—from Vietnam, unite the North with the South, and bring down the Saigon Government. These are not empty phrases from propaganda pamphlets, but genuine aims, for which they are willing to lay down their lives. . . . There is no similarity between [the] . . . the mine-layings and quick return to Arab territory [of El Fatah terrorists] (where they are paid for these "raids") and the life-and-death struggle of the Vietcong. . . .

The Arab leaders claim that . . . Israel's Jews . . . are foreigners, Europeans who have succeeded in occupying an Arab country but will be compelled to evacuate it again. Their fate, they assert, will be like that of the Crusaders who were in the end driven out by Arab forces, or the French, pushed out of Algeria.

This political and military analogy fails to take into account a basic fact—that the Jews are not foreigners in Israel. This is not only true as regards their own feelings and their historical links with the land. While Israelis may be Jews who came from other countries, they did not remain tied to them. The decision to evacuate the French from Algeria was taken in Paris, and the fate of the Crusaders was decided in the capitals of Europe. But it is the citizenry of Israel who make the decisions on the security problems that plague them, and this they do from the point of view of Jerusalem, not that of Jews from New York or London. In the Arab-Israeli dispute it is the Arab guerrilla fighters who are the strangers; the native inhabitants of Israel are the Israelis. The entire question of the war against Israel and the way in which it should be waged is decided in Cairo and Damascus.

In this remarkable document, Dayan concluded by cautioning against the intoxicating rhetoric of guerrilla insurgency: "The Arabs seek to wrest Israel from the Jews. This can be achieved—if at all—only by means of total war. Acts of sabotage and terror do not lead to this end, and in fact have the opposite effect—they tend to strengthen the nation that is attacked.

Guerrilla warfare can achieve its aim when it is used as an instrument of national struggle against a government imposed from the outside, but it is rendered ineffective when it is used to assault a people settled on its own land."

It should be appreciated, however, that Dayan's commentary on guerrilla warfare was written prior to the Second Sinai campaign. This means that with the acquisition of vast new territories, irrespective of their de jure status, in which Arab majorities prevail, guerrilla organizations are now in fact quite feasible. For in these newly conquered regions the special circumstances for the conduct of permanent underground violence do exist. It will thus become a prime focus of Israeli management to prevent the conditions of insurgency from emerging. This can be done in either one of two ways: treatment of guerrillas as gangsters (in which case the Israelis will be making the same mistake that the British committed in the '40's), or treatment of Arab opposition as normal and even legitimately expressing authentic national sentiments. But a settlement of the tactical issues obviously depends on a resolution of the policy questions—a settlement which is made terribly remote because of the ideological shallowness of an Israeli policy that yet manages to bridle the organizational sophistication of the Israeli armed forces.

ISRAEL AND THE SOVIET UNION

The Arab-Israeli war has turned into a post-war confrontation between Israel and the Soviet Union. Clearly, the Soviet Union must be shocked by Israel's behavior. It has a fifty-year history of treating Jews as Russians have been accustomed to treating Jews—and getting away with such treatment. This gap between stereotyped expectation and Jewish performance is what partially accounts for the violent response to the Israeli victory.

The Israeli military victory was a Soviet political defeat. More significant, it was a defeat for a foreign policy based on illusions and on alliances with incompetent regimes. In one sense, however, the Soviet Union has gained by the Arab defeat. It has made these regimes far more dependent on her than they were before their military defeat. This has given her even greater political leverage in the Arab world than an Arab victory might have. Nonetheless, it was a blow to Soviet prestige, a defeat for Soviet military planning and weaponry, and an event not likely to inspire the confidence of other countries which may require her material and political support.

There have been shock and hesitancies on both sides. Israeli political leadership, drawn so heavily from Ashkenazic sources, from Eastern Europe and Russia, at one and the same time seemed intimidated by Soviet military might and convinced that this might would be used with restraint. After all, if Ukrainian anti-Semitism is deeply rooted in Russian rural history, so too is Socialist condemnation of anti-Semitism. The war against Nazi Germany fused Soviet and Jewish interests for at least the War epoch. And this was but the most recent chapter in a history of socialism that drew profound sustenance and gave equal support to an "emancipated" Jewry from Marx and Bebel to Luxemburg and Trotsky. Even in the most bitter days of Stalinism, yesteryear, the support of the Soviet Union for the establishment of the State of Israel, however tepid and hesitant, was genuine. Furthermore, it was a compromise of the Soviet position on the "national question" consciously taken in the name of humanitarianism. It was made in the name of the Jewish people along Zionist rather than Marxist lines, not to mention an end to British dominance in the Middle East.

The extent to which the Soviet Union preserved the remnants of European Jewry from destruction and supported the rights of Jews to a nation-state should not be forgotten. However, the Israel leadership could not be expected to accept the realities of post-Stalinist Soviet policy—the extension of Russian power to the Middle East on the shoulders of Arab backwardness. Socialist dialectics and Marxism-Leninism have given way to the pragmatism of geographical determinism. Nonetheless, it is evident that the Israeli authorities were taken by surprise, were in fact stunned by the severity of the Soviet condemnation of Israeli "aggression." They were unprepared for the lopsided Soviet support of Arab military sheikhs and feudal landlords (including many who had persecuted Communists), all in the name of supporting the Third World. As recently as 1966, the Israel Government Yearbook referred to the Soviet public utterance calling for the settlement of disputes by peaceful means as a neutralization of the Soviet foreign policy toward Israel.

So careful has the Israeli government been not to offend the Soviet Union that more than one voice sympathetic to Israel has accused her of a policy of calculated indifference toward the fate of the three million Russian Jews. The most recent, and perhaps sharpest, voice is that of Elie Wiesel, who, in *The Jews of Silence,* stated categorically that "Jewish solidarity extends to everyone in the world but Soviet Jews. The Jewish State has even begun to help nations of Asia and Africa, but toward them it displays an attitude of vague and hesitant indifference." Now these calculated hesitancies have been destroyed, along with the memory of past associations. The Israelis, too, then, have had their own shock of recognition.

ISRAEL AND THE WEST

To some extent, Israeli foreign and domestic policies have probably contributed to the view that she is an "imperialist gendarme in the Middle East." The frequent charges in the United Nations debates by Arab and Communist spokesmen alike, concerning the "Hitlerite" character of the Israeli armed forces, were replied to with profound outrage by Israeli delegates and her foreign minister. However, the extensive militarization of Israel, its reliance on military force from the outset of its existence, cannot be seriously denied. But no commentator has demonstrated that the Israelis had any real alternative. This military determination of events has made it extremely difficult for Israel to carve out an independent foreign policy. With notable exceptions, her position has been identified in practice with the United States. It has acted in collusion with Britain and France against Nasser's "anti-colonial" regime. It has carried out systematic reprisals against Arab terrorist attacks, many of which have gone well beyond even the most generous definition of mere "defensive forays." In fact, Mapam and Achdut Ha'avodah, the Israeli Socialist parties, have consistently opposed these policies, as have leading non-Socialist figures such as the late social thinker Martin Buber and Nahum Goldmann, head of the World Zionist Organization.

Even Ben-Gurion, who was to be the architect of Israel's pro-Western leanings, recognized the rationality of nonalignment for Israel. In a speech at the Knesset in 1948, he flatly declared:

The state of Israel is not concerned with the internal affairs of other states. We want to live in peace with all. We are compelled to do so because we have hostages in every country, and we desire their migration to Israel. This is our orientation, and I am not ashamed of it. We shall persist in it. If some should give this orientation the foreign name "neutrality," I shall not be ashamed of that. This is an orientation based on the unity of the human race, on peace between nations, on the desire to live in peace with all peoples.

Despite its neutralist protestations, Israel did not remain idle in the Cold War. Israel became involved with policies which, perhaps expedient in the short run, could not help but alienate her from the Third World and also permit the Soviet Union to rationalize its anti-Israeli posture as progressive. Until the outbreak of the Korean War, Israel did not identify with either bloc, and emigration of Eastern European Jewry was permitted, even encouraged, while most Jewish communities in Eastern Europe joined the World Jewish Congress. Israel's alignment with the United States in the Korean conflict put an end to this era of good feelings between Soviet Union and Israel. This was followed by the irrational anti-Zionist campaigns in the Soviet Union and the notorious anti-Semitic trials in Moscow and Prague. The policies which Israel pursued in the next several years of attempting to obtain a mutual security pact with the United States, or as an option join NATO, clearly put her in the anti-Soviet world, which in the context meant, or appeared to mean, pro-colonialism.

Since Israel was caught in the Cold War, it is not at all clear how relevant a different foreign policy would have been. In 1955, the United States' attempt to impose the Baghdad Pact on the Middle East was resisted by Egypt and Israel. This did not stop the Soviet Union from giving unequivocal political and military support to the Arab regimes, nor the Czechs from concluding a major arms deal with Egypt. The Sinai Campaign of 1956 followed this arms build-up. The Skoda works in Czechoslovakia were supplying Israel with weapons, just as Great Britain shipped military hardware to Egypt up until the seizure of the Suez Canal. It was after the successful Israeli "campaign," however, that the geopolitical lines hardened into their present mold. For there could be no question that, if Israel's goals were internal security, those of England and France were to conduct a preventive war for the purpose of punishing and, if possible, destroying Nasser's regime. His government had just nationalized the Suez Canal and seemed to be an emerging stalwart in the anti-colonial wing within the Arab bloc. By participating in this action, Israel placed herself, as Martin Buber reputedly viewed the Sinai Campaign, on the side of the reactionary part of the world.

Even given certain historical perspectives, it is still unclear what choice was open to Israel, since Egypt was constantly threatening her with destruction and seemingly was growing in military strength. The historic irony is that the Arab regimes aligned with the West (Jordan, Iraq, Saudi Arabia) were as inflammatory and threatening in their anti-Israel pronouncements as Egypt. (Ahmed Shukeiri, then the Saudian United Nations representative, demanded the dismemberment of the State of Israel and the expulsion of the Jews.) Had these regimes then presented the same dangerous military threat, Israel probably would have acted toward them as she did toward Egypt. The retaliatory action in June 1967 against a pro-Western Jordanian regime ruled by a king, whose legion was trained by the British and armed by the Pentagon, had no effect, however, on the cries that she is an "imperialist tool."

The constant propagandistic din over Israeli policy drew attention away from Israeli decisions that demonstrated its relative independence from the Western bloc nations and the World Zionist community. Israel's failure to support the Algerian liberation struggle against France strained relations with the Socialist bloc. Her abstentions in the United Nations debates on Algeria, which in fact put her on the side of France, came not out of ideological principle (even for the ruling Social Democrats of Mapai) but out of necessity. By condemning France, she risked losing her only major source of military hardware, thus making her vulnerable to Arab attack. When the risk to her existence was less, Israel acted unequivocally against colonialism. She voted in the United Nations for sanctions against the South African regime, siding with the most militant Afro-Asian governments, despite the large South African Jewish community and past diplomatic support by South Africa.

There is the demonstrable distance Israel put between itself and the United States Vietnam policy. She did this by a measured rejection of close ties with the South Vietnam regime and by complete neutrality in the matter of war support. Like nearly every major power, it has provided token medical supplies as a show of humanitarianism rather than as support for the war effort. Earlier, in 1962, having abstained in the past so as not to affront the United States, Israel voted for admission of China to the United Nations, although she did not support

the Soviet demand to replace Formosa's seat with China's. Israel has maintained a friendly stance toward the new African
States, providing a modest but important program of technical
and economic assistance that encompasses some thirty-five Afro-
Asian nations and which received warm praise, for instance,
from Ghana's Kwame Nkrumah when he was still considered
Africa's most important anti-colonialist leader. Despite this,
the Casablanca Third World "summit" in 1961 unanimously
resolved to condemn Israel "as an instrument of imperialism
and neo-colonialism not only in the Middle East but also in
Africa and Asia." In the showdown over the General Agreement on Trade and Tariffs, and, more important, in the United
Nations Conference on Trade and Development, Israel continually and consistently supported a Third World posture,
and in so doing opposed United States policy. There was also
the support officially tendered on May 15, 1966, for Polish
claims on the Oder-Neisse territories. And lest this be viewed
as a means to gain an ideological foothold in Central Europe,
it should be understood that in so doing Israel threatened its
fragile cordiality with West Germany.

The long effort of the Israeli government to achieve recognition in the eyes of the non-Arab portion of the Third World
bloc has paid significant dividends. The assumption that the
Israeli government is a Western outpost, an enemy in the Middle East, has not been convincing, particularly for many sub-
Saharan African nations. Despite production and employment
fluctuations early in 1967, Israel serves as a model of a small
country effecting a healthy import-export balance and a high
degree of economic autonomy despite the presence of foreign
capital and industry. The Arab representation of the Israeli
military victory as a huge defeat for the Third World assumes
a stability in that world that is nowhere to be found.

Guinea was the only one of thirty-one African nations to
break diplomatic ties with Israel after The Five Day War, and
even Julius Nyerere, President of Tanzania, made a public

statement emphasizing Tanzania's recognition of Israel as a State with a right to exist. But more than this, there is an unofficial support for Israel that in effect points to a common suspicion of Egyptian aims in particular. Kenya and Ethiopia fought undeclared wars against Somalia, an Arab sympathizer. Uganda, Chad, and Ethiopia were having their troubles with Sudan, which declared war on Israel and was supposed to be Egypt's channel to black Africa. Ghana, which even under the regime of Kwame Nkrumah maintained an extensive set of economic and cultural ties with Israel, did not support Egyptian claims. The present Arab-Black African rapprochement must thus be seen as a very recent development.

Israel as a small nation has limited room for maneuvering at international levels of power. However, if the charge of "lackey of imperialism" is to be treated seriously, one would have to demonstrate that any other nation of comparable size and status has fared nearly so well in developing an independent foreign policy. In a world of big power blocs, Israel has suffered from its intense isolation, yet it has also derived the advantages of turning its isolation into independence, and has not been quite so conservative or timorous in its foreign policy posture as its detractors continue to claim.

Like in Dante's consignment of the Jews to the "First Circle" or "Limbo," wherein the "virtuous heathen" hover between heaven and hell, Israel belongs neither to the highly developed nor to the underdeveloped sector of the world political economy. The dilemmas and contradictions of Israel's world status are such that it is by no means clear what the pragmatic gains, in terms of a peaceful national existence, would have resulted from a consistent anti-colonial stance and of nonalignment in the Cold War. Even those governments, like those in Africa, with which she has established ties of friendship, have often scorned her advances while accepting her favors. She exists in a limbo which wins her genuine friends in no camp, and resentment, or at least suspicion, in all.

From yet a different perspective, to view Israel as a pawn in the hands of United States foreign policy contradicts the effect Israel has had upon Arab unification. The French commentator, Jean Daniel, writing in *Le Nouvel Observateur,* has stated this fact most cogently:

The kings of Saudi Arabia and Jordan are the ones who are deliberately supporting and serving the imperialist designs of the present United States foreign policy. But any support for Israel does not divide the Arabs; it unites them. The goal of imperialism, as everyone knows, is to divide. Israel has long survived, thanks to United States "charity" and French arms. It has never been a factor balancing or tipping the scales one way or the other. When we see King Faisal and President Nasser united against Israel, knowing how these two men hate each other and how each is preparing the extermination of the other, no one can conclude that the existence of Israel favors the battle of a pro-American king against a pro-Soviet president.

If such facts help to demonstrate that Israel is not the "lackey" of United States foreign policy, they do little else. Funds from American Jewry have long given Israel a special economic situation in the world of finance and business. The international character of Jewish voluntary organizations has given Israel an inordinately large voice in the councils of world Jewry.

Finally, the quality of the immigrants entering Israel (at least those who came from Europe) and the high level of their education provided the young nation with the kind of developmental expertise absent elsewhere in the Middle East. Israel may be the last new nation to develop along Capitalist or neo-Capitalist lines. This is a fact of paramount significance, and one that is hardly likely to inspire confidence or respect among those who define industrial development and political independence in terms of one or another form of socialism. All of this raises anew, at the international level, the specter of the Sombartian Jew—the Jew as a creature of capitalism, who cannot survive the death of capitalism. The "inference" of some "Socialists" is that anti-capitalism is, in its very essence, a struggle against the Jewish State rather than for socialism within it.

ISRAELI SOCIALISM

Socialism was interwoven with the web of Israeli politics long before Israel's actual establishment as a State. It came as the vision of the *chalutzim*, carried with them from the *shtetlach* and ghettoes of Eastern Europe as well as from the centers of "emancipated" Jewry from France to the United States. Socialism was fundamental to the dream of the Jewish State, and the physical labor of the *chalutz* aimed at one and the same time to re-create a homeland and transform the individual Jew from *luftmensch,* petit-bourgeois intellectual, trader, and Talmudist, into a citizen rooted in the soil of his own nation. The kibbutz movement of collective agricultural settlements, the cooperative *moshavim,* provided the foundations of Israel. The Histadrut, the central labor organization that is cooperative enterprise and trade union fused into one, implanted a Socialist consciousness in the political culture of the Israeli working class, linking the task of nation-building and Socialism into an inseparable vision.

Dream and reality, however, have often conflicted. The Arab-Israeli war and the continual state of siege Israel has been compelled to live under—a "nervous peace, a dangerous peace," as Mapam's Yaakov Chazan put it—have created a climate wherein the most obdurate and least flexible policies, having nothing in common with either Democratic or Socialist principles, continued to be put forth.

The Israeli Left-Socialist party, Mapam, since its inception welcomed Arabs as members, and sought Arab-Jewish understanding on the basis of common class interests and Socialist principles. However, it was not until 1959 that the Histadrut first gave Arab workers the right to full membership. Military government in Israel's border regions subjected its Arab citizens to persistent harassment and infringement of their individual liberties, until such policies were lifted under Levi Eshkol's administration. Their general conditions of life continue to be inferior, even taking into account the composition of the Arab community, most of whom are new wage-earners, and certainly new to the money economy. The State's use of eminent domain has been disproportionately directed against the Arab-Israeli community. This resulted in the expropriation of 250,000 to 300,000 dunams of Arab-owned land between 1952 and 1965, and the reduction of the per capita dunams owned by Arabs from 6.0 to 4.2 dunams.

THE ARAB DIASPORA

On the question of the Arab refugees, Israel may have in many ways had a rational and correct posture, but it was one also infused with the military ethos and the conception of the Arabs simply as a "fifth column." If the right wing believed merely in the imposition of a victor's solution on the Arab refugees, with regard for their fate, Israel's government did, at least, pledge compensation for abandoned lands and express the willingness to participate in rehabilitation and resettlement programs elsewhere in the Middle East. She also allowed many Arabs to rejoin their families who had not left Israel in the great exodus.

Yet, in general, especially under Ben-Gurion, Israeli policy has been summed up, in his words, as the return of "not a single refugee," with little or no attention to the possible resettlement within Israel's borders of some refugees, within the limits of her means and absorptive capacity. (Leading spokesmen, like Egypt's Foreign Minister Salah e-Din, demanded "the restoration of the refugees to Palestine as the masters of the homeland, not as slaves." More explicitly, they intend to "annihilate Israel." This could not help but stamp the issue in its most cruel mold.) The imprisonment on trumped-up charges of "dealings with a foreign state" of so respected and nationally known an authority on the Arab peoples as Aharon Cohen, a major spokesman for Arab-Jewish rapprochement (and leader of Mapam), indicated how the internal situation stultified the search for alternatives and solutions other than military ones. Israel had her own Thermidorean reaction, if not against a revolution then against a legacy that seemed irrelevant in the context in which Israel was compelled to live, and in which, in the name of socialism, the Soviet Union and many Third World nations attacked her sovereignty.

The Arab refugee problem has become magnified precisely because of Israeli military victory. Whether the exodus of Arabs in the wake of the 1948 and 1956 wars was stimulated as a deliberate part of Arab military strategy to maintain a vanguard anti-Israeli force, or whether it represented a spontaneous resistance to Jewish majoritarian state, has become largely academic. Since the extensive victory of the Israeli army involved the total occupation of Palestine, from the banks of the Suez on the West to the River Jordan on the East and the Gulf of Aqaba in the South, the question of the Arab refugees has magnified. It can no longer be argued that the Palestinian Arabs are simply moving from one part of their cultural continuity to another.

Israel has achieved a degree of security that only borders of water can provide. But, in turn, it has inherited a degree of danger that only an "enemy within" can provide. In some measure, the one million Arabs now on United Nations Relief rolls, joined as they are by at least an equal number of Arabs caught in the net of the Israeli victory, potentially offer an acute case of the "left" or "right" substance of Israeli politics. A left solution would have to allow for the equal rights of the Arab peoples. Based on a population nearly equal in size to the Jewish inhabitants, the possibilities are there for a policy based on full enfranchisement of the Arabs in the political processes, bilingualism as an Israeli national policy, and restitution of Arab property which, by default, fell into Jewish hands at the end of the three-part Arab exodus. What is increasingly being urged by the Israeli political right is an adaptation of the original United Nations policy of making the portions of territory occupied by Israel (but lived in by Arabs) an "autonomous republic." The same conceit is urged of imposing a condition on Arabs that was imposed by the Soviet Union on the Jewish people in the '30's: they were "given" the autonomous Republic of Birobidjan, in an area and under conditions which guaranteed its ultimate failure. In this sense, the Zionist idea can issue into a Stalinist policy.

THERMIDOREAN REACTION?

The solution to the Arab refugee problem is contingent on the solution to the Jewish refugee problem. For in some measure, the question to be settled is: What kind of society is Israel, theocratic or democratic? From a sociological perspective, a great deal can be brushed aside in search of an answer. Israel is not a theocratic state, since it does not have as its ruling political directorate religious leaders. Yet the potency of the religious "zealots" can hardly be minimized, given the cultural stamp they implant on the nation.

The Thermidorean reaction may have been inevitable in a State surrounded by enemies determined on Israel's destruction, ruled by the same political apparatus since its founding, and for much of that time by one man as its hallowed national symbol. The incorporation of theocratic elements in the State's political structure, and the inclusion of religious parties in Israel's rule, also made such a reaction highly probable. There were, of course, other factors contributing to a general conservatizing of the State. Among these were the disquieting partial absorption of hundreds of thousands of refugees from Arab lands having neither political traditions nor the skills of mass participation; the remnants of a European Jewry psychologically unprepared and socially unwilling to support policies which would separate them from the policies decreed by the political leadership; the gradual identification of the Zionist movement with its most potent economic source, the American middle-class Jew; and, finally, a kibbutz movement gradually relegated to a marginal role in the enbourgeoisement of Israel's industrialization.

Nonetheless, a nervous peace had endured for ten years between Arab nations and Israel. For example, there had not been a major incident between Israel and Egypt until the June 1967 War. Shimon Peres, Moshe Dayan, and Ben-Gurion above all, the architects of the Sinai Campaign and of Israel's pro-Western and inflexible stance toward the Arabs, had left the government. In the confrontation between the new Rafi Party of Ben-Gurion and the old Mapai led by Eshkol, the latter won a clear electoral victory. Relations with the Soviet Union were improving; Eshkol had lifted military rule of Israel's Arab citizens; new initiatives and openings on the international scene were being explored.

Habib Bourguiba's hesitant but significant call for "realism" and re-examination of the Arab position on Israel, and similar statements in editorials appearing in *Jeune Afrique,* were the slightest indications that Israel might finally become a sovereign reality, an integral part of the Middle East, allowed to pursue a peaceful national existence. The June 1967 War and its aftermath have put an abrupt end to such hopes. The Arabs have become intransigent; the Israelis imperious.

The position we have taken leads to the ineluctable conclusion that Israel cannot possibly put forth recommendations for direct negotiations with the Arab belligerents that would be tolerated, much less entertained. Nonetheless, if Israel has made plain its desire for direct negotiations with the Arab States on a parity basis, it also served to weaken its case in the rest of the Third World. This it did as a result of its precipitous transfer of captured Soviet weaponry to the United States armed forces. *Time* magazine reported:

At bases in the Sinai and in Israel, the Israelis have been showing off some of the weaponry of Western technicians and, on at least one occasion, even lending it out. The United States sent transport planes to Israel to pick up three captured MIG-21's, the Soviet Union's best fighters. Two MIG-21's, the first ever to fall into United States hands, are being test-flown at Edwards Air Force Base in California. The third is being evaluated in laboratories at Wright-Patterson Air Base in Ohio. Since MIG-21's sometimes challenge United States pilots over North Viet Nam, the Air Force hopes to learn things that will be useful in the air war there.

Just why this loan or sale was made, whatever the quid pro quo may be, remains unexplained. Indeed, a rejection of the United States request for Soviet hardware could have performed two functions at one stroke: point up the genuine independence of the Israeli government from United States control and indicate the solidarity of Israel with the peoples of the Third World.

The entire Middle East is now on a vicious treadmill. The intransigence of the Arabs creates countervailing intransigence in Israel. The unbridled campaign conducted by the Soviet Union against Israel causes the Israelis to embrace United States economic aid even more fervently than before the Second Sinai campaign. Two decades of United Nations indifference to legitimate Israeli complaints has created an internal attitude in Tel Aviv to "go it alone." Under such circumstances, it is perhaps time for a transvaluation of values: let Jewish world opinion concentrate on imperatives for settlement (including a vigorous defense of Arab human and property rights), while Israeli political life would do well to begin an "agonizing reappraisal" of the obligations imposed on it as a result of its military successes. The rational ordering of geographic boundaries is one thing; the rational taming of passions quite another.

This is a time for testing. As the Soviet-German Pact of 1939, so, too, the Arab-Israeli War of 1967 separates out those who believe in a radicalism of slavish subservience to big-power ideologies and maneuvers from those whose radicalism is rooted in the destiny of free men to define their own future.

2 ISRAEL:
A SOCIAL AND
POLITICAL OVERVIEW

Judgments about the State of Israel are both easy to make and difficult to prove. The society represents a continuum with the ancient traditions of Judaism, yet at the same time it is one of the newest nations in the world. Under the circumstances, this excursion fare overview of Israel can only be an attempt at ethnography, a delineation of the context and characters I encountered when first traveling there in 1969, to deliver a set of lectures at the Hebrew University in Jerusalem.

I came to Israel and Jerusalem by way of Italy and Rome. A sharper contrast is hard to envision. In Rome, one can hear the night people, the seekers after *la dolce vita,* stumbling to bed at 6 A.M. in the morning—precisely the time when people in Israel are getting up to go to work. In Rome, in contrast to Northern Italy, it is unusual to find anyone who subscribes to the principles and premises of the Protestant work ethic, but in Israel one is hard pressed to find anyone who does not. What Werner Sombart once remarked of Jews in general seems particularly applicable to the Israelis: They are the last great embodiment of Puritanism.[1] Rome and the Via Veneto have no counterpart in Jerusalem; there, night clubs are few and far between, and late evening drinking establishments can be counted on one hand. If the maturity of a civilization can be measured by the amount of frivolity provided for, Israel is a very young society. With the exception of some desultory "tourist traps" in Tel Aviv, gambling, gaming, and gaiety are not characteristic. On the contrary, Israel has a seriousness and a high-minded purpose that one associates with revolutionary regimes, such as present-day Cuba, rather than with well-established European civilizations. Although one finds among Israelis a certain sophistication about the nature of revolution and about the limits of social change, this is the consequence, in large measure, of links to an ancient Hebrew civilization rather than the rapacious regime in modern Israel. To be sure, one finds in this land an ancient civilization and a modern nation-state standing not only side by side but engaging in an uncomfortable dialectic. This coexistence produces a national nervousness making Israelis more certain of their present than of their future—not an uncommon Jewish affliction.

ON THE "JEWISHNESS" OF ISRAELIS

The Israelis make much of their distinctiveness from the Jewish tradition, and stylistically there can be no doubt that Israel represents an amalgamation of peoples very different indeed from those typically considered Jewish types—usually European Ashkenazic immigrants. The Sabras, or native-born Israelis, are not so much a type but an anti-model—a direct assault on the representation of Jewishness as a hot pastrami on rye smothered in a mother's loving embrace.

Despite the ethnic plurality of the Israelis, certain characteristics of the Jewish tradition remain. (One hastens to note that these may also be characteristics of other peoples, not the least of all the Germans.) Like Jews, Israelis are noteworthy for their sobriety; they are serious and scholarly, almost self-consciously dedicated to the premise that upward mobility is guaranteed through education. Familialism and kinship ties are extremely strong among Israelis, as they are among Jews. In a city like Jerusalem, almost all "night life" goes on within the family circles or in the interpenetration of families sharing a common work life or kinship ties.

Since Jews may also be characterized by what they are not, abstinences among Israelis are also worth noting, primarily the absence of alcoholism and drug culture. The only "drug problem" is at Hebrew University in Jerusalem, and seemingly it is the result of the American Jewish contingent, one thousand strong and eight thousand miles away in spirit. Jerusalem has few drinking bistros; those which do exist are generally for tourists and foreign service diplomats who have tasted the joys of "cosmopolitanism" in other developed lands.

Aside from personality, more generic traits stamp Israelis as Jewish. Probably the most apparent, at least in my conversations, is their dialectical uncertainty of the future. Strong tendencies toward historicism abound in the everyday speech of ordinary people. There are also the customary and by now well-grounded Jewish trepidations and fears concerning annihilation and liquidation. Jacob Talmon has said that the Jews of Europe went to Israel to escape the ghetto, only to find that in a sense Israel is a monumental ghetto, surrounded by hostile Arab peoples who will not even recognize her national existence.[2] Stylistically, the gap between Israelis and Jews is wide and growing, but underlying continuities do seem present. As has been true for thousands of years, the ambiguity of Jewish existence is mitigated by the single-minded dedication of their enemies to annihilate Judaism as a whole.

ON JEWS AND SECULARISTS

There is a strong bifurcation between Hebraists and secularists. The Orthodox Jewish population seem only marginally concerned with the fate of Israel. A better way of putting the situation is that, although they are centrally concerned about Israel, they consider it a contaminated national State yet to be redeemed. From their point of view, the Redeemer has not arrived, either in Jerusalem or elsewhere. A clear manifestation of this attitude is the tendency of Orthodox Jews to train their children to speak Yiddish or any other European language rather than the sacred language. From the extreme orthodox point of view, those often found in the Religious League (*Agudat Israel*), speaking Hebrew as an everyday language is profane and represents a sinful rather than a necessary linguistic identification of religion and State. Yet, one is surprised by the paucity of visible theocratic overtones in the country.

The attitude of Israelis toward war and peace is opposition to war in principle and support for government policies toward the Arab nations in practice. The overwhelming majority of Israelis support the regime's "annexationist" approach. Major differences arise over what portion of the occupied lands should or even could be returned to Arab national sovereignty, but very few people seriously entertain even the possibility of "returning" Jerusalem to its pre-1967 status. Ordinary Israeli attitudes toward its right and left "ultras" is not atypical. Israelis see Orthodox Jews and Maoist Jews as people who want to live in and benefit from the Promised Land, but who at the same time, seek to escape duties to the State, and to impose minoritarian theological or political points of view upon the whole society. Most Israelis resent the Orthodox Jews for implying that Israel is not the sacred land, and for the unwillingness, particularly of the young Orthodox Jews, to enter into the mainstream of Israeli life, especially the "universal" military obligation. And still, the existence of such religious extremists serves to warrant the pluralistic nature of Israeli society.[3]

Strangely, Israel will accept the idea of cultural and national diversity but finds it extremely difficult to accept religious orthodoxy. I heard stronger anti-theological conversation during my stay in Israel than in any comparable period of time elsewhere, at least with respect to the religious commitment of Jews. It would be absurd to describe the Israelis' attitude as "anti-Semitic"; on the other hand, it is almost as difficult to define it as anything else.

If the intelligentsia will not accept the idea of binationalism or bilingualism with the Arabs, it also firmly rejects Jewish orthodoxy. Being an Israeli and a Jew still go together, but more tenuously than the outsider might imagine. Orthodox Jews are accused of everything from cowardice to betrayal; on the other hand, Orthodox Jews fire off equally sharp retorts about Israel. They resent Israel's propensities toward materialism and nationalism and all of the various twentieth-century secular frivolities that they feel have caused the deepest grief for Jews. Perhaps over time the sharpness of the controversy between Orthodox Jews and secular Jews will diminish. Many problems in history have been solved or resolved by an exhaustion of vitality in the controversy itself. To the degree that orthodoxy in Israel seems very much on the decline, or at least no longer able to exercise any profound political role, a resolution by obsolescence rather than by decision is likely to result.

The recent electoral combination of two major secular parties, *Mapai* and *Mapam,* has eliminated the religious parties from dominant political contention. They no longer provide the leverage that they have had in the previous twenty-five-year period, when the two major secular parties were separated and when the ruling *Mapai* was itself split into factions. Under relatively total mobilization, particularistic elements in Israel political life have diminished in importance. Even if religion continues to exercise a certain cultural domination, at least in terms of the formal rule system, the role of religious leaders is more analogous to the role of the Vatican in Italian affairs than of the clergy in Spanish life. Israel is not a theocratic state; but it does display a theocratic-veto effect over tendencies toward undiluted secularism.

The economic holdings of Orthodox Jewish groups are similarly limited. The real power of Orthodox Jews in Israel derives from their connection with Orthodox Jewish centers elsewhere in the world. Religious appeals abroad generate a considerable amount of financial support for Israel. Therefore, certain forms of direct support to the Orthodox sectors are still provided. But again, as a secular State, a sharp distinction is drawn between Israeli citizenship and the entirely volitional participation of Israelis in religious activities.

ON JEWS AND ARABS

The relationship between Jews and Arabs within Israel is a difficult matter to cope with at the observational level, especially for the outsider. One must first distinguish between the official Arab population in the new areas which were occupied by Israel after the Six-Day War in 1967 and the more established Arab communities that never left after the establishment of the Jewish State in 1948. The Arab population was estimated at a quarter of a million people prior to the Six-Day War, but would be closer to one million if the territories now held were incorporated into the State of Israel.

The Arabs of Israel are the blacks of the country. They work as laborers, menials, domestics. They play an important role in the building trades industry and in areas where heavy labor is a requisite. The Arabs represent "hard labor" just as assuredly as urbanized Israelis represent "head labor"—a class distinction not relished or even acknowledged by many Israelis, especially by the Labor Zionist groups which rest on socialist doctrine.

The avant-garde of the Jewish population is beginning to fear the growth of ethnic stratification within Israeli society. From the time of Chaim Weizmann to that of David Ben-Gurion Israel has been almost pathologically egalitarian, and even now one sees few either extremely poor or extremely wealthy people. This new phenomenon of a lower-class culture in the midst of Israeli "affluence" is a problem the society has not faced before.

The Arab nations' insistence on their Third World status makes one overlook the fact that, not only in rhetoric but also in basic forms of economic mixture, Israel is largely a socialist society. It is a society dedicated to principles of social egalitarianism as well as to a high degree of public ownership of basic means of production. The Arabs within Israel engendered a serious crisis of conscience even prior to the Six-Day War. Now, they represent a potential crisis of economy, since they are a greater asset in the private, Capitalist sector than in the public, Socialist sector.

Among the articulate liberal spokesmen for the Arab position—and there are surprisingly large numbers in journalism and in the Israeli Parliament (the Knesset)—there is the demand for full-scale egalitarianism and economic opportunity on a par with all other Israelis. Among the separatists, the minimum demand is for a distinct Palestinian state in which the Arab population would not only prevail in ecological and demographic terms but would assume control of state authority. This issue evokes bitter political disagreement, since in point of fact some Israelis would almost welcome and be relieved to see the formation of an independent Palestinian State in the occupied Jordan territory, or the Gaza Strip, or the Sinai Desert region. An independent autonomous Palestinian state, with friendly and cordial relations with Israel, would eliminate many Israeli fears about the future of their country as a Jewish State. On the other hand, those who argue for Jewish supremacy in Israel not infrequently oppose any move to divest what are referred to as the "new territories" from Israel.

And here we return to the paradox that one would have thought was resolved when Israel was established: namely, are Israelis different from Jews? With respect to the Arab "national question," being Jewish is of transcendental importance to the very definition of the Israeli state. Israelis want to have a secular State and do in fact have a secular society, yet they want to build into that definition of the secular State a religious criterion for participation. This problem has arisen in the past, and reappears continually in regard to Israeli citizenship, and what in fact constitutes organic statehood. This problem is unresolved in part because the larger question of the size, shape, and structure of Israeli society remains to be determined. Until that formation can occur in a less hostile environment, ambiguities will certainly continue to plague the State of Israel, as indeed they plague their Arab adversaries within Israel to almost the same extent.

ON MILITARY LEADERS AND POLITICAL LEADERS

Israel is certainly one of the most militarily mobilized societies that I have ever seen. The number of soldiers observed in the streets of Jerusalem is larger than in any country of Latin America or Western Europe. Not only is Israel a highly mobilized society, it is a society under arms. Soldiers walk around with *uzis,* portable, light sub-machine guns, made in Israel, clearly earmarked for immediate use if necessary.

On the other hand, despite large-scale show of military force, the amount of juvenile delinquency and illegal use of fire weapons is probably lower in Israel than in any other country in a comparable military position. One ministerial informant told me that there is not a single case on record of the personal abuse of weapons by any member of the Israeli armed forces, male or female. Since nearly every youth serves in a military capacity, this is a remarkable record. Though the comparatively huge numbers of weapons in the hands of ordinary people indicates a high degree of mass mobilization, the absence of illegal or unauthorized use of such weapons indicates the degree to which Jewish civilization underwrites Israeli society.

In this sense, Israel, like Cuba, is a society in which there is a democracy of the gun. The number of people under arms is a remarkable tribute to the solidarity of Israeli society, to the underlying unity of the population despite apparent cultural and religious diversities. For no society could dare arm so many of its citizens with such potent weapons if there were any fear of counterrevolutionary guerrilla activity. Al Fatah must reckon with a unified nation that provides little internal support to a counterinsurgency force. The Arab minority is sufficiently "convinced" by Israeli militancy; and the Jewish majority —even most of the small nationalist wing of the Communist Party—will reject any crude guerrilla war strategy focused on the Israeli nation.

One must describe Israeli society by the incongruous and almost ideologically apologetic phrase—military democracy. The State is firmly in the hands of civilian rule. Indeed, the Israeli Workers' Party, now simply the Labor Party, insures such a continuation. On the other hand, just as clearly, the military definition of the Middle East situation does contribute in no small part to the tempo and the style of Israeli society. This seemingly does not disturb Israeli politicians such as Levi Eshkol or Golda Meir, as long as military postures stimulate the Herculean labor effort of Israeli citizens.

A major by-product of Israeli militarization is accentuation of the overwhelming sense of a youth culture. One associates the military with the young. Whether the demographic characteristics are as youthful as they seem is hard to determine, but the degree of high morale and youthful determination is indisputable. The military culture helps define Israel as a young society and a modernizing society, precisely the characteristics that are attributed to developing countries in the Third World. This is particularly important in a political context where a virtual gerontocracy akin to China continues unabated. Thus Israel shares with Cuba the distinction of being a society virtually free of "rebellious" youth.

ON THE ROLE OF FOREIGN CAPITAL
IN ISRAELI SOCIETY

The amount of Jewish money that has been poured into Israel obviously has had a major impact on its development. Hardly any public building, Israeli monument, or any part of the physical plant of university life is untouched by Jewish funds, mainly collected in the United States, South America, South Africa, and in other parts of the world where Jews are permitted to make and export profits.

Those societies that have achieved rapid development during the twentieth century have all had to receive large foreign "donations" of money. The Soviets have supported Cuba as surely as American Jews have supported Israel. Yet, in many instances, foreign capital has been thrown in to support developing countries, and these nations have nonetheless been unable to develop. Soviet support for Egypt is at least equal to the contribution of American capital to Israel. Yet the growth rate and the quality of development in the two leading contenders for power in the Middle East are radically different. It is characteristic of societies that have developed in the twentieth century that either today or in the past they, like Israel, admit to a sense of being surrounded. The psychology of the minority, the desperation that the ordinary Israeli feels about his future, is also an enormous developmental input. It makes the people willing to accept lengthy working hours, a condition not typical of middle-class Jewish societies and just as clearly atypical of modern societies per se. The sense of being surrounded characterized Japan and the Soviet Union earlier in the twentieth century. It now characterizes Israeli society. The external factor may well be the most important element in the rapid development within the society. One cannot deny the role of foreign capital in Israeli development. But foreign capital can only be made developmentally productive and fruitful when the people involved feel threatened in, but content with, their society as a whole.

Even more important than foreign capital has been foreign sources of sophisticated labor. Israel is an immigrant society, and many immigrants who came to Israel brought with them all kinds of highly developed industrial skills and highly refined educational backgrounds. The slow but steady influx of Eastern European immigrants provided a sophisticated body of proletarians absent in other parts of the Middle East, and even in many parts of fully developed nations. If foreign inputs are viewed in a broad developmental perspective, it is evident that more important to Israel than foreign capital is sophisticated labor drawn from foreign "brain drains." But as has been noted, of supreme importance is Israel's sense of being surrounded and under constant threat of annihilation. This is, after all, how development takes place in the twentieth century—when models of the fully developed nations are a constant sore point, indeed a constant reminder, of how far one can get with technology and with ease of labor in place of raw labor power and long hours for the working class.

ON ISRAELI DEMOCRACY OF THE GUN

If one means by democracy the formal apparatus of a party structure subject to constituent constraints, then Israel certainly qualifies. It has regular elections; its system is unicameral and based on proportional representation within the multiparty system inherited from an English rather than an American model, which is natural enough, given the length of British occupation of the country. On the other hand, at the formal political level, Israel is also a nation which has been ruled from its inception by one party; and in this sense Israel is indeed a single-party State rather than a multiparty State. Israeli elections are not so much intended to bring about changes in the power structure but rather to legitimize the system.[4] Just as the Congress Party dominates India and the *Partido Revolucionario Institucional* also dominates Mexico, the Labor Party (created out of *Mapai, Achdut Avoda-Poalei Zion,* and *Rafi*) controls Israel's political fortunes. Other parties are tolerated and even appreciated, since at the same time there is no clear mandate for lasting one-party rule. Indeed, the limits of politics are determined by the intense changes in public opinion which take place after the elections. Although charisma is resented at a personal level, after so many years of dramatic figures at the top, the party charisma phenomenon is more entrenched than ever in Israel. The party apparatus, while easy to penetrate, remains the only means of achieving political influence either in Parliament or in extra-parliamentary military circles.[5]

There is an aspect of Israeli democracy which provides a much broader base. This is related to the kibbutz movement, democracy of the land, the egalitarian notions that have been embodied in Israel from the time Herzl announced a fusion of agrarianism, socialism, and Zionism. Not having seen many kibbutz operations, I find it difficult to speak of this part of the Israeli experience. However, even in the cities, there is an apparent egalitarian mode, a spillover from the kibbutz ethic, which goes far beyond the *Mapan* Party that is identified with the kibbutz. Even the wealthy are characterized by inconspicuous rather than conspicuous consumption. I think it is fair to say that there is more economic equalitarianism in Israel than there is political democracy. This is underscored by the military factor in Israeli society. No State could have such a large number of men and women under arms without thorough conviction that these arms will not be turned inward but will only be used against the external enemy. On the other hand, no State can be so heavily armed and yet tolerate the sorts of radical changes that are permitted under a democracy.

Democracy in Israel has to be measured against democracy elsewhere in the Middle East. By such a yardstick, Israel is the most democratic society in the area. It does not have the kind of feudal dictatorship that characterizes Arab countries such as Jordan; it does not have an elitist socialism that induces mass participation by coercion or excludes it nonexistent for the bulk of the people, as in Syria. The class differences that exist in Arab countries do not obtain in Israel. Indeed, the irony is that Israel is the only Middle East nation with not one but two Communist Parties, a Soviet wing and a Chinese wing; other countries in the area, the Arab countries outside of Iraq, apparently cannot tolerate even a single Communist Party.[6]

If democracy signifies libertarianism, an absence of terror, Israel is certainly a Democratic society. Nowhere in Israel is terror against the citizenry manifest, nor is there any fear of people being herded around and awakened at night or subject to forms of illegality and nightmarish brutality and corruption suffered by the Arab neighbors of Israel. Israel is a country where futuristic planning principles have been incorporated without overwhelming either the individual or the group.[7] I attended various left wing and university functions that clearly had the government's disapproval—all without incident or without fear of intervention. Indeed, post-electoral policy-making is far more significant than pre-electoral politics in Israel.

Here, too, one should probably make an exception of the Arab population. They do not seem to share either the general spirit of affluence of Israeli civilization or the general political democracy. The Arab population represents the low end on an economic stratification model, and it also represents a nonmobilized political sector of Israeli society, a constant source of the enemy from within. The refugee problem of Palestine Arabs of the Islamic faith only exacerbates this problem of the nonintegrated, non-Jewish sector. Until this problem is solved—and it looks as if it will be a long time before it will be recognized as a problem, much less resolved—one cannot say that the tasks of democracy in Israel have been or will be fully realized. A central pressure upon Israeli politicians to argue against rapid annexation of the newly won territories is precisely the widespread fear that the expansion in land would not be worth the increase in the Arab population within Israel. Only the counterpressures from Arab lands prevent this view from receiving more widespread attention.

ON ISRAEL AND THE THIRD WORLD

Israel is schizophrenic on the question of the Third World. It is a significant training ground for middle echelon personnel from throughout Africa, and yet maintains an exceedingly low profile about such support.[8] Perhaps, equally, the Third World is schizophrenic about Israel. At one level Israel shows all the hallmarks of a successful case of Third World development, the small nation succeeding in the empire of big nations. It is also an ethnically solidified nation succeeding in a world of dominant cultures that are always threatening to engulf it; finally, it has been able to establish an industrial base and a degree of economic autonomy that is the envy of many Third World nations; particularly in black Africa, which has a vested interest in a pluralistic North Africa in which the power of Islam does not go unchecked.

However, if Israel is envied by the Third World, it is also the scourge of that World, for it exposes the weakest segment of one of its largest chunks, the Middle East. The ambiguities of Third World response to Israel stem largely from Israel's realization of a modern technology and a modern scientific army that cannot only withstand pressures from large masses in the Third World but can actually emerge supreme in any military engagement. The three victories that Israel has chalked up against her Arab neighbors are a particular source of embarrassment and frustration for the Third World, since they have had the opposite effect of what the war in Vietnam has done to the United States. The war in Vietnam has exposed the weakness of a very advanced nation against an underdeveloped nation which has a single-minded, dedicated purpose; inversely, Israel has demonstrated that a single-minded, dedicated small nation is quite capable of handling its internal affairs and foreign affairs, of not only withstanding the informal pressures of its Third World neighbors but of pointing the way to the rest of the Third World as a developing area.

The Israeli handling of their success has been most encouraging; they are constantly going to Africa, India, and other parts of Asia and offering themselves as a model, at least to any of the parts of the developing world willing to listen. The African nations in particular have benefitted greatly from their relationship with Israel. Since there is no love lost between the black Africans and the Arab Africans—after all, the Arab sheikhs were the slave traders and the exploiters of black Africa for many centuries—one would have to admit that Israel wisely is making a great effort to link up with areas of the Third World that are not themselves directly menaced by the Israeli presence. What adds to this sense of Third World tranquility with respect to Israeli assistance is that such "aid" is based on personnel and expertise, not outright fiscal support or economic intervention.[9]

During my stay in Israel, I was unable to meet many of the people who interested me professionally for uniformly the same reason: they were in various parts of the Third World on teaching assignments or research expeditions or involved in educational activities with Third World nations that would hopefully be mutually beneficial to both societies. Israel is very much a part of the Third World, although it is hypocritically denied member status by many of the nations who themselves employ Israel as a model of success in a world of neo-colonialism. And while this denial of Israel in legitimation, but not in operation, is a major policy irritant to conservative Israelis identified with "America," for the most part Israeli officials are sophisticated, patient, and above all secure in their support of most sectors of the Third World.

ON SOCIAL SCIENCE IN ISRAEL

The social sciences are flourishing in Israel, for social scientists are uninhibited in their creative activities. The problems are the usual ones—great demands for increased teaching time and the paucity of funds for research. Also, there is a considerable number of students in the social sciences and not enough adequately trained professors, certainly not enough top quality professors. The social scientists I spoke to were quite disconcerted by anomalies and incongruities in their educational bureaucracy. University officials, at the Hebrew University at least, expected its professoriate to maintain a level of work and a performance in publishing typical of any topflight professor at an American university; yet their course load is considerably higher and their salary scale much lower. Furthermore, their research funds are at least half of what their American counterparts receive. Another problem is that Israeli scholars have few scientific journals in which to display their scholarship. They are therefore compelled to enter the international scholarly market to write and publish in English, which for some is extremely painful and difficult. Although Hebrew is the national language, the need to speak English, to write English, to read in English is so overpowering as to create considerable frustration for any but top, linguistically secure scholars; indeed, even among top scholars one senses a strong feeling that this Americanization of learning will end as the younger generation of Israelis learn Hebrew not only as a first language but practically and exclusively. The new generation are seemingly more concerned with Americans learning Hebrew than they are in learning English.

Many sociologists I met were deeply involved in problems of applied research and far more active in the general tasks of society than their American counterparts. At the highest level, people like Elihu Katz, an expatriate from the University of Chicago, is not only a professor of communications at Hebrew University but a former director of Israeli television—a fledgling of one year. His knowledge of communications from an applied perspective of day-to-day programming is quite different than what it once was on a purely theoretical and survey research level. Indeed, he confided that the problem he then had was applying any of his social science knowledge directly to his work as the Director of Israeli television. On the other hand, he typifies the spirit of applied social research one finds throughout Israel. Others, like Moshe Lissak, were involved in interrogation of Egyptian prisoners of war both after the second war in 1956 and the third war in 1967, while still others like Yonina Talmon combine theoretical concerns in social psychology with experimental activities on new kibbutz groups. Throughout the social sciences one finds top men and women engaged in applied research to a degree not found in the United States. Certainly anyone who desires to implement social science at the innovative level is encouraged to treat Israel as a wide open change laboratory. And the number of American social scientists of Jewish extraction who have taken up permanent residence in Israel is indicative of the openness of social science opportunity, at least as much as any general concerns over resettlement.

If some Israeli social scientists reveal alienated forms of work styles, this is not a consequence of any general separation from the tasks of Israeli society as much as it is the need to emulate certain standard values of professionalism largely taken over and internalized from the American social science establishments. The task of adapting professionalism to Israeli needs, and at the same time relating such goals to applied social research, is indeed the challenge of the moment. As things now stand, the publish or perish (in English, no less!) system is as rigid in Israel as in this country; while the work or worship system is as rigid in Israel as it can be anywhere else in the world.

ON THE ISRAELI LEFT WING

It is really difficult to speak of the Israeli left and right in the conventional way that one speaks of left and right elsewhere, since from left to right, with the exception of the solitary Maoist member in the Knesset and The New Communist List *(Rakach)*, it is taken for granted (even by the Israel Communist Party founded in 1919), that Israel society must be defended at all costs against "Arab aggression," or at least anticipated Arab aggression. Once the assumption is made about the national needs and unity of Israeli society, the rhetoric of the dominant parties, being socialistic, can at the same time be considered as representing the left wing position.[10] The alignment of centrist and left wing parties, embracing the *Mapai, Mapam,* in conjunction with the General Confederation of Labor *(Histadrut)*, has retained power in Israel for fifty years. Parties come and go, but the "government of national unity" remains the chief coalitional force ruling Israeli political fortunes.

Israel professes a labor core. Therefore, to speak of its left wing is not to refer to a marginal group outside the social system, such as teachers or professors or retired members of the Socialist Party, but to the dominant wing of the government. In this sense Israeli society is a left wing society; and its difficulties in absorbing atavistic militarism are as much a consequence of Socialist ideology as of Hebrew theology.

Israel is also a left wing society for fundamental economic reasons: the vast redistribution of wealth in the country and the absence of a financial oligarchy that carries any political weight. Men of wealth in Israel run hotel chains and newspaper combines, but they carry far less political influence proportionate to their wealth than the wealthy group in nearly any other society in the Western world. Beyond that, the progressive tax structure also acts as a real brake on the amassing of individual or familial fortunes.

Thus, in defining the left, as in all other issues concerning Israel, a paradox emerges. On one hand, a left characteristic of the new student movement in the United States or of the Maoists in China hardly exists in Israel; on the other hand, given that the entire society defines itself primarily in laborist terms, the Israeli left is the dominant wing of the society. But underneath the labels is an essentially conciliatory spirit more characteristic of British political institutions than American consensus politics.

The Israelis have nowhere to retreat and nowhere to run. For them, the holocaust is a living memory, but not a future possibility. Only they and the Japanese know the emotional turmoil brought about by near total destruction. For such a people death is simpler than defeat, and tragically, for such a people victory is less meaningful than survival. Each citizen of Israel has a story of personal tragedy and triumph. Israel seems a collective representation of these personal biographies. That is why each death in an encounter with guerrillas cuts so close to the marrow. The pragmatics of survival have a way of transcending in importance the incongruities of nation-building.

ON ISRAELI NATIONAL SURVIVAL

The issue of survival is moot. If it refers to short run survival, the answer is clearly that Israel can, does, and will survive. Indeed, it displays by all odds an expanding economy and an expansionist polity. It has moved great numbers of people into desert regions, occupied territories, disputed regions, and it has sought to establish clearly defined and clearly defensible boundaries. In short, Israel behaves like any other nation—particularly any other Third World nation in search of the "mark of sovereignty"—the military; the "symbol of sovereignty"—the State. If anything, Israel can be faulted far more readily for behaving like the rest of the Third World than for being a puppet of the United States or any other colonial or imperial interests.

Like the rest of the Third World, Israel tends to disguise united political rule behind the facade of multiparty democracy; it believes in nationalist solutions rather than spiritual ones; and it suffers from export-import deficits characteristic of the Third World in general. The costs of becoming a nation have been particularly severe for Israel, because the Jewish people have a long, well-articulated tradition of existing outside of national forms. The recognition that nations—especially new nations—behave in ways not always to the liking of the leaders much less the followers comes hard—and is hard to accept by ideologists. Like India in 1948, Israel began life as a nation with a traditional philosophy scarcely suited for national existence in the second half of the twentieth century. As a result, critics of Israel have a peculiar quality, be they left or right, of demanding exceptional behavior precisely because of these traditions.

This may well work to the long-run detriment of Israel. That is to say, the separation of Israeli Jews from Diaspora Jews may become so complete, and so irrevocable, that the gap cannot be any longer minimized. Indeed, even now differences are obvious. On the way to Israel (via Rome) I found it hard to discern Jews from Israelis. On the return flight, not only was I able to discern differences between the Tel Aviv Jew and the New York Jew; I found myself taking pride in the ability, along with others, to make the distinction. It was a difference in the psychological aspects of nationhood that for want of a more adequate phrase we sometimes called "national type." The Israeli has worked hard at creating a national type. He changes his name, alters his living habits, takes on mannerisms and *macho* conceits that clearly separate him from the classic

models of European and American Jewry. Indeed, it sometimes seems that the "rest of the Jews" are an anti-model, a
negative ideal type. In place of meekness, arrogance. In place
of talmudic dialectics (on the one hand and then again on the
other) an air of decisiveness and scientism prevails. In place of
a moral premium on survival by any means is a new emphasis
on the warrior instincts. That these traits can be and are dif-
ferentially weighed is one thing—that the Israeli has undergone a radical transformation is quite beyond conjecture.

As for long-range survival, I would also say that Israel possesses many advantages over those Arab adversaries who wish
to see Israel perish. We are in a period of history when numbers no longer uniquely determine power. And hence, what
Arie Eliav refers to as the Arab "crusader complex" of their
numerical superiority of 100 million vs 3 million, no longer
works.[11] Quite the contrary: large numbers may invoke large
responsibilities and unfulfilled dreams. Israel is a compact,
closely knit society. This provides advantages from military
logistics to shared psychological perceptions. Israelis sense that
they are alone—and share uniquely in past Jewish tragedy.
They also differ from Jews of old in that they possess a unique
destiny as well.

Temporary difficulties in the Israeli economy notwithstand-
ing, the growth in export and trade, in national per capita consumption, in commodity production, in the amenities of life,
have all been stupendous over the last twenty-five years. If ad-
versity is the handmaiden of modernization, there can be no
doubt that Israel will survive; and if perversity is the hallmark
of the Israeli citizen, there can likewise be no doubt as to national survival. Perhaps the real question of the moment that
takes on tragic dimensions with the passing of the twentieth
century is whether the Jews can survive as a religion *and* as an
ethnic group distinct from all others.

It is high irony that at a time when the rest of the world is
asking itself whether Israel can really survive in a hostile en-

vironment of nonrecognition and constant defiance, the Israeli is asking himself whether the Jews can survive in an environment of quasi-Jewish celebration, and celebration for the wrong sorts of things (such as middle-class life styles and educational upward mobility).

The existence of Israel has made the lot of the non-Israeli Jew more paradoxical, rather than more difficult. He must always take into account profane estimates of what any given set of political parameters means to the survival of a foreign nation, yet he must also become aware that the very survival and expansion of that foreign nation may in fact fossilize the Jew (in ways Toynbee never dreamt of) with a greater finality than any past tragedies suffered and endured. The Jew remains a dialectical creature. In the past, his survival depended upon the good will of non-Jews and other nationals; now it depends upon the good sense of Jews and foreigners. Thus, just as the survival of the Arab peoples ultimately depends upon their own activities and attitudes, the survival of Israel depends on the activities of all the peoples of the Middle East. They will live together, or they will perish together. It is nonsense to imagine that they will conquer each other or vanquish each other. The passions of nation-building are too deep for this to happen, while the reasons adduced for mass slaughter are too shallow for mutual annihilation to occur.

3 THE ARAB "NATION" AND THE JEWISH "STATE" CONVERGENCE AND CONFLICT IN THE MIDDLE EAST

The integrity of the Middle East and the morphology of its problems are defined by the interaction of Islam and Israel and not just by the economic systems or military maneuverings among the nations in the area. The Arab-Israeli dispute is a question of the politics of nationalism and the delimitation and delineation of the Third World as a whole. Ultimately, the dispute is over dependence and independence, a feeling shared by both Arab nations and Israel that entirely too much history of the area is determined by big-power manipulation and management. In a strange way, Israelis and Arabs both have a powerful sense of betrayal by the European powers, and it carries over into a hearty disdain for settlement of current disputes by outside forces. What makes the situation less than attractive is that, despite this shared animus for big-power domination, there remains a fear that Arab powers are directed from Moscow, while Israeli activities are managed from Washington. As a consequence, neither side is especially prepared to enter direct negotiations without hesitation, although for Israel this posture is a strategy, whereas for the Egyptians, Syrians, and Jordanians it is a firm principle.

Moses, the deliverer of the Hebrew children from Egyptian bondage, was himself an Egyptian prince. Whatever the special conditions concerning his origins, background, and ethnic identity, this duality is not without its symbolic meaning in defining the relationships between the Islamic and Hebrew peoples. And despite the patina of humanism attached to the Ten Commandments in later times, the Mosaic Laws are not that remote from the Egyptian Laws of Rameses. The sense of law prevailing over justice, of severity of punishment rather than forgiveness for the transgressor, of quite diabolical forms of the principle of an eye for an eye are too well known to require documentation or to invite repudiation.

What we have in terms of symbolic history, and perhaps actual history as well, is a contest of wills between two peoples with one idea of statecraft. It is a fallacy to assume that the Arab cause is representative of authoritarian modes, while Hebrew law sanctions democratic modes. There was never any contest between authoritarian and democratic political styles, only whether the Hebrew peoples were fit subjects to endure slavery. That slavery was a mixed blessing for the conquering Egyptians is documented by 400 years in which the Hebrews conducted an active resistance and passive and active sabotage. In this sense, the victory of Moses was a natural outcome of an untenable situation for masters and slaves alike. The problems of a slave society were burned deep into the Jewish consciousness, not as a response to democratic ideals but as a response to the pragmatic breakdown of slavery in Egypt. Thus, from the outset, Arabs and Jews confronted each other in a double interchange system, representing competing forms of national liberation but with a shared belief in strong leadership, chiliastic purpose, and a political stratification system guaranteed to tease out a bare existence from arid lands.

Any serious discussion of the political dynamics of the Middle East must extend beyond considerations of geopolitics, and even beyond an overall consideration of the Third World. It must deal specifically with Arabs and Israelis. This said, there are certain links between Israel and Arab nations, whether or not they like to think they share them. They share in common a shopping-center attitude toward political systems of the West. The entire area is rich in religious and cultural tradition, but the Middle East is new to nation-building and sovereign political rule. Although there is a long and strong tradition of Arab political theory and practice, the problems of modern rule have been complicated by an ill-defined class structure and by extremely uneven types of socioeconomic development. Thus, while there exists a rich variety of political analysis and political theory, the Arab world, because of the colonial experience, did not really have a nation-building problem until the twentieth century; and in this, Arab nations have a similar problem to that of the early Zionist settlements: what should be the structure of government?

The Israelis and the Arabs have purchased their model of government from different places. The Israelis bought a multiparty system, which in fact is a uniparty kind of government, whereas many Arab states reveal a tendency toward uniparty rule and multigovernment activity. Israeli political parties show clear differentiation along class and religious lines, yet they maintain a relatively strong degree of internal cohesion, whereas the Arab states tend to have a single-party apparatus but severe innerparty differentiation—in part derived from the socialist model. Therefore, each side has purchased political theory and political systems from abroad.

This political purchase has had different consequences for Jews and Arabs. The Jewish community, uprooted from other areas throughout the world, set about creating social conditions that could accommodate such inherited diversities. The parliamentary style was thus a consequence of new social relationships that were best met by a system that guaranteed both mass and popular support and that left intact the continuity of Ashkenazic leadership in the new terrain. The Arab situation was quite different: new political forms were superimposed on traditionalist socioeconomic structures. As Don Peretz pointed out, "Although the new nationalist leaders were eager to use Western political forms—often perhaps because they indicated a 'modern' approach—few desired to alter fundamental social relationships. Thus Western-type parliaments, political parties, and other institutions were adopted not only to increase the power of the rising middle class, but also to keep political power from the hands of the peasantry and urban proletariat."[1]

There is a special sense in which the terrorism of Jewish guerrillas conducted during the Mandate period was dictated by regional considerations. One writer notes that Jewish groups "tore a page out of the Arab Nationalist Manual and launched a campaign of political terrorism against the persons and property of the mandatory power."[2] What one repeatedly finds among the Israelis is a powerful isomorphism with their Arab adversaries at the level of strategy and tactics. A basic source of frustration is how this utilization of shared strategies and tactics has benefited Israelis more than Arabs. And here the superior level of Israeli economic industrialization and social organization have had a telling effect. There is simply no substitute for the sorts of industrializing impulses, commercial values, and social egalitarianism displayed by Israelis and lacking in Arabs. The treatment of Arab women—the wearing of the veil, their seclusion in the home, a lack of social roles outside the home—contrasts markedly with Israeli women, who have a shared sense of common destiny in every area from military to political rule.

One cannot exaggerate the claims of ideological similarities without falling prey to Panglossian excess. There is an emotional layer of reality quite beyond formal criteria. And at this level the disparities between Israelis and Arabs are greatest. At the core, Israeli society is "Western" in social structure and value system, whereas Arabic societies are much less linked to such Western values. Whether this is indeed a terrible loss for the Arabs in terms of their ability to withstand Israeli might

is debatable. Westernization is certainly easier for a complicated, sophisticated system of military commitments to absorb
than for a society still clinging to traditional class and caste
divisions. Yet, it remains the case that nothing intrinsic to the
area or its peoples necessitates mutual destruction, and much
argues for mutual cooperation.

A peculiar unifying thread between Arabs and Jews is what
might be termed political restorationism. Both these peoples
were involved in the re-creation of civilizations once greater
and more sweeping in power than those in the present century.
The restoration of cultural glory is, however, but one aspect
of the peculiar State institutions they have created. Putting
aside for the present the debate concerning "Israeli democracy" versus "Arab socialism," it is clear that for both a theocratic element is present in State authority. Unlike the European post-medieval tradition in which the "King's Two
Bodies" of Church and State became firmly and finally separated, both Islamic and Hebraic traditions disallow such a complete isolation of religious ethnicity from political rule. And if
this very common thread sharpens the specific antagonism between the two cultures of the Middle East, it does have the
reverse impact of linking the two in an alternative vision of
the political society as carrying a potential for a good society.
Here the restorationist element, while serving as a clear break
on a simple gathering together with the Semitic flock, indicates
that some sort of international twin-track coalition is at least
possible, when seen in terms of the respective political systems
now existent in the Middle East.

An isomorphism in fundamental values between Arab national and Zionist claims extends beyond politics to ideology.
The degree to which moral law determines Arab consciousness
is matched point by point by Israeli "exceptionalism," which
is likewise a product of a special fusion of nationalism and the
religious consciousness. The statement of Muhammad Asad,
on "The Principles of State and Government in Islam," could

just as readily summarize a considerable sector in Israeli thinking about the moral center of the political State:

It has become evident that none of the contemporary Western
political systems—economic liberalism, communism, national
socialism, social democracy, and so forth—is able to transform that
chaos into something resembling order: simply because none of
them has ever made a serious attempt to consider political and
social problems in the light of absolute moral principles. Instead,
each of these systems bases its conception of right and wrong on
nothing but the supposed interests of this or that class or group or
nation—in other words, on people's changeable (and, indeed, continuously changing) material preferences. If we were to admit that
this is a natural—and therefore desirable—state of man's affairs, we
would admit, by implication, that the terms "right" and "wrong"
have no real validity of their own but are merely convenient fic-
tions, fashioned exclusively by them and socioeconomic circumstances. In logical pursuance of this thought, one would have no
choice but to deny the existence of any moral obligation in human
life: for the very concept of moral obligation becomes meaningless
if it is not conceived as something absolute. As soon as we become
convinced that our views about right and wrong or good and evil
are only man-made changeable products of social convention and
environment, we cannot possibly use them as reliable guides in our
affairs. . . . No nation or community can know happiness unless
and until it is truly united from within; and no nation or community
can be truly united from within unless it achieves a large degree of
unanimity as to what is right and what is wrong in the affairs of men;
and no such unanimity is possible unless the nation or community
agrees on a moral obligation arising from a permanent, absolute
moral law. Obviously, it is religion alone that can provide such a
law and, with it, the basis for an agreement, within any one group,
on a moral obligation binding on all members of that group.[3]

One might argue that such absolutisms are the curse and not
the cure for both Israel and Islam. But that is hardly the point.
The main aspect of this isomorphism is how similarities between Islamic and Hebraic doctrines about the State do in fact
enter into the ideological mainstream. This is itself a cause of
fanaticism, since neither side is especially prone to "pragmatic"

thinking about State and society. The continuation of the theocratic tradition as an element in Islamic and Hebraic traditions is thus a root factor in the proximity of Arab and Jewish consciousness, and also a cause for apprehension, since just such moral absolutism creates the seeds for intense rivalry and protracted conflict.

Arabs and Israelis pay homage to the idea of socialism, but both groups have a much more theocratic conception of the public ownership of the means of production than was formerly deemed realistic. The large private sector, the utilization of personal gain, and respect for individual limits is important to both Arabs and Israelis. The main difference is that for the Israelis the idea of socialism is largely connected to tasks of economic, especially rural, reconstruction, while for the Arab States the idea is largely political—to maintain a political dialogue from within rather than changing anything externally. Socialism thus becomes a long-range demand for equity in human relations rather than a series of immediate demands connected to national class struggles. Of course, in both Middle East sectors, socialism as class struggle is raised by various and sundry parties and groups, but it is plain that "socialism" becomes a term of consensus and integration rather than a rallying cry for revolutions yet to be fought.

A political issue common to Israel and Islam is legitimacy itself. The problem of legitimacy for Israel is that, in theory or in fact, Israel views itself as a ghetto surrounded by states that do not recognize her sovereignty. Israel is the only nation in the world whose common borders are with nations which do not recognize her sovereign right to exist. On the other hand, the Arabs have the problem of establishing legitimacy in a more grandiose form. The Arab "nation"—considered as a single entity by many—represent a long and large land mass which is being constantly humiliated by the "ghetto" most pointedly on the battlefield. Arab nations must also deal with national borders often set by colonizing European powers rather than ones based on natural cultural distinctions. Thus both sides in the Middle East struggle consider themselves subject to political and military indignities; and both sides view themselves as the true source of area-wide liberation. The fact that within the Arab World a "third force" Palestinian view has arisen only sharpens the intensity of feelings, but it does not lessen the common legacy of defeat.

Then, too, there is the staggering problem in the area of the inter-connection of politics and religion. It is impossible to talk about the Middle East without recognizing that at one and the same time we must contend with problems of religion and problems of the State. The recent chain of Israeli Supreme Court rulings "liberalizing" the official definition of Jewishness; and the countermanding of those rulings by the Knesset under the impact of its religious orthodox segment, indicates that the question of Jewish identity, both on a personal level and at a policy level, is sobering and difficult to establish with precision.[4] The quality of secularism in Israel, the character of the State, and the integrity of its people are constantly at stake and constantly being reviewed. Similarly, the problem of religion in politics plagues many Arab states. The Ba'athist Party is perhaps a classic example of the relationship between religiosity and socialism in the Middle East—between the socialism of a whole people, based on certain religious premises, and the character of socialism, which, after all, involves a kind of highly secularized and modernized process. Both Israel and the Arab powers have similar contradictions between their secular and clerical factions. The attacks on the Muslim Brethren by the late Gamal Abdel Nasser were at least as strong and deeply motivated as the attacks on the National Religious Party made by Moshe Dayan. The experience of modernization in a cultural milieu that displays mixed feelings about how "far" sexual equality or the rights of marginal groups can be carried without destroying the presumed moral-religious basis of such states is similar in both Islamic and Hebraic contexts—although with special nuances in each instance.

There can hardly be any doubt that this emphasis on "consensual" elements between Arabs and Israelis flies in the face of dominant ideological persuasions held by influential Islamic elites. Two myths in particular deserve to be laid to rest: first, that the sum total of common language, literature, customs, traditions, and character somehow add up to "an Arab nation" with a common interest.[5] Whatever else might be said about the Middle East, the idea that being an Arab is sufficient to determine an Arab State is belied by the existence of diverse States with distinct interests. The other myth is that Arabs "are unanimous in considering Israel as the first danger, and Arab nationalism today is emphatic that Israel is a mortal peril, not only because it usurped a vital part of the Arab homeland (the Holy Land), but also because it is a real menace threatening other parts of the Arab homeland."[6] The idea of a Greater Islam, like that of a Greater Israel, serves no peaceful purpose; and in fact, is simply unrealistic in terms of the overall needs of the Middle East.

The emergence of a special Palestinian element, with claims against Israel and the contiguous states within the Arab orbit, has further served to throw into sharp relief the difference between cultural claims to organic unity, and political and economic claims to distinctness. Egypt, Syria, Jordan, Lebanon, no less than Israel, represent recognized sovereign States—with a common monetary, legal, and military framework. The Palestine Liberation groups confront the Arab nations with a serious threat to the monopoly of coercive authority that has always been an identifying hallmark of the State. The crisis in King Hussein's Jordan was even greater in 1971 when challenged by the Palestine exile groups than by the 1967 reintegration of Jerusalem under Israeli rule. If Israeli military pressures provided the impulse for Jordanian military action, it also provided the ruse whereby the Al Fatah threat to Jordan's State power was successfully countered. This is not to pass judgment on the claims of Palestine's Arabs on a place in the Hashemite empire; it is to say that the Palestinians become a "problem" to Arab nations precisely because they do not share the essential characteristics of State power. Raw military strength is a necessary, but not sufficient, part of such State power. It is small wonder that for Arab militants, specifically the Fatah type of insurgents, the "priority" of doing away with Israel sometimes seems less imperative than the elimination of traditionalist Arab states.[7]

It is difficult to argue with Vatikiotis' conclusions that in the early seventies the Palestinian guerrillas underwent a self-imposed disintegration. The act of fighting Jordan was "an act of self-immolation." In lacking both a mass base and State authority, the Palestinian guerrillas were traumatized and fragmented.

One of the original obstacles to the success of the Movement was that it tried to operate in an actively inhospitable environment; in states which were determined not to make room for it. It was also obstructed by trying to operate in an equally inhospitable *popular* milieu: in Lebanon, Jordan, Egypt, and even the West Bank. Without a massive popular commitment to the Movement's objectives by Palestinians in Lebanon, Jordan, the West Bank—anywhere—let alone the massive popular commitment of other Arabs to it, the chances of its success as then constituted were almost non-existent. Unfortunately for the Palestinians their Liberation Movement after June 1967 did not only fail militarily. It rashly forgot the lessons of their earlier performance in the conflict, particularly in the thirties and forties: it failed to constitute itself as a *political* movement with clear, realistically defined interim objectives, which could eventually pre-empt the representative role for all Palestinians in any confrontation or dialogue with the Israelis. In that way it could have hoped to command the serious attention not only of the Israelis but also of the regional and international parties involved in this tragic conflict. For it should be pointed out here that at no time between June 1967 and 1971 did the Palestine Liberation Movement enjoy the support of the pro-Arab super-power, the Soviet Union.[8]

But in this very fact the basis of area rapprochement increased considerably. The pressure for overt military action by the Arab nations against Israel declines precisely to the degree that the Palestinian Liberation movement fragmented and became reduced to isolated enclaves in Lebanon—picking targets of attack remote from Israel and even counterproductive to Arab efforts at garnering world opinion for its own cause.

A central problem of the Palestinian insurgents is that they identify both with the "Arab nation" as a whole and with village life inside Israeli-held territories. The sense of a firm Palestinian national identity has thus been absent in the past, and it is hard to create in the present. In the forging of a Palestinian ideology, in part to overcome this lag effect, the terrorist leadership has chosen a rhetoric of zero-sum game, in which Israel is provided no alternative to self-liquidation. Under the circumstances, Israeli dismissal of Palestinian Arab claims is part of a larger effort to prevent any sort of disintegration of the idea of Israel as a Jewish homeland (wherever those Jews originally emigrated from). Ronald Segal[9] has aptly pointed out that even in a narrowly defined Palestinian context there are sharp differences between Moslem Arabs living in the Gaza Strip and their more affluent brethren living in the West Bank region, and that there are huge gaps between Bedouin bureaucrats in Basman Palace and guerrilla pronouncements from the street of Amman. His conclusion is sobering: "Nearly all Palestinian Arabs may yearn for the disappearance of Israel and the restoration to them of all the lands that they once inhabited. But experience has taught many of them that this yearning may prove a trap, in which the refusal to accept any less becomes the occasion for losing even more."

The problem of sovereignty is endemic to the dilemmas faced by the Palestinians. For in addition to flying in the face of existing realities, that there is an entity called the Israeli State, the very existence of a Palestinian movement with national ambitions threatens the Arab States. As Quandt[10] recently noted: "A guerrilla movement with a substantial popular base, an activist social political program, and a viable military force would present an intolerable challenge and threat to the existing political systems in Jordan, Lebanon, and

Syria, and is therefore bound to clash with the central authorities. The stronger the movement grows, the more destabilizing a factor it becomes, both as a radical, militant challenger on the internal political scene, and as a potential trigger of large scale Israeli reprisals against the host country's territory."

The "Palestinian Question" is illustrative of the limits of Pan-Arabism, and of the continued compelling power of national claims in the Middle East. Palestinians have become "wandering Arabs," not entirely certain of their place within the larger Islamic universe and locked out of the Israeli universe; or, more accurately, they are permitted participation only to the extent that existing forms of sovereignty go unchallenged. The Israeli posture is not to deal with the Palestinians because they have no legal status, whereas the Arab governments deal with the Palestinians as "visitors" in a "host" nation and not as equals. For the Palestinian enclave to achieve special rights within the Jewish State is possible, but only to the extent that Jewish minority groups have their rights reestablished, or better restored, in the Arab lands. This in turn would undoubtedly be coupled with a general peace settlement. And because it is highly unlikely that either Egypt, Lebanon, or Syria will move in this direction, it is likewise unrealistic to expect any overtures to the minority Palestinians for a restoration of their special claims. In short, precisely because firm claims of sovereignty have not been assured to the parties involved, the political problems of the Middle East become exceedingly difficult to resolve.

Even were the last guerrilla insurgency camp in Lebanon to be eliminated, the Palestinians would remain a living, suffering reality. Jordan has no more intention of divesting itself of any legal claims over the West Bank region than does Israel intend to simply restore the status quo ante by divesting itself of any military claims over this area. But in a sense, this makes possible a Palestinian place in the sun—either through the establishment of a binational state in Israel or of an independent

Palestine which would not involve military armaments.[11] It is significant that the "Arab nation" like the "Jewish nation" is a symbolic entity; that in fact there are many Arab *States* and one Jewish State—Israel. The tortured rhetoric in this area reflects precisely the inability to translate de facto into de jure—into legitimacy. But when such a larger understanding is reached, then the question of the Palestinian Arab people can be resolved without resort to yet another round of armed hostilities.

Without assuming the burdens of geographical determinism, the fact does remain that the Middle East is a real entity that embraces Israel no less than the Arab States.[12] The discussions often are in terms of presumed analogies. And while these structural similarities are real enough, so too are the differences. But what is overriding are the quite real needs that can only be met by the area as a whole: dam construction, irrigation, expansion of farming lands, water resources generally.[13] Military tensions in the area prevent such forms of cooperation. But should priorities be radically exchanged for both Israel and the Arab States, then far greater attention could be given over to methods for achieving significant economic growth. The composition of investment in a technological age necessitates an increase in know-how and in scientific education. And it is in these areas that Israel might yet prove most helpful to its Arab neighbors. It has the highest proportion of skilled manpower, expertise, and specialization in the Middle East, while the Arab States have the physical terrain and mineral riches with which to convert such skills into modern communities. The reality of past wars and the rhetoric of future wars obscure the elemental fact that Israel and its Arab neighbors have not only a common past but a shared destiny.

That this sense of commonality was understood by the inhabitants of the area in the past is attested to by the fact that prior to the emergence of the State of Israel the feelings of Jews and Arabs, while perhaps not intimate, were nonetheless cordial enough. Basic forms of economic and social cooperation did exist during the Mandate period. And there are few gleanings in the Zionist literature of the earlier era that would indicate even a dim awareness of crisis and conflict between the two Semitic peoples. In part, this was a function of Jewish blindness to the real and felt rights of Arab inhabitants of the Palestinian terrain; but in larger part it was a widely shared belief amongst the settlers that Zionism and Arabism were compatible ideological styles for reaching the same institutional aims: entrance into the industrial world of the West.

While it may seem a serious exaggeration to emphasize similitudes between Israelis and Arabs, the historic fact is that the early Zionists, and not a few Arab leaders as well, perceived Jewish resettlement of the Palestinian lands as a blessing for both peoples. It is a remarkable fact of history how few members of the early rural Zionist settlements even perceived of the Arabs as potentially hostile, much less the main danger to Jewish migration. There was a general feeling, even a consensus, that, once the approbation of European powers were obtained, then the rest would be axiomatic. It might be argued that this very imperviousness to Arab sense and sensibility was itself a contributing factor to the ferocity of the conflict between Arabs and Jews for the land of Palestine. From the Arab side, it was not so much the peopling of Palestine with Jews that proved an irritant as it was the transformation of Jewish peoplehood into Israeli Statehood. For at this point the antagonism became quite modern, even European, involving State power and national liberation. On this matter, Arabs and Jews were agreed only on the importance of the subject, not on the nature of the political resolution.

The relationships between the Arab States and the Soviet Union and between Israel and the United States are certainly vital questions for all nations in the area, because they define the thirdness of the Third World as the problem of nationalism: that is, the right of these nations not only to exist as sovereign States but as autonomous in their development process. The deepening of the Arab-Israeli military crisis stimulates a political crisis of identity, a crisis of who rules and the terms of rule in these nations. The physical departure of the older European powers from the Middle East created a void in which the Soviets were able to penetrate the Arab world in a fundamental way, while the United States was compelled, often against its will to underwrite the survival of the Israel State.[14]

Even the fact of mutual antagonism between Arab States and Israel has a peculiar binding effect. There can be scarcely any doubt that the high degree of cohesion among Israelis is artificially supported by the sense of immediate and direct threat. The normal tendencies of Jews to disagree and divide into groups have been prevented from taking place and thus have dampened the democratic political processes. The present seem frozen in respect to parties, political coalitions, and the relative absence of broad based new mass social movements. And if this is the situation for Israel, it appears to be even so for the Arab States, for the very assumption that the Israeli question must take an a priori precedence over the Herculean tasks of economic development and social integration leads to a condition in which sheiks, militarists, religious leaders, students, and the new bourgeoisie develop forms of collaboration that are as artificial as they are unworkable. These coalitions have the effect of freezing Arab societies at a point in time when the degree of their dependency on American, Soviet and European capital is more urgently required than is Arab oil in these more advanced sectors.

The Arab-Israeli dispute, by its very intensity and all consuming nature, leads to an artificial freezing of social and economic processes, the consequences of which are mutually disastrous and dangerous. The possibility of an end to the Cold War in the Middle East must thus be linked to the possibility for a major renovation of social classes in the Arab lands and new openings in the political and social structures in Israeli society. The growing recognition that the current situation has the potential for progressive as well as destructive changes may yet serve to soften the contours of conflict and lead to an era of reconciliation and reconstruction. As one prominent Arab Israeli put matters:

One key to a better future undoubtedly lies with the Middle Eastern element in the Israeli setup. These Jews, whose historical circumstances spared them the experiences of being cooped up in ghetto-like enclaves, have had a long and firm tradition of dealing and discoursing with their Arab neighbors, and often took an active part in public affairs of the countries in which they dwelt. An Israel in which this important element gets its full shape of responsibility and leadership will have a substantially different image of her neighbors and may thus be the better able to attain a meaningful coexistence and mutually beneficial cooperation with them.[15]

Islam and Israel are two poles of the Semitic tradition. And if this fact may provide slender comfort at the moment, and certainly no sufficient cause for preventing hostilities, it nonetheless represents a factor of considerable significance. For in discussing the similarities of the two peoples, we are not necessarily declaring the impossibility of controversy or conflict. Indeed, sibling rivalries are often the most bitter. Yet, there is the fact that Arabic is the second most widely spoken language in Israel, and that more than one-half million Arabs live and work within the framework of Israel. No authentic solution can therefore neglect this common Semitic element, or the fact that large numbers of Arabs and Jews interact constantly (and at times cordially) within a context of cultural pluralism. The recitation of these variables, rendering the things which unite Arab and Jew, Islam and Hebrew, Semitic peoples all, should not be viewed as an intellectual trick or a denial of the prima facie hostilities which exist. What deserves articulation, if only as a prelude to the potential sources of political settlement, are precisely these unifying factors. Perhaps, peace in the Middle East would then become not so wild a dream.

4 OF JEWS, ISRAELIS, AND THE THIRD WORLD

In Israel there are tasks of religion, tasks of culture, and tasks of the State. The basic aim of religion is to maintain Israel as a nation in which the Hebrew faith and theology prevail over Moslem, Christian, and other belief systems. The primary aim of culture is to maintain Israel as a Zionist system in which secular dreams of a land free to all Jews co-mingle with sacred beliefs in Jewish manifest destiny. Finally, the tasks of State-hood involve the maintenance of a monopoly of power within the borders of the land of Israel. Obviously, these tripartite aims interpenetrate and intersect. Just as obviously, they come close to functioning as an ideal type for the Third World as a whole. Religions, cultures, and States change, but the deep and desperate sense of national autonomy and national libera-tion is a common thread that Israel shares with those other na-tions of the post-World-War-Two period.

Even the morphology of Israel shows stark parallels with the Third World: high militarization, with the armed forces func-tioning as much as the mark of national sovereignty no less than a response mechanism to a threat of any major interna-tional sort; high capitalization, in which every effort is bent toward increasing the Gross National Product toward holding constant individual forms of private wealth; high centralized political authority, in which, irrespective of the particular nu-

ances of the political party and parliamentary network, decision-making is lodged in a well-defined group with long-
standing, firm leadership roles. Israel shares with the Third
World a mixed societal pattern: Keynesian mechanisms of regu-
lation in the economic sector, Leninist mechanisms of domination in the political sector, topped off by strong social welfare
and social reform orientations in dealing with the individual
in the society.

The irony of the present historical moment is that these similarities exist without explicit recognition. Many Zionist spokesmen have sought to maintain the fiction of Israel as a trans-
planted European society, replete with central European
manners, mores, and customs. Others, closer to the American
fiscal support base, prefer to speak of Israel as a political enclave of Western democracy—a middle-Eastern outpost of the
New Deal. Such nonsense only reinforces the misanthropic conviction of those "Marxist" elements within the Arabic world
that seek to deny Israeli existence, much less legitimacy. For
such elements, Israel is an outpost of American imperialism, a
foreign cultural intrusion in the homogeneous Middle East,
European Ashkenazim play-acting at being farmers, and so
forth.

And yet it remains that the very absence of granted legitimacy, the explicit denial of Israel as a Third World leader,
much less member, has perpetrated distortions that seriously
jeopardize the peace of the Middle East. The consequence of
this denial has been to make the entire Middle East a pawn in
the larger East-West struggle and to weaken its bargaining
power as a whole in relation to the West and to Soviet-bloc
countries. It has further led to military escalation, which has
produced inordinately high military budgets and through artificially maintained refugee camps has denied vast numbers of
its poor the right to a normal existence. It is in order to perceive the actual relationship of Israel to the Third World,
these remarks are directed to the question of the relative im-

portance of the tasks of Statehood versus those of culture and religion.

Israel thus far seems to be using a model which is not entirely appropriate to its specific international status. The model of Israel will not be made more useful by a return to parochialism, to a concept based solely on the idea of Jewish community, whether it be a North American Jewish community or a Jewish-Israeli community. Israel needs to move beyond a Jewish exclusivism based on the inverted dialectic of overseas Jews and Israeli Jews. The problems of political, economic, and social formation go far beyond the personal problems experienced as a consequence of being either a Diaspora Jew or an organic Jew. The dialogue, if we must use that kind of format, should try to get beyond the contradictions that exist in the very framework of such a paradigm.

If you look at the academic literature on this country called Israel you will see that it is first defined as the home of a Mediterranean people; in the next paragraph they become a Middle East people; while in the next paragraph still, they are a Westernized people; for scientific and sportive functions, Israel is linked with Asia; and finally, they are said to be a people of all continents. Any four paragraphs of any popular Zionist brochure can arouse considerable doubts as to the very nature of the people or nation with which we are dealing. These confusions will never be resolved until we can examine Israel on its own terms as a developing nation.

The State of Israel is increasingly a model for developing African peoples as well as some Asian peoples. Indeed, Israel is one of the rare examples in the twentieth century, outside of Japan, of a "properly" developing young nation. The model of a "properly" developing nation tends to reveal the primacy of political economy over inherited status considerations such as religion and ethnicity. This sort of developmental model involves non-Jews as well as Jews and establishes a definition of Israelis quite apart from their conception as Jews.

As a development model, Israel's history of struggle against colonialism in the 1940's was essentially a prototype of guerrilla warfare. Second, Israel's unity is based on ethnicity, religious values, and a strong egalitarian background. Whether you call this exclusivism, triumphalism, or anything else in the arsenal of contemporary theology, it is a necessary mobilizing component for most economic development.

Third, as with any successful economic development of the twentieth century, Israel has had very strong external support for this development. In this case, the support base is an overseas religious group. Many of these overseas Jews have prospered in the advanced nations; hence they are able to provide both material support and technological know-how at a low cost and on a temporary or permanent resettlement basis.

There is nothing wrong with these facts. They indicate the ways nations develop, in some measure the way nations *have* to develop, in the twentieth century. Israel exhibits strong characteristics of Third World membership in its political structure. The country formally has a multiparty structure but actually has a uniparty operational apparatus that runs the country within the framework of almost socialist dimensions of democratic centralism. There may be more Leninism in Israel than there presently is in the USSR—if one takes seriously the intention of building a democracy based on class rather than party—and Israeli politicians certainly take class consciousness seriously.

Israel also has a strong professional military group that has a political interest in the maintenance of the national status quo. It also faces the same dilemma many other nations do today: namely, the place of militarism in its society.

The relationship between Jews who live in Israel, a State and a nation with the obligations of a State and of a nation, and Jews who live elsewhere, in the United States, South Africa, or where have you, may be important precisely because each group has its own special mission and vision.

The test for a State is its ability to maintain its power. While suffering may be a value and a positive attribute to Jewish solidarity, it comes perilously close to making powerlessness an equivalent to virtue. As a nation, one cannot celebrate powerlessness; as a people, one can; and as a religious group, one should. This is where the dialectic is located. For example, many American Jews had an atavistic response during the 1967 Arab-Israeli war. The martial spirit overtook American Jews momentarily. It was, to be sure, a heady euphoria. But some also had a feeling of disquiet over this very euphoria. That kind of psychological response, as it were, reflects the confusion between the reality of Israeli State power and the concerns of the Jewish people in their community, wherever they are in the world.

The relationship between the Jewish State and Jewish culture overseas, or for that matter in Israel, becomes the essential pivot for Jews. But whether it should be central to the State of Israel is another matter. The tasks of Jews, in contrast to those of Israelis, are tragically becoming separated; they are very different. It is more important, for example, that a Uganda ruler opens up a legation in Jerusalem than that ninety conferences between American Jews and Israeli Jews are held in Israel. The State needs legations more than conferences, needs Africans at least as much as Americans, needs support from poor nations no less than from wealthy Jews.

These kinds of considerations should be placed on the public agenda and not made part of a hidden agenda. We must remember that what we have is a dialogue, not so much between Israeli and Jewish intellectuals as between Jews who happen to be spending four days or four weeks in another country. Unless Jews outside of Israel come to terms with these facts, there is going to be disillusionment of a high order, the kind that could easily ensue if Israel develops diplomatic relationships with the Soviet Union or the People's Republic of China, or establishes cordial ties to the Falangist Republic of Spain, or does any other things that a State has to do to survive or expand. Israel may not meet the needs of liberal Jews or Orthodox Jews in the United States who may not approve of the State's actions, but such considerations must become less vital as the power of Israel becomes autonomic and independent of private foreign capital.

Like it or not, the tasks of Statehood are sometimes Hobbesian—nasty and brutish. If the rights of a State to exist are distinct from the moral claims for the superiority of a particular State, then one of the grand anomalies of being an overseas Jew is dissolved, if not resolved. The overseas Jew can thus recognize the special task of his own nation. Many will return to the United States and face tasks that are uniquely related to this country—an election battle one year, war in Southeast Asia every year, making a living in the face of a deteriorating economic situation.

As a Jew, one is expected to be a shareholder in Israel as a nation. Yet every adult realizes that some stocks which may be very good at one period of time may turn sour at another period of time. Being a spiritual holder of volatile national stock, I am fully aware of the risks as well as the rewards of marginal stock participation.

One often hears that all American Jews are shareholders in Israel, without the parallel assumption that Israelis have to make a side bet or an investment in world Jewry, not simply as a residual category but as that human and economic force which uniquely can and will support the Israeli State. To maintain that all Jews are shareholders in Israel is a risk as well as a reality. Israel has all religious Jews and all of world Jewry with which to contend. God help Israel if it makes a tactical mistake at any given time. Most nations have to confront pressure groups, including narrow interest groups, only within their own boundaries. Israel must contend with international pressure groups whose power is sizable but whose commitment is somewhat unsteady.

At some point, the Israeli position has to be a national position; further, at some point Israel has to recognize that if it wants moral leadership as well, it will have to give up some portion of its national sovereignty. The history of Western political theory, from Hobbes and Rousseau to the present, indicates that few nations will yield their political power or military advantages to the ethics of others. It is hard to believe that Israel will prove an exception to this rule of nations. My point is that Israel should take this for granted, and probably does so already; thus we should all move on to real issues.

We often hear fine scenarios for the Jewish future, but they usually leave out the most outrageous hypothesis, one that none of us would hope for, but nonetheless must be included; namely, one which includes the fall of the State of Israel and the survival of Jews throughout the world, and even in the Middle East. What could possibly happen in that kind of totally negative scenario? One possible outcome is that the religious zealots, of whom there are many in Israel, would say, "The fall of Israel was predetermined by a certain error, a religious error, a sin of pride," ignoring certain factors in the religious credo. Yet, Jews must go on in their search for the true "Zion." In other words, the very fall of the Israeli State would serve for such zealots as a warranty of the "moral decay" of the nation.

Another survival response might be that of the nonreligious Jews to whom the fall of Israel would be a tragedy, such as the fall of Biafra was a tragedy; "It is a terrible thing. We should make sure immediately that the U.N. feeds these people." It is unfortunate, but it has to be said: Among these Jews the fall of Israel would be like the fall of other small nations; or the latest Pakistani schism in which federation is no more important than separation. Drawing upon the American Civil War experience, some Jews might advocate a confederation of greater pan-Palestinian unity: "Not the nicest thing in the world, but nonetheless, you see, they are not starving the Jews and they are able to survive." What would happen to the people of Israel in that kind of scenario? Admittedly, all this is highly conjectural and hopefully will never come to pass. Yet, there is a need for a sober assessment of overseas Jewish behavior that does not take fundamental loyalties for granted.

My personal opinion is that world Jewry could not sustain another holocaust. Jewish community life would disintegrate, except for certain Hasidic sects for whom this disaster might not be the monumental tragedy it would be for most other Jewish people. However, the Jews of Israel might be absorbed into a larger Palestinian confederation. Slowly, they would develop integrated community patterns and re-establish community forms of life. Or there might be a protracted period of United Nations or international supervision. If the velocity of defeat were slow, then Jewish overseas survival might be less impaired than the utter destruction of Israel through war or conflict would initially suggest.

I am trying to point out, in an admittedly harsh way, that the tasks of Statehood are different from the tasks of peoplehood. The problems of Jewish religious and cultural survival are continuous. They take special forms under conditions of a powerful Israeli State apparatus, and they would take special forms should the Israeli State falter. It is evident that the survival of a nation is not uniquely tied to the survival of that people. The great Simon Dubnow said in the last century that there is a certain peculiarity rather than uniqueness about Jews. They have a nationality of the mind. I dislike sounding idealistic, but that nationality of the mind has a certain functional capacity to survive even the most powerful and protracted nationality of the land. Perhaps this point has been obviated by the rise of Israel. Perhaps Jews will never again have that particular sense of spiritual continuity. It may very well be that the condition of world Jewry is inexplicably tied to the fate of Israel; but this is not necessarily to the benefit of Jews as a religious entity or Jews as a cultural entity; although it is of a distinct benefit to Jews as a national and ethnic identity.

It is dismaying that any Israeli citizen can speak in a cavalier fashion about the Third World, or about the Arab world, or about the African world, or about the Sephardic problem and the Black Panthers in Israel. Certainly a sense of justice is an integral part of any definition of what it means to be a Jew, and a sense of universal peoplehood that embraces all oppressed peoples is a part of such a definition. Too many people, it seems to me, with the support of established Jewish organizational life, assert the need for a definition of Jewishness and deny the extension of Jewish concern for the condition of the Third World, the Arab population, and the black population.

That does not mean that, as Jews, all the people of Israel have the same kind of response mechanism or the same kind of reaction time to what goes on in the world. But to speak blandly and blithely about Jews who see themselves as Israelis, and Israelis as Jews, is to talk within terms appropriate to the nature of the State viewed as an organ of power, but it is a denial of the Jewish religion and the Jewish people as organs of morality. It is not that politics and morals lack any connection. They *are* connected. What makes Israel special is that there are many moral Jews in it, not that it is a State of a special moral sort. There are people who have a moral conscience living in Israel, as Israelis. Israel as a nation-state, however, cannot be said to embody all virtue. After all, even in Israel Machiavelli's dictum exists: it is only the combination of fortune, opportunity, and virtue that can permit the State to service the nation.

I would like to hear my Israeli colleagues express what they perceive as the future of their society and civilization. When they talk about minorities and majorities I would like to understand what minorities they are talking about and what majorities they are talking about. I myself do not feel terribly "minoritarian." On the contrary, I am somewhat taken aback and nonplussed by the sense of militant "majoritarianism" as an ideology that lurks behind much that is discussed in Israel. As Jews we have the requirement to transcend nationalism and to outlive all nation-states. The recognition of the sovereignty of Israel does not mean the celebration of statism. Quite the contrary, only such recognition allows Jews elsewhere to once again behave "naturally"—as the marginal people of the world; as the moral guardians of principles of equity and ethics.

I would like now to present some low-risk proposals for Israel and for America that could help American Jewry. I say low-risk because they should be considered in the context of present-day Israeli foreign and domestic policy.

First, American Jews have a tremendous problem with American black people. These are not historic problems or inevitable problems; there was a long period in which blacks and Jews were close to one another, certainly closer than they are now. I think that if the Israeli government were to change its "low profile" of ties with African states, giving them an even higher priority than they now have and publicizing those ties, it would help American Jews generally. The stronger the ties between Israel and black Africa, the stronger the ties between American Jews and American black people, not automatically, not ipso facto, but it would help to a considerable degree.

Second, it has become plain that the concept of a multiracial, multinational policy which does not repeat the homilies of our own American forms of separatism and our own forms of superiority is very much needed. Again, this is a matter of reshuffling priorities, and such changes are in the wind in any event; this is bound to happen within the next ten years—there can be no question about it. The semi-Western Oriental Jewish population is so extensive that a legislative as well as an educational reshuffling has simply got to be pronounced so that this group is given proper attention within the Israeli

State. Otherwise, Israel cannot serve as a moral model for another land or other peoples.

Third, to help American Jewry, there must be an end to the theocratic State. Pseudo-apologists—those who would use repressive regimes like Pakistan as a theocratic model of the Third World that might be emulated by Israel—cannot be taken seriously any longer. Pakistan has fallen apart, and obviously Pakistan is no model for the Third World or for Israel. It seems to me, if one is going to reach young American Jews, the theocratic aspects of the Israeli State must be taken into account; and more, simply overcome. Israel will always be under siege. So let the inevitable come. For the secularization of the State of Israel to take place, many of the problems that have been raised—uncomfortable, embarrassing problems— must once and for all be confronted.

These are relatively low-risk items on the historical agenda. I am not talking about long-range, complicated, ideological problems. If even these risks cannot be taken, it seems to me that fundamental issues will never be addressed, much less resolved; and thus the unique place of Israel in the covenant of nations will become sheer myth, lost in the rubble of geographical determinism.

5 FORCED COEXISTENCE: THE SOVIET STATE AND ITS RUSSIAN JEWS

Whatever else the condition of the Jews in the Soviet Union proves or disproves, it underscores beyond a shadow of a doubt the essential "peoplehood" of international Jewry. This may be viewed as a positive force by the Jews themselves or a completely negative cosmopolitan and even conspiratorial tendency by Soviet authorities. But the essential loyalty of Jews to each other, especially in their misery, is simply no longer questioned. There was a period in the 1950's when the Israelis were quite willing to shut their eyes to the conditions of Jews under the post-war Stalinist terror in exchange for diplomatic neutrality, if not overt Soviet support. Even so, the Jews of the Soviet Union were hardly willing to shut their eyes to the promise of deliverance held out to all of world Jewry by the existence of Israel. The irony of Israeli foreign policy is how, in a span of two decades, it has gone from an acceptance of the separation of Soviet Jews, on the grounds that the Soviet Union could not permit any portion of its population to maintain contact with an international community that had a foreign policy of its own, to a position which now seems to hold that Jews have absolutely no future within the boundaries of the Soviet Union, and, for some, that Communist authorities have no rights whatsoever in relation to the Jewish population because they have offered no real right of self-determination.

In a strange way, Israeli policy reflects a tendency to over-compensate as a form of political expiation of guilt for the be-nign neglect of Soviet Jewry during those long years of Sta-linist and post-Stalinist coercion. Just as Jews within the Soviet Union could not possibly remain oblivious or immune from Israeli society, especially after its stunning military success in three wars; so too Israeli authorities must now confront the realities of continuing Jewish life inside the Soviet Union not only as a distant possibility but even as a distinct reality. The position of the Soviet Jews, even more than that of the United States Jews, demonstrates the continued realities of Diaspora Jewry: a chain of agonies that are deeper even than those en-countered by American Jews, precisely because of the risks and threats one encountered even by a declaration of being a So-viet Jew. American Jews may have been irritated and irked by the remote possibilities of having to bail out Israeli military adventures, but they never had to pay the price of victory as did the Soviet Jews. In other words, Israeli ecstacies have cre-ated a source of Jewish agonies in the Soviet Union more se-vere than that suffered by any major bloc of Jews elsewhere in the world.

While the substance of international Jewry reveals special dimensions within Soviet boundaries, the attitudes and behav-iors of Soviet authorities reveal quite typical dimensions. As Talmon[1] properly notes, the exceptional characteristics of Jews and special treatment toward them was repeated and replicated with a vengeance in the Soviet experience. "The ex-perience of the Communist countries goes to confirm a 'law' of Jewish history: a new society, regime, or economic system wel-comes Jews as pioneers, but thrusts them out unceremoniously as soon as the 'natives' are ready to take over Jewish functions. This was the case in the early days of urban colonization in Europe, in the first stages of laissez-faire capitalism, and the same development appears to have taken place in Russia since the October Revolution." We are presented with the strange situation of a revolution intended to abolish all forms of exploitation and economic oppression and which furthermore guarantees in principle the rights of national self-determination, performing the same role which proved disappointing in relation to Jews as previous revolutions that were made in the same universal principles of equality and fraternity. In the Socialist case, as in the bourgeois case, such equality was bought at the expense of Jewish liberty; and the fraternity insured by modern constitutions was denied by traditional customs.

Among the recent deluge of writings on the status of the Jewish community in the Soviet Union, a modest effort entitled *Perspectives on Soviet Jewry*[2] ranks in the forefront. Social analysts like Nathan Glazer, Moshe Decter, William Korey, John Armstrong, Alex Inkeles, Hans Morgenthau, Maurice Friedberg, and Paul Lendvai have joined to draw a collective portrait of Soviet Jewish misery. The social science commitment of many of these scholars gives their contributions a reserve and caution, but their collective effort also displays a genuine passion for justice that has been characteristic of those concerned with Soviet Jewish affairs, Jew and non-Jew alike. In short, this is the best overview of the situation yet available, far superior to the polemical literature that now abounds and confounds this problematic area. The volume examines the actual status of Soviet Jews with great fidelity and a strong sense of contemporaneity. It does so minus the usual bombast surrounding the subject.

The volume, particularly the essays by John Armstrong and Alex Inkeles, shows that Soviet anti-Semitism is an instrument of Soviet foreign and domestic policy and not simply an irrational assault on a small minority group within the country. This collection shows how, in fact, the needs of Soviet foreign policy, dictated in some measure by a response to its commitments to the Middle East, are mitigated by domestic factors. Thus, the Soviet Union shares with the United States a Jewish factor that it must account for, if not answer to.

The condition of the Jews in the USSR has been complicated by Marxist ideology, by the insistence that the Jewish question is a national question rather than a religious phenomenon. When it is combined, as it is, with the importance of Jews as an economic resource, Marxism partially inhibits anti-Semitic excesses. This may explain why the Soviet Union has reacted more extremely than any underdeveloped nation on the subject of the Jewish "brain drain"—demanding payment for the education of its Jews as the price of departure. Furthermore, the Socialist system of planning, in the very act of eliminating small private entrepreneurial activities, has also dislocated and even derailed many traditional forms of Jewish economic existence. Both at the ideological and social levels, specifically Jewish existence was made more complex by the elimination of forms of economic exchanges that made marginality possible, even tolerable.

Historically, anti-Zionism was directly linked to the destruction of intermediary classes. Wherever Soviet life penetrated, the universalist claims of socialism led to a decimation of Jewish life styles. It further led to an attack on Jews as perennial dangers because they were carriers of marginality and particularistic values. The Soviet position was simple enough: first, expropriate Jews; second, demand that they work; and third, assume that they were living on black market proceeds if they did not work.[3] But in the very character of Bolshevik formulations of the "national question," a demand for differentiation between Soviet citizenry and Jewish nationality, a certain ambiguity was permitted to Jews in the Soviet Union that allowed some room·for maneuverability by Soviet Jewish citizens, albeit within a narrow and highly circumscribed area of political activity and social mobility.

In the same volume the papers by Moshe Decter and William Korey, who are co-workers on The Academic Committee on Soviet Jewry, deserve special commendation. Decter traces the history of Jewish national feeling in all parts of the Soviet Union, thereby building a strong case for the unity of purpose of Jews within the Soviet portion of the Diaspora. The demographic contribution of this paper is significant, as it provides a basis for upward correction of official Soviet statistics on the size of its Jewish minority. I do not think Decter need have portrayed such a renaissance of consciousness as a "mystery," since the very dialectic of oppression and liberation and the inability of the Soviet regime to return to the Stalinist era of terror or advance beyond the Khrushchev era of safety-valve liberalism, this interregnum itself provides a significant clue as to why Soviet Jews have selected this moment in history to assert their claims within the USSR and their connections to Israel. Add to this Israel's solid victories in three successive wars with the Soviet-supported Arab states, and it is easy to account for the present militant mood of Soviet Jewry.

William Korey's essay and the accompanying documents on legal and extra-legal pressures against Jews of political prominence are a grim reminder that the show trials of an earlier era in the Soviet Union and Eastern Europe are by no means simply a memory of the past. For Kremlinologists, there is a special value to Korey's essay, documenting as it does that the Soviets, in order to deflect from their aggression against Czechoslovakia, were preparing another big anti-Jewish and anti-Zionist show trial in that beleaguered and blighted satellite. The resistance to this by former Prime Minister Dubcek prevented such a further aberration from happening. However, the pattern of legal harassment is shown by Korey to be part of a continuing Soviet policy toward its Jewish minority and not simply a feature of the Stalinist era. But this too has to be placed in the larger context of Soviet jurisprudence, which, as Julius Jacobson has ably documented in his book *Soviet Communism,* has enshrined political partisanship into legal theory, no less than legal practice.[4] That Jews have uniquely been victimized by this condition is unquestionably correct, but it is also true that all Soviet citizens suffer legal terror even more acutely than physical aggression. That is why the present wave of civil liberties issues in the Soviet Union, affecting psychiatric practice, literary rights, and direct expression of political opposition, are also of deep moment to Jews; here the general interests of Soviet citizens most positively connect with the special claims of Soviet Jews. Moreover, the importance of Jewish demands to exercise their right to emigrate can scarcely be lost upon the millions of other minority people seeking greater freedom (including the right to emigrate), nor is it lost upon the Soviet political hierarchy who see the Jews' demand for rights of free travel as a prelude to internal reform, or, failing that, internal rebellion.

It is understandable but regrettable that so much of the argument on the condition of the Jews in the Soviet Union seems to ignore their profoundly Russian character. Everything from the twentieth-century novel to the marching songs of the Red Army reflects the Jewish contribution. Indeed, the traces of this Russian impact are profoundly apparent throughout Israel. The beat of the Palmach marching songs derives from the Red Army chorus; the impact of the Ashkenazic and primarily Russian strain on Israeli political and economic structure has been too well articulated to need further repetition.

Nor are we dealing here with simple cultural artifact. The Russian Jews are close to the land, certainly far more so than their American counterparts. The Kibbutz movement, the intense desire to frame Israeli socialism in predominantly rural terms, the spirit of collectivization all have sources in the Russian agrarian reform movements of both pre- and post-Bolshevism. And from the Israeli side, we witness the intense desire of its political leadership to maintain this European-Russian strain in its emigration policy. It is not simply European versus Oriental pre-eminence which is at stake, but the distinctly Russian character of leadership in Israeli political life. Of course, any such point can be stretched too far. But as the intensity of anti-Soviet feeling has mounted, so too has the tendency to denigrate distinctly Russian aspects of much Jewish life in Israel. And such a denigration can lead, not just to the falsification of history, but to very practical damages to the millions of Jewish citizens who continue to live and work in the USSR through choice, or at least not through any overt display of compulsion.[5]

Jews are not just exiles in Russia; they are after hundreds of years the practical and intellectual sources of Russian strength. Bolshevism ranks second only to the psychoanalytic movement among the contributions largely made by the Jews. Under the circumstances, it is simply absurd to suppress the eminently Russian character of the Jewish question. What is involved is a shift in the policy of the Communist movement, of Bolshevik foreign policy commitments, that has created an opportunistic assault on the Soviet Union's own Jews. But not everything Russian is Communist; and not everything Jewish is separated from the Russian tradition. Indeed, the great irony, which Simon Dubnow long ago uniquely appreciated, is that the Jews, in the vigorous pursuit of secularization and enlightenment, saw in the Socialist Bund and in the Communist Party movements new forms for the liberation of all men and hence their own liberation from Judaism. In a sense, the current malaise of the Soviet Jews is traceable to their own sixty-year history of self-denial as a people with a tradition, no less than a people with a conscience. Birobidjian was, after all, not just an imposed Soviet policy, but to some degree the agreed upon course of action of those Jews who desired a national identity without a concomitant religious identity. It is by no means certain that the majority of Soviet Jews would still not prefer such a truncated solution to the more total experience of being a Jew in Zion.

The Birobidjian project, admittedly an exercise in futility and failure, nonetheless highlights the special nature of the Soviet Jewish condition. Following the Bolshevik Revolution, the Jews, numbering then as now, about three million persons, were in the peculiar situation of having supported many of the policies and aims of the Revolution, as well as supplying a considerable portion of its leadership. One weakness of this Jewish leadership stratum is that they stemmed from the "petty bourgeois" sector of the population which the Revolution was sworn to eliminate. This factor, added to the traditional animus of Ukrainians and White Russians for its Jews, led to a simulated form of Zionism within the bowels of the first successful Socialist Revolution. To be sure, most of the impulse for resettlement of Jews came from the People's Commisariat of Agriculture, and some Politburo members such as its President M. I. Kalinin. The rhetoric was from the outset heavily anti-Zionist, but the emphasis on separate State and national power, Jewish language education (in contrast to Hebrew, not Russian), collective styles of work, resettlement on class terms, that is, the transformation of the petty bourgeoisie into agrarian proletarians, indicate how powerfully entrenched the idea of resolving the Jewish question had become.

Birobidjian failed, and failed miserably. Despite being declared in 1934 as a Jewish Autonomous region, by the end of the thirties more Jews were leaving than arriving in Birobidjian. Post-World-War-Two efforts at revivication failed with equal grandeur. And by the 1959 Soviet census, there were but a total of 14,269 Jews out of a total population of 162,856 living in Birobidjian. The area was unattractive for Russians generally and in equal proportion unattractive for Jews. Birobidjian was a response to the special conditions set in motion by the October Revolution but without any understanding of the special history of the Jewish people. So it remains one more tragic failure in the efforts to "resettle" Jews in an artificial homeland. The Soviet Jews demonstrated a great preference for the Diaspora condition rather than the nationalities resolution. This, of course, led to further forms of anti-semitic denunciations: Jews as cosmopolitans, individualists, petty bourgeoisie. The failure of Birobidjian only underscored the tensions of Soviet Jews: either a push toward assimilation into the Russian mainstream or a pull toward Zion and Israel.

The failure to take seriously the Russian origins and sentiments of Soviet Jewry flaws *Perspectives on Soviet Jewry* in a very special way: none of the contributors are able to put forth a set of proposals for the solution of the Jewish question within a Soviet context. There is the unwritten assumption that the USSR is a place of timeless oppression. But the inevitable fact is that the Jews of the Soviet Union still comprise a population equal to that of the Jews in Israel; yet they are being written off as much as being written about. Surely the contributors and the many antagonists of the Soviet regime do not expect an immigration wave of between two to three million people to take place; surely they cannot entertain the idea that only the 5 per cent who manage to immigrate are entitled to be called Jews or to survive as Jews.

The contributors to this volume are not unique in their unwillingness to deal with the fact that had Soviet policy on the national question been more than a bag of empty promises, and were the regime of a more democratic and tolerant nature, there might be no Jewish question. Indeed, the Soviet Union could have provided an alternative to Zion no less (or no more) meaningful than that presented to Jews living in the United States. The sources of Jewish discontent in the Soviet Union, I would suggest, do not stem exclusively from a magical or miraculous rebirth of Jewish consciousness, but from the quite commonsensical consciousness that escape from the Soviet system is perhaps only accomplished by strongly identifying with Israel. The problems of such identification are acute—and they have been fully and accurately portrayed in the volume as well as in other works (especially *Soviet Jewish Affairs*) —but it is palpably more pragmatic to put in a claim for immigration to Israel than, say, to the United States. Whether the lure of Zion or animus for the Soviet Behemoth is predominant remains to be explained, if the fate of Soviet Jewry is not to be prematurely sealed by the friends of Soviet Jewry no less than by its enemies. Underlining its current policy of pricing Jews out of the export market, is the implicit acknowledgment by the regime that the Jews have uniquely tested the Leninist doctrine of the rights of nations to self-determination—and have found it wanting. Other national minorities of course have also felt the burden of doctrine without practice, of the assertion of the rights of people to cultural equality and denial of the rights of these same people to economic equity. But these historic burdens of flight and resettlement have traditionally fallen to the Jews; and it is to them that the other national minorities now look as they wait for their own turn. The Leninist principle of self-determination has always been a charade; it is a theory without practice. To attempt to put it into practice is either damned as bourgeois nationalism, as in the case of the Ukrainians and Georgians, or doomed as rootless cosmopolitanism, as in the case of the Jews and Armenian minorities. Under such circumstances, the Leninist doctrine of self-determination has easily been transformed and converted into the Stalinist practice of Great Russian chauvinism.

There is another element involved that can hardly be avoided; and, yet, it is the most difficult to pinpoint. This is the classic Russian belief in the Jewish stereotype: in the Jew as cowardly, clannish and, above all, conniving. In the Soviet Union this image of the Jew, stamped most profoundly by its Ukrainian minority, has been elevated into an approach to the Jew. As so often happens, the actual practice of Soviet Jews did in part conform to these stereotypes—if for no other reason than as a mechanism of survival—a practice not unknown to other minority groups and other cultures. But in accepting this stereotype, the Russians lost their ability to understand Israeli Jews and their militant and even martial spirit. The idea of militant Jews, of Jews who talk back—even in English accents— is so unheard of that in their statements at the United Nations the Soviet delegation has betrayed signs of disbelief no less than disfavor with Israeli practices. Hence, you have the spectacle of the Jew, who formerly was viewed as the most cowardly member of the human race, being portrayed by the Soviets as the successor of the Fascists, with the bloodthirsty instincts of primitive Huns. The Soviet recognition of the fact of Israel has not enabled them to comprehend the difference between an Israeli Jew and the traditional Russian Jew. In a sense, their anti-Semitism has worked to prevent accommodation, because to do so would mean a recognition of the awful failure of Soviet Jewish policy to create a Soviet man—at least in relation to its Jewish population.

A question that arises with increasing frequency is that of Jewish response to anti-Semitism in the Soviet Union; and here, the book mentioned, it seems to me, is at its weakest. Despite the quarter century of Israeli history, steeped in guerrilla insurgency and military battle, none of these writers seem to take seriously the tactic of Jewish violence. The Jewish Defense League is simply nonexistent for the contributors of this volume. Nathan Glazer points out in his own essay that one reason why it is hard to maintain interest in possible ameliorative techniques for dealing with Soviet Jewry is that we are at a loss when we consider the mystifying question of how public opinion in the United States—and elsewhere in the Western world—can influence the leaders and rulers of Soviet Russia. In the absence of exact knowledge as to how Soviet public opinion influences its own political structure, it is hard to get beyond economic sanctions as a core approach. Alex Inkeles, in his thoughtful contribution, dissects the problem of existing Soviet Jewry. He perhaps adds to frustration rather than to a solution when he indicates he wants to emphasize that Soviet policy in the realm under discussion lies outside our capacity to make any significant difference in how the decision goes. Indeed, the maximum influence we can exert, I think, would result from our maintaining a dispassionate and analytic attitude rather than from an attempt to create an environment in which we call for a "holy war" to prevent another kind of holy war from going its course.

Whatever the counterproductive aspects of terror, its selective use is hardly a stranger to world politics. The whole thrust of the Jewish Defense League and its slogan of "never again" is to open up Soviet foreign policy and internal practices directed at Jews to new channels of pressure. Boycotting, storefront bombing, kidnapping, all highly reprehensible acts, and particularly so when launched by Palestinian Arabs against Israeli Jews, can nonetheless not be ignored as factors in the current debate of the means to alleviate the situation for Jews in the USSR. To think only in terms of low profit approaches is to sanction only elitist styles of political mobilization, and the success and failures of such low profile elitism can perhaps be measured by the most recent tactic of Soviet authorities—to impose taxes of astronomical sums for the ransoming of its Jewish citizens. Even in a world grown weary of further violence, but also a world in which the Jews have been uniquely victims of such violence, it still falsifies the options for Jews, outside no less than inside the Soviet State, to rule out violence.

In an unusually fine essay on Soviet anti-Semitism, Mikhail Agursky points out that the new wave of anti-Semitism "represents an extreme reaction to the very real national conflict between the Russian and Jewish populations of Russia." His substantive position is that the Bolshevik Revolution signified above all, the triumph of the border territories against Great Russian chauvinism and that the Jews were in the forefront of such national aspirations. He also notes that at the same time Jews had a strong role in the campaign to de-Christianize Russia. And although Jews as well as Christians were put to rout in this "trial of God," the fact that a Jewish ethnic minority, with Trotsky himself in command of this assault on traditionalism, took the lead makes Soviet Jews today peculiarly culpable in the minds and hearts of many in the rural masses who retain a lively interest in Christianity. The conclusion offered, and one heard with increasing frequency among the Jewish intelligentsia of Russia, is that "the only real way to end Russian-Jewish conflict in Russia would be to allow mass immigration by Jews to Israel."[6]

Several dilemmas are present, beyond the obvious one that the population of Soviet Jewry is still approximately the same as that of Israel Jewry; and that assimilation even at current levels (27,000 per/annum) are sufficiently large as to occasion deep trouble and discontent. First, the major troubles of Jews have been with the Ukrainians and not with the Russians; hence to speak of Russian anti-Semitism is to ignore the simple fact that it is precisely among the nationalist sectors that some of the greatest reaction against Jews has occurred. It might well be that the breakout of nationalist separatisms, far from ameliorating the Jewish condition, would actually intensify such problems. For example, the Bolshevik Revolution was accompanied by a wave of mass pogroms by Ukrainians, with over 200,000 Jews massacred, over 300,000 children left orphans, and over 700,000 rendered homeless.[7] After the Revolution it was again in the Ukraine that the most ferocious anti-Zionist crusades developed;[8] and under the Nazi invasion, the process of Ukraineization was employed by the Nazis to destroy Jewish people and convert Jewish schools into Ukrainian schools. It was the nationalistic elements with anti-Semitic backgrounds that had a monopoly of public office.[9] Thus, the argument that anti-Semitism is somehow directly linked to Great Russian chauvinism simply does not hold.

Second, it may well be true that Christian belief leaves a residue of anti-Semitism. Yet, the fact is that the Jews attracted to and attached to the Bolshevik movement were extremely marginal to Jewish life. And it is well known that after the Revolution was concluded the Bolsheviks had to begin a heavy recruitment drive among Jews to gain their support and their allegiance beyond the marginal portions of the intelligentsia that was attracted to Bolshevism on secular and assimilationist grounds. It is also important to realize that Jewish demands for the right to emigrate serve as a test case for other Russian minorities to articulate their demands, and hence, certain nationalistic animosities are muted, or at least blunted, by this peculiar experiment in true national self-determination.

The history of Soviet anti-Semitism is indeed of a piece with Russian history, particularly its takeover of Polish territories and its westward expansion. But this history is marked by extreme sensitivity to charges of anti-Semitism; great pains are taken, however demagogically, to separate out anti-Semitism from anti-Zionism. And beyond that, every Soviet leader has paid lip service or more to the rights of national identification. The constant glare of publicity, the steady erosion of Soviet Jewish loyalties, the shock of emigration, the awareness of an absence of Soviet life styles for a big and important minority sector may indeed intensify Soviet animosities toward Jews, but it may also lead to a softening of attitudes, toward greater pluralization, toward a search for new grounds of accommodation. And for the sake of the nearly three million Jews still residing in the Soviet Union, and the more than two million willing to make Judaism their primary national identification, researchers and intellectuals should be extremely cautious in assuming the impossibility of accommodation without assimilation. It is the height of mechanistic thinking to treat Soviet anti-Semitism only as a question for Jews; it is equally a question for Russians, and beyond that, for the survival of the Soviet Union itself as a multinational and multilinguistic nation-state.

A recent thoughtful essay by Jonathan Frankel[10] has pointed out that the Soviet political apparatus, even at this stage, has not made up its mind what its posture should be toward its Jewish community. Frankel points to a genuine contradiction within the Politburo between the faction dedicated to Leninist internationalism and Stalinist ultranationalism. What makes this debate especially intriguing is that internationalism has time and again proven to have a mass appeal among Jews and is, in effect, a powerful countermagnet to Zionism, whereas the neo-Stalinist anti-Zionist campaign has proven to be largely counterproductive and has only stimulated a desire for migration. That is to say, the Soviets have learned through experience that a hard-line attitude toward the Jewish question is by no means guaranteed to silence the Jewish minority, but quite the reverse; it compels Soviet Jewry toward migration, even though many may have relatively well-paid and interesting jobs in the Soviet Union and would have to exchange these for the hard life which Israeli circumstances impose on East European immigrants. In other words, it is by no means the case that the crude intimidation practiced by the neo-Stalinist wing is either the exclusive or even at this point the paramount impulse behind Soviet policy toward its Jewish minorities.

Some indication of the ambivalence—indeed, what might be called the contradictions—within Soviet policy toward its Jews is reflected in the decision to enhance the attractiveness of Birobidjian in the eyes of Soviet Jews as an antidote to bourgeois nationalism and Zionism.[11] What we have then in the Soviet Union is a simultaneous campaign, which in effect is an implicit acknowledgment of the strength of Jewish national sentiment to make the Soviet Union more attractive for the less ideologically oriented Jews while permitting the more ideologically oriented Jews to leave. This campaign thus creates a safety valve effect, in which the bulk of Soviet Jewry can be kept within the Soviet family of nations, while at the same time that segment which obviously has become either too marginal or too alienated to remain within the Leninist fabric of Soviet life can be eliminated. To understand the contradictions of the Soviet Union on the Jewish question is to understand the contradictions of Bolshevism toward the national question as a whole. The question is whether the rights of nations to self-determination have a genuine limiting effect at some point on the rights of the Soviet Union as a whole to dispense and dispose policy at will.

Affairs of politics move rapidly in this day and age, and what we have witnessed is the rise of Jewish militancy within the Soviet Union and of a corresponding demand by the Soviet authorities for greater allegiance and adhesion to the Soviet State. This is not exactly a new situation in Jewish history; on the other hand, it is a new situation for a society which claims socialism as its system and equality for all as its goal. Whatever the long-range outcome, that is, whatever the long-range potential for Jewish survival within the Soviet Union may be, this situation makes the short-term dialogue on the national question a much more viable, a much more lively, and above all, a much more serious question than it has been since before the Russian Revolution.

6 JEWISH ELITES, ELECTORAL POLITICS, AND AMERICAN FOREIGN POLICY

In the United States in the 1970's the Jewish community, somewhere between five and six million people, has a unique challenge and opportunity. The presidential election provided a focal point, not so much in relation to the position of the candidates toward Israel but in relation to the attitudes of Jews toward the United States. Much conventional Jewish analysis has thus far been couched in terms about how hard or how soft the Republican Party or the Democratic Party is on the Israeli issue, which seems to be remarkably wide of the mark. It is not that American policy toward Israel is not a real issue, but rather that such policy ultimately is distinct from the Jewish question in America.

The election prompted discussion of widely reported and much-heralded defections from the Democratic Party by prominent Jewish elites who in the past had contributed heavily to Democratic Party funding, if not to policy. A sample list of economic brokers who either openly supported the president and the Republican Party, or, more characteristically, simply did not support the presidential aspirant of the Democratic Party, makes impressive reading: Stanley Goldblum (chairman and president, Equity Funding Corporation); Eugene V. Klein (Board chairman, National General Corporation); Meshulam

Riklis (chairman and president, Rapid American Corporation); Davis Factor (Board chairman, Max Factor & Company); Irvin J. Kahn (San Diego Industrialist); Stanley Beyer (Vice chairman of the Board, The Pennsylvania Life Company). Whether this flight of political capital is temporary or permanent is less important than the permanence of the ideological shift.

Less impressive in wealth but equally significant as a cultural force are the political brokers who in the 1972 presidential elections defected from the Democratic Party, thereby clearly breaking with the Jewish position of near monolithic support for the Democratic Party. These included Irving Kristol (former editor-in-chief of Basic Books, and co-editor of *The Public Interest);* Leo Cherne (Executive director, The Research Institute of America); Herschel Schacter (Former chairman, Conference of Presidents of Major American Jewish Organizations); David Luchins (chairman, Jewish Youth for Humphrey); Leonard H. Marks (former director, United States Information Agency); William Wexler (chairman, World Conference of Jewish Organizations).

United States/Israel relationships, unlike others, cannot simply be bilateral; they are intrinsically multilateral. That is to say, the policies affecting the two countries are filtered through the nearly six million Jews living in the United States and their special role both with respect to America where they live, work, and have citizenship, and Israel to which they feel profound historic and religious attachments. Of course, this is partially true for United States policies toward Poland, Italy, Ireland, and other countries of which large blocs of "ethnic" peoples reside in this country. But assimilation of Jews is tripartite in character (religious, cultural, and national), whereas with other peoples the assimilation process, while incomplete, at least does not involve the same degree of religious and cultural differentiation as Jews exhibit.

Israel is a special case of a Third World nation, cut off from its geographic base in the Middle East, and therefore its natural economic and political allies in the area. Thus, Israel is tied to the United States artificially and at times even against its political will—as for instance its begrudging neutrality on Vietnam. Israel must forge its own domestic and foreign policies to suit United States interests, and the extent of this can be gauged by the similarity of its voting patterns to the United States in the United Nations. To some degree, the natural inclination of Israel to move toward alternative policies is thwarted by this need for continued United States support.

The artificiality of this linkage is of particular interest, since American Jews, often of middle-class backgrounds and upper-class interests, linked to Israel through Zionist organizations, serve artificially to restrain dealings with the rest of the world, especially the developing areas and at the same time dampen enthusiasm for much needed Israeli internal reforms. Hence, the special conditions and contradictions of Israel are accentuated and made manifest not only by those dependent dealings with the United States as its exclusive powerful ally but no less by a lingering feeling of double dependence upon American Jews, who are perceived (not always correctly) as helping to shape American foreign policy.

Considerable problems in the relationship between the United States and Israel are inherent in the inability of either to accept a third-party coalition in Middle Eastern affairs. Israel falls victim to the small nation–big nation dichotomy. It simply cannot abide by, or accept, arrangements between, for example, the United States and the Soviet Union settling by superpower fiat the fate of the Middle East. Israel has had to forge its own future for so long that it cannot easily accept manipulation by others. This underscores the recalcitrant nature of the alliance between the United States and Israel. The fact that Israel can call upon a hidden Jewish constituency, overt in the United States and covert in the Soviet Union, does indeed give weight and substance to the Israeli claim that it is not simply a small power which can be regulated or mortgaged at the behest of the major powers but a force of international socioeconomic weight as well as national interests.

The United States does have vital oil interests in the Middle Eastern Arab countries, and these fundamentally economic interests act as a restraint and a brake on any overt manifestation of support for the "greater Israel" position; that is, a permanent peace settlement based roughly on the de facto boundaries forged after the 1967 War. The burden of the Rogers plan, of the Sisco initiative, and of the McCloskey proposals are all based on the trade off of Israeli rollbacks for Arab settlement. And this burden proved too heavy for the Israeli Labor Party leadership to accept.

The position of the United States, whether the Republican Party or the Democratic Party is in charge, is quite simple: normalize relationships in the area; achieve a peaceful settlement between the contending parties; maintain an American presence in Israel, but also maintain the American economic presence in the Arab Middle East; at the same time, permit a modest Soviet presence in the Mediterranean, and a land and air presence in Egypt, Syria, and elsewhere as the Soviets and their Arab associates deem necessary. In this, it is impossible to detect a shred of difference between the position of the two parties or their leadership. This party isomorphism is a consequence of fundamental American political requisites, not short-range personality quirks between candidates.

In a world dominated by the force of arms, the United States role as the primary arms supplier to Israel has increased over time. Unlike economic assistance, Israel's dependence on United States military sales credits has become overwhelming, particularly in 1971 and 1972, as the United States assumed the role of sole foreign supplier for most types of advanced military equipment since the Six-Day War.[1] In part this represents a deepening commitment. But beyond that, this commitment itself is a reflection of the United States assessment that the power balance was in danger of being upset by virtue of declining Anglo-French support to Israel during the late 1960's. The United States has been in a position of having to step up its own arms support or run the serious risk of upsetting the military as well as political balance in the Middle East. Nonetheless, it is doubtless true that for Secretary of State Rogers and for Under-Secretaries McCloskey and Sisco this stepped-up role was always felt to be a reluctant admission of American needs in the Middle East rather than an enthusiastic assertion of Israeli rights. With the decline of the Soviet presence in Egypt, one can expect United States bargaining with Israel to become even tougher as it seeks a political settlement as a trade off for military supplies.

This brief overview serves to indicate that the current debate in American Jewish higher circles of whether to diversify its support for the Democratic and Republican parties or continue its traditional Democratic Party allegiances is largely devoid of any empirical content, at least as regards to relations with Israel, and reflects instead a serious shift in the social condition and political position of the upper strata of American Jews. This special class, unable to face up to the challenges of American life, chooses a convenient rhetoric of support for Israel. The issue of party loyalty is instead a posture in relation to the future of America as such.

Jews are as frightened and nervous over the black population and minority-group violence as any other ethnic middle-class suburban sector. Beyond being aware of the fact that there is more inter-group minority violence than intra-group violence, they not only have the right to be scared, they have the obligation to declare that fright. Polish and Italian city-dwellers and middle-class housewives on city shopping sprees are quite candid in expressing their fears. They do not raise the Italian question or the Polish question with regard to political party affiliation. Ethnic politics is authentic enough, yet it clearly is hyphenated politics—Italian-American, Irish-American, etc. Such politics are as foreign to the "old country" as the values left behind in the great migrations of the late nineteenth and early twentieth centuries. Jews for their part have tended to substitute Israeli survival for Jewish-American politics—at one and the same time a snare and a delusion, but also a special source of strength within American Jewry.

The various attributions of Israeli support for the Republican Party, and conversely, fear of a Democratic Party victory, are built on sand and manufactured of whole cloth. The few preferential utterances that have been made are reported as informal and off-the-record. They have had the nature of diplomatic correctness. For example, exchanges of telephone pleasantries between Richard Nixon and Golda Meir on the opening of a new television channel in Jerusalem were interpreted as a veritable campaign pledge. The actual statements of Democratic Party candidate George McGovern and other Democratic campaign spokesmen offered the identical support to the continuation of the State of Israel and its sovereign right to existence as that of Republican officials. On the Israeli issue, differences between candidates and parties are virtually non-existent. Thus, the alteration of American Jewish voting patterns, which are real enough (albeit quite modest), must be largely explained either by mass Jewish disaffection or class Jewish disaffiliation. While these factors coexist, my own belief is that the bolt to republicanism remains a class phenomenon, specifically American in its substance.

A cluster of powerful Jewish businessmen on Wall Street and their commercial counterparts throughout the country are deploying the Israeli-Arab struggle as a disguise for their own profound shift of class interests. They have real economic fears (which they share with their fellow entrepreneurs): higher taxes on business to support new welfare and work programs, multinational challenges to the American economy, German and Japanese capital, an ever deepening inflation, affirmative action in federal and state level that might change existing social and educational patterns, and a winding down of military spending that might result in smaller profits and greater short-range labor discontent. That the Jewish masses do not share these concerns is shown by the continued support given to the Democratic Party by unions such as The Amalgamated Clothing Workers, The United Automobile Workers, and the Meat Cutters Union, where Jews remain an important factor at the rank-and-file and/or administrative levels. That Jewish "defections" from the Democratic Party ranks have taken place is unquestioned, but that such defections amounted to more than a fraction of the American Jewish electorate is untenable. Indeed, the ability of the Republican Party to increase its base of Jewish support from 10 per cent to 30 per cent has proven to be a notable political fact, but in and of itself this has not reshaped the character of American foreign policy. It has, however, given substance to the broad base of disenchantment with social welfare programs in which Jews are not major participants.

It is a fact of American political life that neither the Democratic nor the Republican parties have clearly delineated policies toward Israel—at least not beyond the convenient canard that both parties stand solidly behind the right of Israel to its national survival and sovereignty. The question of how this lofty goal is to be implemented remains, however, a cause for difference within each party, rather than between parties. In terms of recent American political history at least, a good case has been made that Republican Party indecisiveness rather than Democratic Party softness provided the essential ingredient for a diplomatic isolation of Israel even from its own former sources of support in the United Nations.[2] It is a curious fact, in the light of the present conservatization among affluent Jews, that very few, if any highly placed Republican officials have been willing to drop the Rogers formula of supporting only "insubstantial alterations" in the 1949 Armistice lines and substituting in its place a formula that recognizes the primacy of establishing defensible borders for Israel. Thus, in terms of long-range policy considerations, the issue of party allegiance has not materially altered the conduct of United States foreign policy.

The Jewish community of the United States has traditionally voted for the Democratic Party not as an act of contrition or faith but rather in the belief that that Party expressed the best interests of the American political commonweal in its search for universal justice and complete equity. The Jews have proven to be a unique force in American politics in that, despite their class backgrounds or interests, they have exhibited the capacity to vote and act beyond their class and interest group constraints. The critical decision then in the current decade, and perhaps beyond, is whether this historic sense of equity, built up by strong and powerful identification from the New Deal to the New Frontier, will yield to a sense of fear and a sentiment of loathing for the newer minority groups, particularly the blacks and Spanish-speaking groups who have gone beyond philanthropy in their dealings with Jews, and for the large deviant marginals who clearly represent a threat to traditional Jewish ethical and cultural credos.

The issue for Jews in the 1970's is not Israel but their survival as an ethnic group in their own right, one which will permit them to join with blacks, poor Catholics, Poles, Slovaks, urban labor, and college youths. This "new politics" will probably turn out to be a losing coalition in the short run, but nonetheless this coalition shows the face of the future if not to American society as a whole, then at least to the Democratic Party. The alternative is to have the Jews become part of the dominant national culture—that largely Protestant culture which in the past was most hostile to specifically Jewish aspirations.[3] What is at stake then in this process of long-term party realignment is not the Jewish identification with the "national culture" but its identification with the dominant social classes that are represented by the Republican Party and the more conservative elements in the Democratic Party.[4]

To pretend that Jewish political behavior is guided on the basis of what is best for Israel is simply a cruel disguise and a form of misanthropic humor. Everyone knows that it is the fate of housing projects in Forest Hills or affirmative action in Los Angeles which will be the actual determinations in Jewish political preferences rather than the supposed postures the two national parties take toward the State of Israel. The current situation is of special interest to the Jewish community, which now faces a pivotal and long-standing decision whether to join the ranks of the middle classes in politics as they have in economics by voting for conservative candidates in both parties, or whether to display a continuing fusion of Jewish interests with the working classes and the lower-middle classes, that spectrum of people involved in the urban sprawl who comprise the backbone of The New Politics in the Democratic Party and Ripon Society Politics in the Republican Party.

To put the matter metaphorically—or perhaps even metaphysically—will Jews remain loyal to their historic faith in universal justice, or shall they become just one more link in the great chain of Protestant Bourgeois Being that constitutes the dominant sectors of both major parties? If this question puts the matter somewhat simplistically, it at least has the advantage of being infinitely more accurate than the current "soft or hard on Israel" debate. At least it is fair to the principles and premises upon which electoral decisions are made: how they affect the citizens of the United States, who after all, are the only ones who vote in American elections. Beyond that, the seventies have displayed a break with party affiliations, but a break which strangely intensifies, rather than weakens, fundamental value decisions as these are reflected in the political process.

The presidential elections of 1972 witnessed a remarkable demonstration of the accuracy of the polls. This precision extended to the degree of religious and ethnic shifts as well. It was, for example, the case that the Jewish vote for President Nixon more than doubled from the previous national elections, moving from approximately 15 per cent to 35 per cent. Yet, it was also the case that as a voting bloc the Jews scored second only to the blacks as supporters of a national Democratic ticket that could not hold other segments in the traditional New Deal coalition intact. To be sure, any determination of religious and/or racial voting preferences are difficult to obtain; yet, if we draw upon the relatively homogeneous areas of New York City, a sound indication of the myths and realities of Jewish voting preferences can be readily established.

The overriding fact in examining New York City Assembly Districts is that the Jews voted much more like the blacks and the Puerto Ricans than they did like the Italians, Irish, and Polish voters—the so-called "ethnics." Indeed, the shift to Republican voting on the presidential line by esesntially Roman Catholic voting groups was pronounced. Most of Nixon's borough-wide plurality came from four districts in Western Queens, which he carried by small margins in 1968. This time, these same "heritage" areas of Queens and Richmond went to the president by a three-to-one margin. Similar patterns seemed present in Brooklyn, but the large numbers of both Jews and Italians in the same assembly districts make any exact analysis difficult to establish.

Where poor Jews congregate in the city, as in the Crotona Park and Southern Boulevard district of the Bronx and the Springfield Gardens and St. Albans area of Queens, the continued extended solidarity of Jews with the national Democratic ticket was evident. The five-to-one and four-to-one ratios in these districts inhabited by poor Jews and new ethnics compares favorably with the ratio of support manifested in the Bedford Stuyvesant, Bushwick and Brownsville sections of Brooklyn and with the Harlem districts in Manhattan. It was precisely in these poorer areas where the defections were least in evidence.

Working-class Jews, unlike their Polish, Irish, and Italian

neighbors (and unlike their own elite), did not abandon the Democratic national ticket nearly as widely as expected or predicted by conservative Jewish organizational spokesmen. Elites within the American Jewish Congress, for example, have tended to argue that a redefinition of political alignments is in order, one that would lead to the creation of a broad-based ethnicity to counter the growing demands of racial minorities in the city. Indeed, the ethnic vote and the middle-to-upper-class stratum of Jews proved far more interest-group oriented than did the poor Jews. It was among these ethnic and middle-strata Jews that electoral defections from the national ticket were manifest, while their local interests kept them on the Democratic Party line for congressional and local offices. Poor Jews, like poor blacks, those who intersect most pronouncedly and directly in such places as Co-Op City in the Pelham Parkway district, still delivered a vote for McGovern over Nixon by a three-to-two ratio.[5]

This data confounds the currently fashionable thesis that it is the poor Jews, those in fearful contact with the black community, that have accounted for the major defects from the Democratic Party ranks. Nothing could be further from the case since available information reveals that it is the middle- and upper-income level Jewish areas, those with the least contact and the most stereotyped attitudes about blacks, that shifted most in their party preferences from the Democratic to the Republican lines. This might well have been anticipated, given the avowed change in allegiances, however temporary or permanent, by the economic power brokers and political opinion leaders among the Jewish establishment. It turns out that it was not the liberal and radical Jews who were "out of touch" with the "new realities" but, rather, the new conservatives and self-declared Jewish ethnics who were out of touch with the broad strata of Jews who continued to feel that the Democratic Party and its presidential standard bearer remained the most articulate voice for equity and justice in America. The elite defections were real. But the mass allegiances were just as real.[6]

There is, however, a larger consequence of the 1972 presidential elections that cannot be reduced to quantitative or community terms. That is the ideological realignment of the Jewish community in the United States. No longer is the "dialogue" along a liberal to radical axis, with a certain amount of confusion between labels and actions. The rise of Jewish republicanism has strengthened the impression that Jewish interests are not irrevocably tied to social change in America but are linked more firmly to the social structure of America. This conservative trend is not likely to diminish in any post-election euphoria. Indeed, Jews, like their counterparts in other religious and ethnic blocs, have had to make fundamental commitments either to the United States and American culture or have had to reassert their beliefs in the values of political and ideological marginality. That this is now a choice is indicative not just of changing national pictures but of changing Jewish fortunes as well. We now have a situation where Jewish centrality is a distinct possibility, whereas in the past Jewish marginality was a fact of social reality and not a cultural choice.

Thus, the 1972 political watershed was crossed only to find a fork in the road: one path leading to assimilation into the national culture, the other leading to separation from the national culture. And what decisions are taken depend of course on the evaluation of the worth of that American national culture, and, beyond that, what realistic alternatives exist in that culture. In short, the 1972 watershed was a demonstration rather than a resolution of the Jewish agony, since it sharpened, in dramatic fashion, a choice between conservatism and radicalism, republicanism and egalitarianism. The automatic support of liberalism has finally come to a stark halt, replaced by a condition of polarization that, while not exactly new to the Jewish people, has seriously affected traditional Jewish assumptions about the universal rights to justice and equity. But this only demonstrates that the Jewish problem is, after

all, tied directly to the American dilemma and can only be resolved along with it.

This brings us back full circle to the Israeli Ecstasy; to the
ways in which the internal political struggles of the United
States as they are influenced—one can hardly say determined—
by Jews produce larger ramifications at the level of foreign
policy.

Many questions raised about the current and future status of
United States foreign policy toward Israel are predicated on a
great assumption: that there is such a beast called United States
policy toward Israel. I strongly suspect that this is not the case,
but rather that there exist alternating currents of policy—
indeed, contradictory formulations that express themselves as
vacillating policies.[7] This is inevitable, given the fact that foreign policy emanates not simply from the Department of State,
and not simply from the advisor on foreign policy to the Executive Branch, but also, lest we forget, from Congressional sources
as well. As a result, we should first try to distinguish who is
making what sorts of policy toward Israel and toward what end.

The State Department seems riddled by contradictory factions, but I do believe it is an open secret that the pro-Arab
faction usually holds the upper hand. The reasoning used by
this faction, which favors changing United States policy
toward Israel, is based on the "even hand" concept that the
United States should cease foreign military aid to Israel. Failing
that, it argues equal amounts of military favors should be supplied to Arab nations in exchange for neutrality or support by
the Arab nations of United States foreign policy goals in a non-
Middle East context and for a far more neutral Arab stand-
point toward Soviet foreign policy. The general reasoning goes
that the United States needs a stable neutral Middle East, and
all of the oil supplies that would flow from such stability, and
that they need this far more than they do an Israeli deterrent,
or even its rhetoric about democracy. Arab supporters further
declare that current United States policy will compel Egypt,

Syria, Lebanon, and the other Arab nations to accept Soviet hegemony over the region: thus the United States will lose an enormous chunk of the Cold War by default. The argument further goes that Israel at no point can really be counted upon to support American policy initiatives elsewhere in the world, and that it is doubtful that this support, even were it to be forthcoming, would be worth much to begin with. The various State Department initiatives undertaken during the first Nixon administration, by Joseph Sisco and William P. Rogers, and their support for the Jarring Commission, clearly indicate that the United States interprets the United Nations cease-fire formula of 1967 far more in terms of an Israeli territorial roll-back than in terms of guaranteeing Israeli sovereignty and legitimacy through secure boundaries.

The pro-Israeli faction in the Department of State is far more amorphous and seemingly less well organized than the pro-Arab faction. Indeed, it is not so much a group favoring Israel as a coalition in favor of "balance of power" politics. Old-line anti-Communists based at European desks and many other people of humanistic and democratic persuasion some-how feel that the existence of Israel provides a counterforce in the Middle East that no amount of overt United States military aid could possibly equal. In effect, the argument is that historical conditions are such that the Arab nations, whether of the more traditional bourgeois variety or of the newer socialist variety, cannot be expected to support United States policy initiatives or roll back Soviet penetration, except where the latter becomes excessive and overtly interferes in the domestic affairs of the area. Hence, the theory goes, Israel provides a balance and leverage for United States foreign policy at a minimal cost in men and materiel.

The Israeli faction in the State Department is primarily supported by such Congressional figures as Henry Jackson and Senator Jacob Javits of New York. The makers of politics, un-like the makers of policy, are acutely sensitive and responsive to the large, so-called Jewish vote, and, indeed, more so now that that vote is more evenly divided between Democratic and Republican figures. Now that this bloc is up for grabs, declarations in favor of even greater economic and military aid to Israel serve the natural constituency of many Congressional figures—especially from industrial Northern and Western states, where there is a large and influential Jewish population. Insofar as effective initiatives must themselves reflect legislative currents, one can expect United States policy to remain firmly anchored in limbo. That is to say, it will provide guarantees for Israeli survival and even overt military support on a modest scale for that one nation in the area which clearly represents an isomorphism with American democratic society. Even if the formal structure of Israeli politics differs sharply from that of United States politics, the sentiments are there in common as well as the constituents back home. On the other hand, one can expect the State Department Realpolitiker to become increasingly concerned about demands emanating from the OPEC oil-producing countries, and increasingly willing to sacrifice Israeli ambitions in favor of Arab neutrality. The popularity of this position with militant minority groups and so-called anti-imperialist groups in the United States should not be discounted as a factor lending a certain constituency of its own to this pro-Arab posture within the State Department.

The national security bureaucracy, which is an amalgam of the Department of Defense, the United States military as an entity unto itself, and the foreign policy apparatus attached directly to the White House, shows a similar degree of ambiguity in its dealings with Israel. The impulse toward reconciliation with the Arabs is quite strong within the White House wing. One close student of the Middle East sees this rapprochement as coming in four distinctive stages: the resumption of diplomatic relations; a massive economic aid program; an arms limitation arrangement worked out in conjunction with the Soviet Union that would establish parity in armaments among the powers of the area; and, finally, a diplomatic and public relations campaign for Israel to return most, if not all, of the lands occupied after the Six Day War.[8] What would weigh against this sort of unilateral big-power approach, aside from Israeli objections that have already been stated well in advance, is the belief of the American military that Israel as a military ally deserves special consideration in the distribution of hardware, and, beyond that, that reconciliation of the United States with China represents a simple political act in contrast to the rapprochement of two bitter rivals in the Middle East such as Egypt and Israel.

Apart from tactical changes, the substance of the situation has also changed. The question of United States foreign policy toward Israel has less urgency now than it did when the ceasefire was declared in 1967. During this six year period, Israeli military might has grown considerably, and, far more important, the capacity of Israeli society to generate hardware of its own has kept pace with this military mobilization. Indeed, Israel produces enough military supplies to make it one of the leading exporters of small hardware ammunitions. This fact alone is enough to shrink the significance of United States policy initiatives in the area. While Arab dependence on Soviet hardware grows deeper, despite current ambiguities about Soviet military personnel and their presence in Arab lands, the Israeli potential for military self-management, for an independent deterrence, has grown enormously.

The real gulf between Israel and the United States on foreign policy questions is over the matter of diplomatic initiatives. Israel increasingly considers itself to be a major small power in the Middle East and would infinitely prefer direct negotiations with the Arab states to settle claims that arose out of the 1967 War and out of the 1948 resettlement of the Palestinian Arabs. Thus, Israel's impulses are to minimize big-power initiatives in general, and, insofar as the United States initiatives are part of that syndrome, to curb its propensity for unilateral big-power settlement of the area's difficulties.[9] Israel is certainly unsure of the contents and substance such initiative could provide; but, far beyond that, it considers that the very act of direct negotiations would go a long way toward providing the sort of legitimacy that would establish its security—and from the Israeli point of view, tranquilize the area for years to come, if not indefinitely.

If the burden of the Israeli question is survivalist in character, then the tasks of Israel are simply to intensify present tactics and trends: high modernization, high militarization, and high mobilization. The effectiveness of this policy can hardly be faulted on power grounds. From a scant beginning —with scarcely a decent road connecting Tel Aviv to Jerusalem, with Israel itself divided by a wall, with a population of barely one million Jews, with only the faint hint of the ancestry of a common language—Israel has become the pivotal military force in the area. A country united—at least with respect to external threat—having defensible borders and boundaries, demonstrating a reunification of ancient and modern capitals, and having a population of approximately three million Jews —Israel is, after all, a nation-state with muscle and might, and a national homeland for millions of displaced Jews throughout the Middle East, the Soviet Union, and Central Europe. And it serves the same function for disenchanted Jews who prefer a Jewish state to a simple Hebrew consciousness and who much prefer the center to the Diaspora. Thus, when Israel is asked to do something different, by implication it is asked to turn its back on the sources of its success. And I daresay that this has become a commonplace among well-intentioned commentators and critics from other nations.

Yet, there is a sense in which the question of the character of Israeli society is of paramount importance and deserves serious response. Israel is and has always claimed to be more than a typical nation-state with typical acts of barbarism permitted to the nation-state in the name of law, wisdom, and tradition.

So the real question comes down to what Israel must do differently if it is not to be despised and hated by members of other despicable and hateful nation-states, and beyond that, maintain its overseas Jewish constituencies as well. That is to say, the hidden agenda behind any question of what Israel must do differently if it is to prevent deterioration in world opinion and world sentiment is precisely the moral component presumed to exist in Israeli society.

And here one must postulate a minimum series of conditions for Israel's moral survival and not just its economic and military strength. The first is a bold recognition on the part of Israeli authorities of the multinational, multiracial and multireligious nature of Israeli society. This would have great benefit for world Jewry no less than for the inner dynamics of Israel. Second is a profound change in Israeli political leadership, to better reflect the demographic and economic role of the Oriental Jews and the Christian and Arab populations of Israel. The continuation of East European Ashkenazic leadership is akin to the persistence of the Virginia dynasty after the start of the United States Republic. The breakup of that dynasty strengthened American society. The same could be expected if Israel makes a similar opening to presently excluded or suppressed sectors within its own society. Third is the unfinished business of the first twenty-five years—and that means an end to the theocratic state. The process of secularization is irrepressible, and it is the last stage in the modernization process. At a time when Arab nations have dangerously turned back toward theological justification and rationalization for political behavior, Israel should serve notice that it does not intend to emulate this turn away from modernism and toward fanaticism. The threat of a "holy war" can best be met by Israel with a firm determination to maintain its identity and its national character without pushing to a new stage of escalation in the current tragedy of Middle East conflict and terror.

To look forward with confidence is thus not to look forward

to an anxiety-free situation, but rather to a morally worthwhile situation. Before imposing solutions in the name of futurology, it should be carefully noted how frequently the Christian world, the Third World, the Democratic World all somehow expect less hypocrisy, less charlatanry, less belicosity from Israel than from their Arab neighbors, or, for that matter, from any other nation. This is both a blessing and a curse, for having assumed the burdens of being *both* the moral vanguard of the Jewish people and the military vanguard of the Jewish state, Israel is attempting a difficult feat indeed. It must in effect square a circle, a feat rarely, if ever, performed by a modern nation. Even the miracles performed from Prince Moses to Prince Metternich have not yet included the great wonderment of fusing universal moral goals with national political claims.

7 JEWISH ETHNICITY AND LATIN AMERICAN NATIONALISM

Our enemies in all generations cry out: "There is a certain people scattered abroad and dispersed among the peoples and their laws are diverse from those of every other people." In modern times they call it "a state within a state." But the congregation of Israel goes on in its historical path and says: "Indeed, a state within a state," an internal autonomous group within an external political group, and the nature of things sanctions it.[1]

The problematic nature of survival for the Jewish communities in Latin America has caused concern for many years. In a demographic and sociological analysis of the Jewish communities of Argentina in 1959-60, especially Buenos Aires, I raised the *Judenfrage* precisely in survival rather than in growth terms. But while the survival problem at that time resulted from the failure of the Jewish community to integrate with a prevalent right wing political culture, the problem has now been greatly exacerbated a decade later by the rise of militant left wing political cultures from which Jewish communities are also largely alienated and estranged.

The problem might be posed in terms originally formulated by a rather unsympathetic social science commentator on Jewish affairs, Werner Sombart. His position, as defined in *The Jews and Modern Capitalism*,[2] is that Jews, even more than Lutherans or Calvinists, symbolize the Capitalist spirit. Jews flourished in the Diaspora in proportion to the degree that the European medieval contract society was supplanted by a modern industrial society based on monetary exchange. Sombart's formulation leads one to speculate on Jewish survival as an ethnic and religious group under post-capitalism. Bluntly, can the Jewish people retain a cultural, religious, and national identity in a Socialist setting, which is defined more in political than in economic terms?

Where Jewish communities of Latin America are largely middle class in character, and the rest of the society has not been able to share, as have their North American counterparts, in the bountiful riches of bourgeois life, these communities have become inextricably tied to the international Capitalist system. More pointedly, the Latin American Nationalist version is that Jews participate in that special brand of post-industrial capitalism, neo-colonialism, that places great store in property and profits but has all but ignored other shibboleths of capitalism such as free market competition and equality of access to personal growth. We are not talking here about Jewish communities in the state of Israel, which from the outset were formulated in terms of an agrarian socialist pattern. My remarks pertain only to the Jews within the Diaspora, and specifically as that Diaspora took Jews to Latin America.

Even in their quasi-radical Communist versions, Jewish communities always retain their lively sense of bourgeois perspectives. In Brazil, Mexico, and Argentina membership in Communist parties of the traditional variety represents, or rather, it did in the past, a secular expression of Jewish aspirations for a just society. Membership in athletic clubs, private banking societies, and generally well-heeled life styles was a bourgeois expression of this same aspiration. Thus when the political crunch has come, Jews—whether as open or closed middle-class members—face a crisis of class membership. The immigrant generation, by any standards, represented a shallow commitment to Judaism; they were concerned with adaptation to the nations of Latin America as a survival mechanism. The second generation that group once removed from the immigrant culture, by all odds represented a shallow secularism since once a modicum of integration was achieved, economic pursuits became dominant. Thus, for third generation Jews to become truly radical means an abandonment of Judaism altogether, while to remain overtly and manifestly Jewish implies an identity with the exploiting middle sectors. This then is the untenable truth faced by established Jewish communities in Latin America. It is little wonder that their rage is directed at their special condition as Jews rather than at their condition as members of a middle class in which they are limited participants. The pressure of the political left in many of these nations further heightens the belief that being Jewish is itself the source of their alienation.

How do Jews fare in such Socialist states as Cuba and Chile, states which have had a revolution against Capitalist social relationships? And how have they fared under neo-Fascist regimes such as those that have been dominant in Argentina, Brazil, and Paraguay, states which have had revolutionary assaults on the classic Capitalist model that incorporates the liberal tradition of free criticism and free choice?

To pose the questions in these terms avoids the new assumption that the Jews are on the verge of catastrophe, and the conventional assumption that, as Latin America develops, so too will Jews prosper and profit. The convergence of ethnicity and nationalism was far greater at an earlier period when immigrant labor was a central ingredient to business and labor expansion in Latin America as well as North America. Now, in the post-industrial era, the need for such labor has given way, and confrontation has replaced convergence as the essential dynamic in Jewish-Latin relationships. For example, if one were to ask how the Jewish community of Cuba fared after the Castro Revolution, the answer would be not very well. According to the latest and most reliable demographic estimates, there were roughly 10,000 Jews in Cuba at the time of the Castro Revolution in 1959; that number has dwindled to roughly 2,000 a decade later.[3] One might argue that the exodus from Cuba was part and parcel of the middle-class exodus and so had very little to do with religious sentiment. But that leads us to Sombart's point that Jews and capitalism are so intimately linked that an exodus of the bourgeoisie implicitly means the exodus of large numbers of Jews.

Yet this neat model does not seem quite so applicable to a nation like Chile. Immediately after the victory of the Socialist Party of Salvador Allende, there was a Jewish exodus corresponding to a by now typical post-revolutionary process: a middle-class entrepreneurial exodus. This was heightened by the pro-Arab views of Allende that compelled many Jews to assume that anti-Zionism was indeed a prelude to a wider anti-Semitism. But before this progressed far, a curious reversal took place. The exodus seemed to taper off dramatically. Some Jews quickly moved from being economic entrepreneurs and began functioning as political entrepreneurs. They performed with admirable loyalty to the new Socialist regime and exhibited a brilliance that has permitted a flowering of a politicized intelligentsia the likes of which has not been seen in South America since nineteenth-century positivism took hold in education. In Chile we have a country in which the Jews have historically participated economically, not politically. There is a residual of anti-Semitism in the new Chile, and Jews must travel with light suitcases and heavy hearts. Yet the expected exodus did not take place nor have Jews been physically or spiritually imperiled.

In Argentina under Perón, in Brazil under Vargas, and in Mexico under Díaz Ordaz the Jews fared exceptionally well economically. There were occasional outbursts against Jewish financial interests, but these became increasingly muted after the defeat of nazism in World War Two. However, Jews have not been particularly prominent in political life, and certainly not in the military life of these countries. There are of course rare exceptions, particularly in Brazil. But the overall fact is that Jews have remained in the economic interstices of these nations without exercising any corresponding political role. And it would seem that prominent Jews felt this form of accommodation to be quite acceptable if not desirable, given the cycle of Latin American political instability.

These distinctions are extremely important. There is a marked tendency to talk in generalizations and abstractions about Jews in the Diaspora or Jews in Latin America, without taking note of different possibilities and changed circumstances over time. The role of politics in the Latin American orbit has always been equal, if not greater, to the socioeconomic forces often considered basic. Given the highly politicized societies in Latin America, Jewish power can be measured as effectively in terms of political power as in terms of the conventional measure of economic mobility. With these kinds of variations accounted for, and frankly acknowledged, some of the undue concerns for the physical survival of Jewish people can be put in clearer historical perspective, where they somehow seem less ominous, if not necessarily less omnipresent.

In part, the Jews of Israel have escaped the dilemma of surviving outside the framework of capitalism (at least in part) because the national aspirations are isomorphic with Jewish aspirations. Israel is, after all, a Jewish State. The Jewish community within Israel links up with problems and processes of the State and the governmental apparatus. The idea of a Jewish State, however coated with religious values, is at the core the idea of a State as such, and that signifies the capacity to direct the instruments of control and coercion within the society.

It is the estrangement, the alienation of Jews in the Diaspora from the sources of State power, that is responsible for their special connection with the spirit of capitalism. For the economic arena alone seems to be hospitable to Jewish talent, or at least does not subject the Jew to the same level of ire and suspicions of other nationals and other nationalities. Now that Israel has existed for almost a quarter of a century, it is perhaps to be expected that the suspicion of Jewish dual loyalty lurks deep in the rising nationalisms throughout the Third World and not least in Latin America. The very existence of Israel, while providing a support and a shield for the Jews of Latin America, also creates problems for these Jews, since it raises the possibility that Jews might never really be integrated into the national aspirations of each nation in Latin America. Now that such aspirations are increasingly framed by the left, not only as nationalism, but as anti-imperialism, the Jewish condition has become ubiquitous. Jews are perceived as marginal economic men in Marxian terms, and even more marginal neo-imperialists who cannot be absorbed into local nationalism, and at the same time refuse to consider nationalism as a salvation.[4]

At this juncture, Jewish organizational fears for survival in Latin America link up with nationalist fears for survival of Latin America apart from dependency relations with the imperial powers. The tragic fate of the Jewish communities of Latin America does not involve a concerted effort of a Torquemada or a Hitler to destroy human life for reasons of religious or political fanaticisms, but it makes them the victim of the rising tide of national liberation movements throughout the hemisphere, to which Jews are remote and residual rather than central and integral. Jews, classically and historically linked to causes of mass democracy and social equity, are now outside the impulse toward national liberation from imperial domination, that is, outside the very source that would provide for the sort of democratic goals Jews have been linked to historically. There are very important exceptions, such as those seen in Chile. And it must also be candidly noted that these liberation movements create a causal nexus moving from anti-imperialism to anti-Zionism to pro-Soviet and pro-Arab postures that make it hard for all but the anti-Jewish Jew to participate in such movements.

To pose the problem of Jewish survival as a question of left wing Latin American nationalism does not absolve the nationalists from anti-Semitism. It does not remove the sting of left-wing radical organizations such as the Tupamaros in Uruguay, whose singular restrictive badge of honor is that no Jew be permitted in its ranks. On the other hand, we can say—poignantly as well as pointedly—that the historical role of the Jew as marginal man, while serving the purposes of liberalism and even radicalism in fully developed and even overripe capitalism, has not had the same radical thrust in underdeveloped nations with unrealized dreams. If anti-Semitism on the left led to a condition of what Bebel termed the socialism of fools, it nonetheless is a fact that the main threat to Jewish survival is indeed now from the left. Therefore, the main response of the Jews must be to that left, and that response must be affirmative no less than critical; otherwise, the confrontation will be ominous, with serious consequences for the Jews of Latin America. Yet, ironically, those Latin American societies which have been singularly appreciative of their Jewish communities have been singularly enriched, economically and intellectually by their presence.

This muted fear that the Jews of Latin America, in their very immersion in middle sector affairs, may not survive the revolutionary onslaught has given rise to a search for alternatives. And in this search, the leaders of Jewish organizational life have worked diligently to move the Jewish masses away from what is after all a far from robust bourgeoisie.

The Jewish leadership in Latin America are plainly worried, not by the possibility of extermination as in Nazi Germany, nor even by the possibility of cultural absorption as in contemporary North America. Rather they are concerned by something at once more subtle and yet evident to any one who has spent time in Latin America. They are disturbed by the potential for class absorption, the destruction of dependent bourgeois societies that have neither the determination of their North American class counterparts nor the traditions of their European bourgeois counterparts. The myth of the bourgeoisie as a bridgehead in Latin America for more rapid development is being dispelled. Too much poverty exists at the bottom and too much dependency exists at the top of society for the myth to be sustained. In the process of inflation, unemployment, and technical dependency, the fragile status of middle sector superiority is in fact subject to severe strains. This is especially so in Argentina and Peru, less so in Brazil and Mexico. Yet with this general deterioration of the bourgeois condition, one notes the breakdown of the Jewish communities.

Jewish organizational leadership in Latin America, often in marked contrast to their own rank and file membership, has taken to heart its own marginality and its need to settle accounts with the countries and nations in which it resides. Such Latin American Jewish leaders demonstrate much less a sense of world-wide solidarity among Jews than a sense of remarkable solidarity, in part as Jews and in part as Latins, with the cause of the Third World and of national liberation as such. This is an intriguing development because it means that leaders in the Jewish community are in an antithetical relationship to the Capitalist sector, and in an ambivalent relationship even to Israel. With such an identification with the goals of the nation and movement away from identification with capitalism, Jewish participation in indigenous and even radical Latin American movements becomes possible, and indeed it is evidently underway. But it also leads to new strains between Jewish bourgeois aspirations and Jewish radical aspirations—not an unusual situation in the history of Judaism.

A number of spokesmen for the Latin American Jewish community have indicated that anti-Semitism is the product of the unique condition of Jews as representative of middle-class and upper-class life in Latin America and their essential distance from the cause of the peasantry and proletariat. While this is a correct surmise, it is only part, the most highly visible part of the problem. For this view expresses the myth of Jewish power without appreciating the degree to which Jews participate in the bourgeois artifact but not in the bourgeois substance. What E. Franklin Frazier once said about the black bourgeoisie of the United States could well be attributed to the Jewish bourgeoisie of Latin America: they represent shadow without substance, good form and good manners without corresponding real power or real wealth. There are many other factors which contribute to Latin American anti-Semitism other than the Jew's marginal persistence in the middle class. These have not had the attention they deserved.

Latin American culture is significantly a Catholic culture, and that means a monolithic culture. Latin America did not have the Protestant leavening of North America. Jews were therefore forced into a much sharper juxtaposition with Catholics than in North America, where just about all religions seem to blend into an *American* religion of the moral economy. One finds the Jew in Latin American culture confronting Christianity as the Church Triumphant, much as he had to do in medieval European culture, rather than as a fragmented and highly parceled series of churches controlled locally. The absence of Protestantism also represented an absence of pluralistic sensibilities. It was the pluralisms in North America and their absence in Latin America, that enabled Jewish marginality to persist far longer in Latin America. This religious dimension helps explain the current tendencies toward anti-Semitism in Latin America. After all, Jews do represent a religious counterforce there, and not just a cultural or economic force.

Latin America has seen a more militant form of "atheism" or "positivism" than has North America. Secularism has confronted religious belief in a vigorous head-on clash in countries like Argentina, Brazil, and Mexico. And here, too, the Jews have found trouble, for as a religious group they shared with Catholics a set of beliefs that put them beyond the pale of positivism. As a result, they were damned on one hand by the majority religion for being a minority religion, and then they were twice damned by the anti-religious forces for being religious to begin with. Positivism, secularism, and modernism all worked to sustain a low-keyed anti-Semitism in the Latin American environment, though it rarely spilled over into overt manifestations of hostilities to Jewish communities as such.

It is important to deal with these considerations; otherwise, we shall become prey to an oversimplified version of the Jewish condition as presented by those who would have us believe that Jews are culturally dominant and not politically alienated. It would be extremely naïve to assume that Jewish power within the intellectual world translates into Jewish power in other sectors of Latin American society.

Jews who perform cultural services in Latin America can not yet translate these services into political power or into economic power. Nowhere in Latin America do Jews share in significant political power. This is the central fact of the hemisphere. We must therefore get beyond formalistic schemes as to whether politics or economics is of primary importance in the modern world. Rather, we are dealing with a group which is not able to participate in managing the affairs of State in any Latin American nation. Apart from its new-found "political broker" role in Chile, Jews lack the strength of other national and ethnic groups who have participated much more fully in the political life of Latin American society. But generally Italians gave up being Italian to become Argentines, and Portuguese gave up being Portuguese to become Brazilian, and Spanish emigres gave up their loyalty to Spain to become Mexicans, but Jews cannot accept or afford this surrender of traditions and the "nationality of the mind," as Dubnow called it. Therefore, Jews cannot expect to be welcome with any fervor into the political process.

The Jewish communities in Latin America must also confront not simply their Jewishness but their ideological and national position vis-à-vis Israel. Curiously, social scientists in Israel have simply exhibited the kind of interest in the Jewish communities of Latin America that a devoted elder might show toward a younger wayward relative. But paternal concern avoids the basic fact that what Israel does in relation to Africa, or in relation to other parts of the Third World, or how Israel confronts American foreign policy with respect to Vietnam, all have great bearing on the capacity of the Jewish communities of Latin America to develop a significant independent "radical" posture.

The sources of anxiety over the Jews of Latin America extend beyond their heavy concentration in the world of middle-class life and their parallel penetration of the cultural apparatus. At its deepest recesses, the very cosmopolitanism of the Jew, his links not just to the land of Israel but more profoundly his stubborn connection to Jews in the United States, England, France, and even the Soviet Union, appear to be more durable than similar sentiments of other ethnics for the old country. In the latter case, such sentiments pass away rather quickly with the second generation; whereas with Jews, such sentiments pass either much more slowly or not at all. Indeed, even among Jews for whom Yiddish is as foreign as Chinese, the revival of Jewish passions has taken place. Of course, there is none of the ruthlessness and hatefulness of the charges leveled by the Soviet Stalinists in the fifties against "rootless cosmopolitanism," but the attitudes are there in the new-found belief by Tacuaristas in Argentina, as well as Tupamaros in Uruguay, that Jewish cosmopolitanism compromises Jewish radicalism at the source, that is, at their unwillingness to surrender their links to the imperialisms of America and Europe. Even those Jews attuned to current stylistic forms of new left sentiment and doctrine find themselves immobilized by anti-Semitism. And hence the rebellion of third generation Jews not infrequently involves intense self-hate taking the form of open repudiation, or self-adulation taking the form of a left-tinged Zionism—but a Zionism nonetheless. And this of course, in the circular world of anti-Semitic reasoning, only reinforces the belief that Jewish loyalty to Latin America—or really to Argentina or Brazil or Mexico, etc.—is weak and untrustworthy.

The spirit of anti-imperialism and of firm independence from American foreign policy exhibited by the Latin American Jewish leadership is mediated by their condition not so much as Jews as their unique sense of responsibility and commitment to Israel. The norm of reciprocity must finally take effect; and that means a much greater responsibility on the part of Israel, not just for the abstract survival of the Jewish community of Latin America or as an expression of sympathy and concern for their brethren in the Diaspora, but a concerted effort in the formulation of Israeli foreign and domestic policy that in the very act of promoting a more radical posture within Israel would contribute positively to the image of the Jew in the democratic upsurge now taking place throughout Latin America.

There are no easy answers. The problems of nationalism and the Jewish condition cannot be resolved by neat expressions of words and language. But we can make explicitly clear the responsibility of each huge cluster, in the United States, Israel, and Latin America, to forge the kinds of political position that will make possible greater pride in being a Jew as well as enforce the Jew's classic expression of concern for the downtrodden and his demand for universal equity—concerns which at least ostensibly are the tap roots of Latin American nationalism as well.

8 ORGANIZATION AND IDEOLOGY OF THE JEWISH COMMUNITY OF ARGENTINA

With a population of approximately one-half million, Argentina, and in particular Greater Buenos Aires and its adjacent provinces, have the largest concentration of Jewish people in the Western hemisphere outside of the United States. Further, in absorbing over one-half of all twentieth-century Jewish immigration to Latin America, Argentina ranks second only to the United States as a haven for the Diaspora Jew.[1] Given this impressive fact, it comes as something of a surprise that serious sociological and demographic analysis of the Jews of Argentina has only just begun.[2]

The reason for this are many and variegated. First, the generally late development of empirical sociology in Latin America and the particular blight of social science research in Argentina during the rule of Juan Domingo Perón (1945-1953)—years which coincide with a widespread growth of interest in community life and the study of complex organization. Second, the extremely powerful nationalistic ideologies which have tended to emphasize the homogeneity of Argentina in terms of Roman Catholicism as a social institution.[3] Third, the tendency of Jewish community leaders in Buenos Aires to accept the ground rules set forth by competing nationalist and statist ideologies and thus to carry on their activities outside the glare of any sort of publicity which might adversely affect Jewish occupational or cultural advances.[4] Fourth, the widespread "assimilationist" Jewish intelligentsia, which has traditionally identified with the positivist philosophic tradition as against Catholic spiritualism;[5] taking the position that being Jewish, like being gentile, is an accident of birth, an ethico-religious credo having no real utility in the post-feudal world, where a new enlightenment and new humanism ought to prevail (if it does not exist in fact).[6]

I shall attempt a general framework for the study of the Jewish community by taking inventory of relevant statistical information now available on immigration, organization, and occupation.

Beyond that, a canvassing of opinions from leading "decision makers" in the Jewish community of Buenos Aires yielded little consensus. Five issues in particular seemed to find informants equally distributed on both sides of the issue:

How well organized is the Jewish community? What role does anti-Semitism play in Jewish-Gentile relations? Does the Jewish community of Buenos Aires exhibit more rapid, less rapid, or the same sort of social mobility as the populace in general? When is the political orientation of the Jewish community different or the same as that of the population in general? Does the occupational-economic ranking of Jews show approximately the same distribution as the rest of the city's population?

To provide useful answers to these questions requires more than public opinion surveys, since matters of fact are involved rather than statements of sentiment. It cannot be emphasized strongly enough that factual data are in short supply. Hence, the hypotheses and conclusions which follow must be considered as tentative, to be modified in the light of changing circumstances and new evidence.

IMMIGRATION: ADAPTATION WITHOUT INTEGRATION

Clearly, Jewish economic, political, and even ideological forms have resulted from the interaction of the group identities which the Jews brought to the "new world" (what we shall call "ethnicity") with the social, political, and psychological complex they found in Argentina (what we shall call "nationality").[7]

The sociological significance of immigration patterns for questions of ethnicity is clear from the connection, either real or alleged, between immigration and economy ("depressions are caused by cheap immigrant labor"; "immigrants prevent the native population from advancing"), between immigration and psychology ("immigrants lower the general cultural level of the old populace"; immigrants reveal high levels of mental illness and insanity"), and between immigration and sociality ("immigrants bring about a lowering of social morals"; "they create the seeds of higher rates of crime and alcoholism"). These canards were evident in Maciel's (1924) concern about the "Italianization" of Argentina during the twenties,[8] and were used a decade later by Julio Alsogaray to trace the growth of prostitution and white slavery in Buenos Aires to the Jews.[9] While such allegations have in general been laid aside by serious scholars,[10] the popular consciousness clearly lags behind the scientific consciousness.[11] Therefore, the position of the Jewish immigrant in Argentina is heavily laden with conflicting psychological drives and ideological loyalties.[12] Broadly speaking, the Jews insist upon ethnic singularity, while Argentines incline toward national unity. An exploration of these contrasting loyalties sheds a good deal of light, not solely on problems of immigration, but also on basic organizational traits of the Argentine Jewish community.[13]

Our first specific task is to survey the demographic and immigration features of the Argentine Jew. The most striking trait of Table 1 is the twentieth century character of the Jewish pop-

TABLE 1

Jewish Population in the Argentine Republic

Years	Established population	Immigration	Births in excess of deaths	Total increase	Composite total
1890-94	2,595	7,159	365	7,524	10,119
1895-99	10,119	4,536	941	5,477	15,596
1900-05	15,596	8,370	1,437	9,807	25,403
1905-09a	25,403	40,006	3,267	43,273	68,676
1910-14	68,676	41,027	6,573	47,600	116,276
1915-19b	116,276	1,607	9,044	10,651	126,927
1920-24c	126,927	33,963	10,513	44,476	171,043
1925-29c	171,403	32,836	14,284	47,120	218,523
1930-34	218,523	17,336	17,612	34,948	253,471
1935-39d	253,471	26,159	25,357	51,516	304,987
1940-44	304,987	8,210	27,212	35,422	340,409
1945-49	340,409	7,505	30,407	37,912	378,321
1950-60e	378,321			41,679	420,000

SOURCES: *ORT Economic Review,* Volume 3 (April) New York, 1942; Jacob Shatzky, *Comunidades judias en Latinoamérica,* Buenos Aires, 1952; and Moisés Kostzer, "Problemas propios de la estadística relativa a los judíos en la Argentina," *Primera conferencia de investigadores y estudiosos judeo-argentinos en el campo de las ciencias sociales y la historia,* Buenos Aires: Universidad Hebrea de Jerusalén/Comunidad Israelita de Buenos Aires, 1961; Gino Germani, *Estructura social de la Argentina: análisis estadístico,* Buenos Aires: Editorial Raigal, 1955.

[a] Immigration of Russian Jews in the wake of pogroms following the 1905 Revolution.

[b] Immigration decline largely due to World War I.

[c] Second wave of Polish and Slavic immigration.

[d] German Jewish migration following the rise of Nazism.

[e] Estimate of current population in Kostzer (1961).

ulation in Argentina. From 1905 until 1940, the main increase came from immigration. Beyond that point, increase in the Jewish population cluster is due to a steadily climbing birthrate from within the Argentine nation.

The data show not only the extent of Jewish immigration but also indicate worsening trends in the economic and political situation in the "old country." Sudden transformation in the political fortunes of Argentine democracy have not had an appreciable effect on conditioning Jewish immigration either upward or downward. The most singular aspect of Table 1 is that Jewish population expansion is increasingly explainable by the Jewish situation in Argentina decreasingly by new immigration waves; and hardly at all by the inner circumstances of Argentina's political upheavals throughout the century.

As a second and third generation of Argentine Jews emerges, problems tend to shift. A movement takes place within the Jewish community from occupational and linguistic issues to mobility and educational problems. The new generation of Argentine Jews is essentially adapted to the new home country, and is indistinguishable by mode of dress, habit, and speech.[14] The issue then becomes the nature of Jewish identity, while the older (and perhaps more basic) theme of Jewish survival tends to become a minor motif. This generational shift from considerations of survival to those of identity has become particularly pronounced with the liquidation of the Nazi Leviathan in Germany. Although the specter of a Nazi resurgence has been revived in the postwar world by outbursts of anti-Semitism in parts of Europe and the Near East, and perhaps equally by the exposure of the monumental scale of the Fascist effort to annihilate European Jewry, the elimination of mass genocide as a current factor has had definite social consequences. The ideological shift from survival (*who* is a Jew) to identity (*what* is a Jew) can hardly be said to be complete. Nonetheless, the essays which appear in Argentine Jewish publications—from *Comentario* to *Davar*—do indicate that a generational shift has been affected.

The concentration of the Jew in the Buenos Aires area is somewhat obscured by the geographical distribution of provinces in Argentina. The census reports of 1934-35 (which closely approximate the 1935 figures given in Table 1) show that out of 253,242 Jews living in Argentina at the time, 131,000 (or slightly more than half) lived in the city of Buenos Aires proper.[15] But to this total must be added the Jewish population of the Litoral region in general—including the three main provinces: Buenos Aires (29,408), Santa Fe (29,946), and Entre

Ríos (28,231).[16] The additional 87,585 living in these provinces, which are geographically, economically, and politically connected to Buenos Aires proper, must be added to the totals. Thus roughly 80 per cent of the Jewish population are concentrated in the most urbanized portion of the country.[17] The Jewish question in Argentina must therefore be discussed in the context of general urbanization and the tendency of immigrants generally to congregate in the cities. Efforts at the turn of the century by wealthy Jewish philanthropists to relocate the Jews in Argentine farmlands and reconstitute the myth of the Jew as a man of the soil as an answer to anti-Semitic charges of the "commercial Jew" essentially have failed.[18] Jewish colonists came upon a combination of poor soil, strenuous competition, and the general impulse of the Argentine to move from the interior to the capital city.[19]

A comment on these earlier figures is in order. The size of the Jewish population has been the subject of wide speculation. The census figures of 1934-35 and that of 1947 report roughly the same number of Jews living in Argentina. This stagnation is registered despite the large scale immigration of German Jews to Argentina during this period, minimally estimated at between 100,100 to 150,000, and the normal population increase in Argentina (swelling from 12,400,000 in 1935 to approximately 20,000,000 in 1960) it is evident that given a normal curve with the rest of the population, the Argentine Jewish community should range between 400,000 in 1947 to 500,000 in 1960. The case of the "missing Jews," that is, of vast underreporting, is partially accounted for by the fears of the Jewish community during the Perón era—not so much as a function of Peronism, but of very proximate memories of the holocaust. It is not without interest to speculate on the number of those with Jewish parentage answering "without religion" (239,949); particularly in the light of the fact that by combining Jewish population totals (249,330) with this "non-religious" total, the number (487,279) is only slightly higher

TABLE 2

Population by Province in Argentina as of 1935
Jewish Population Totals

Province	Total population	Ashkena-zim	Sephardim	Total combined	Per-centage of Jews
Capital Federal (Buenos Aires)	2,228,440	107,000	24,000	131,000	5.87
Province of:					
Buenos Aires	3,282,869	25,151	4,257	29,408	0.89
Santa Fe	1,439,245	25,557	4,389	29,946	2.09
Entre Ríos	669,974	26,940	1,291	28,231	4.21
Córdoba	1,168,649	6,929	2,364	9,293	0.79
Mendoza	468,117	3,415	627	4,042	0.86
Tucumán	493,903	2,810	1,034	3,844	0.78
San Luis	179,778	185	227	412	0.22
La Rioja	104,147	115	132	247	0.23
San Juan	193,568	1,171	418	1,589	0.82
Catamarca	138,035	440	55	495	0.36
Sgo. del Estero	433,174	1,410	1,133	2,543	0.59
Corrientes	473,742	1,677	682	2,359	0.49
Jujuy	103,901	203	176	379	0.36
Salta	192,105	605	693	1,298	0.67
Regions of:					
Chaco	205,000	1,820	470	2,290	1.11
La Pampa	199,162	2,584	359	2,943	1.42
Misiones	150,683	366	277	643	0.42
Neuquén	42,241	219	38	257	0.61
Río Negro	115,000	576	253	829	0.72
Santa Cruz	23,352	33	18	51	0.22
Formosa	30,000	242	143	385	1.28
Chubut	55,644	561	170	731	1.31
Los Andes	6,000	5	22	27	0.45
Tierra del Fuego	3,296				0.00
TOTALS	12,400,025	210,014	43,228	253,242	2.04

SOURCE: Data drawn from *Dirección General de Estadística de la Nación, Estadística de la Municipalidad de la Capital—IV/C.G.C.B.A.*, Buenos Aires, 1936.

than the normal expectancy of Jewish population in Argentina between 1933 and 1947. The most recent estimate places the Jewish population at approximately 500,000.[20]

It is clear from Table 2 and the previous explanation of the provincial structure that the Argentine Jew is primarily rooted in Greater Buenos Aires.[21] He is, indeed, an "economic man" rooted in *Gesellschaft* relations. But what too frequently has been overlooked is that the Jew is also a "community man," having powerful social roots in *Gemeinschaft* relations. This functional duality makes the Jew of Buenos Aires an adaptive rather than an integrative person.

Undoubtedly the commercial and cultural greatness of Buenos Aires was profoundly affected by Jewish immigration. The Jew added a special dimension to the "enlightenment" strain in the city's educational and cultural life. Along with this he had his greatest opportunity for upward social mobility in the city's compelling commercial and industrial activities. He thus accentuated economic and cultural forces already operative in the city, contributing much needed skilled labor and management techniques to an urbanization process. The philanthropic effort to solve the "Jewish question" by turning back to the land was simply misanthropic. The European Jewish bourgeois failed to take into account traditional Jewish social aspirations: educational achievement, economic security, occupational mobility, and cosmopolitan orientation—aspirations which can far more readily be realized in an urban and suburban environment than in a rural setting.

The structure of Jewish voluntary associations follows closely the characteristic types of migration waves. For some idea of the natural history of Jewish life in Argentina, we may divide immigration patterns of the Ashkenazi Jews into five stages, involving three distinct national or regional types of European Jews. The first type was the Western European Jew, Alsatian, and French. Migrating between 1860-85, after the liberalization of the Argentine constitution, they came in search of religious freedom and found it. Occupationally this first Jewish wave was linked to professional and small banking enterprises. The second (1889-1905), third (1905-21), and fourth (1921-30) waves emigrated from Eastern Europe to form the largest bulk of Jews in Argentina. The reasons for the coming of the Ashkenazim[22] are profoundly linked to the alternating currents of revolution and counterrevolution that shook Eastern Europe during this period. The brutal oppression at the hands of Polish and Ukrainian landlords, exclusion from educational opportunities as a result of Tsar Nicholas' scientific quota system, political impotence, and cultural starvation as a result of "pale settlements" in Rumania, Poland, Hungary, and Russia, which limited the number of Jews living in metropolitan areas are the well-known but nonetheless distressing reasons for the outward migration.

The Jew of Eastern Europe came without funds but with a wealth of domestic, handicraft, factory, and commercial skills, all of which were more readily absorbed in Latin America than in Europe. It was the search for economic opportunity and, concomitantly, political freedoms rather than any particularly deep religious sentiment that accounted for the bulk of these middle waves of immigration. The last type of migrant to Argentina was the German Jew. It might be noted that the German Jew came with his "high culture" intact.[23] Generally, this type of immigrant had some adequate means of financial subsistence or had those professional and business qualifications that soon restored his financial position to its status quo ante. Further, the German Jew had a conservative rather than radical orientation politically, and tended to identify with authority and order rather than to "meddle in affairs of state."[24]

Of these five distinct migratory waves, only the first failed to survive with its "Jewishness" intact. The reasons for this failure offer valuable clues as to the nature of Jewish ethnicity. Leaving aside the imbalance of males to females, something characteristic of all population migrations, the Western European Jews who came to Argentina arrived with their *Gesellschaft* orientation intact. Other than setting up a house of religious worship, they tended to improve their occupational roles by consolidating their social prestige within the larger gentile society. The process of absorption was enhanced by the relatively excellent opportunities for early Jewish settlers, their rapid linguistic adaptation from one Romance language to another, and by a highly "Protestantized" self-vision of fulfilling providential will through commercial and business enterprise. In brief, and to paraphrase Dubnow,[25] this kind of Jew had a religious conscience without having a national conscience. As such, when the Alsatian-French Jew lost his religious beliefs in the general fervor of the enlightenment-positivist revolt against traditionalism, he lost even the traces of Judaism.

The East European Ashkenazic Jew represented an altogether different specimen. First, this Lithuanian-Polish-Ukrainian Jew was born and reared in ghetto life and tended to see himself as part of a solid phalanx against the outside (hostile) world. Second, linguistically, he was far removed from the Romance language tradition, with Yiddish as his first language and the particular national languages of his mother country, Russian, Polish, or Hungarian, as his second language. Third, the new immigrant was organized on a *Gemeinschaft* basis in Europe and, therefore, upon arriving in Argentina, thought of the reestablishment of his "total community" patterns, with voluntary associations for every form of social activity from banking to baking. Jewish credit agencies, hospitals, schools, welfare centers, and orphanages were established around the *Kehillah* as the central institution.[26] Thus, the Jew was identified as such, not simply by his special place of worship but by a reference set brought with him from the old world.[27] Without a powerful counteractive culture or ideology to inhibit ethnic centralization (such as the "melting pot" ideology in the United States), Jewish national ideals and ideas flourished.[28] The importance of the *Kehillah* as an organizational counterpart of the "community of fate" ideology can hardly be overstated. Precisely the totality of Jewishness rather than any single aspect united the Jewish immigrant to Argentine society and served to focus anti-Semitic feelings against this special cultural and social substructure.[29] Typically enough, hostility to Jewish feelings of separateness only served to reinforce the intimacy of Jewish social bonds.

We might note here that Slavic, Polish, and Russian immigrants came with strongly felt separatist ideological leanings. The Jewish substructure tended to conflict with the dominant culture. While the ideologies of the French enlightenment and continental liberalism were outside the normal reference set of the East European Jew, he could accommodate to them. Far more difficult was his adjustment to the military-economic coalition or political *caudillaje*. Conversely, such powerful ideological factors in Jewish life as Zionism, agrarian socialism, and trade unionism may have revealed superficial points of contact with the humanistic tradition in Argentine culture, they were too sectarian and too ethnocentric to be either serviceable or welcome to Argentine versions of the *Führerprinzip*. Traditionalist and nationalist alike saw in Judaism an uncomfortable kind of radicalism that would only deepen the sociocultural schisms of the country.

Even the Jewish view of socialism revealed ethnic strivings, as is made plain in the Jewish *Bund* movement of tsarist times and now in the *Hashomer Hatzair* groupings. This relative disinterest in the nationalistic strivings of either the Argentine right or the left, and the contrary identification of socialism with specifically Jewish goals, continues to divide Jewish "interests" from Argentine "national" interests in general. Socialism, like Zionism, was thought of by the Jewish Community as valuable insofar as it was a guarantor—and not the grave digger—of Jewish interests. In this fashion the East European Jewish immigrant developed over a period of years an ideological superstructure which operated as a functional reinforcement of the *Gemeinschaft* structure against the first furies of Argentine industrialism, nationalism, and urbanism. Political detachment was thus a form of resistance—a strategy of survival through disengagement.

A paramount difference must be noted between immigration to an underdeveloped country and one to a highly advanced industrial complex. In this case it marks a distinction not in the type of Jew (since he was essentially uniform in ethnic stock and cultural background—Ashkenazic, East European, Slavic, ghettoized, etc.) but in the society to which he came. The Jews entering an advanced industrial society are self-conscious and very concerned when they do not blend quickly into the new nation. According to an observation made in France, the immediately preceding peer group to the new country tends to reinforce this need to belong as a means of getting along. The urge to be "accepted" is pronounced.[30] This applies with equal if not greater force to the United States where the market-orientation attitude contributes greatly in defining social mobility. For the East European Jew in the United States "this might mean that he could adjust his 'artificial self' to the outside world by leaving his internal 'idiosyncrasy'—a part of his heritage, his sympathies and his group attachments—for his 'home consumption.' "[31]

Precisely the absence of such affective relations and drives characterizes Jewish immigration to Argentina. For the introduction of a group with a relatively high state of "cultural achievement"—herein signifying everything from hygienic habits to educational perspectives—into a society which does not have that high a level of culture and is unable to offset this cultural differential in material wealth, is bound to foster a clash that perhaps most important, tends to cut away any common meeting ground between the new group and the society. In short, ethnicity does not simply become self-liquidating in the face of a new cultural milieu unless or until the national culture holds out very substantial advantages that cannot be guaranteed in any other form. Nor is this a specifically Jewish "neurosis" since a similar pattern can be observed for English, French, and German communities living in Buenos Aires over a span of several generations.

The middle-class character of the Argentine Jews places them in an anomalous position of having relative economic security without any significant voice in the political process. With the possible exception of Hipólito Irigoyen's regime (1916-30), twentieth-century Argentina has been ruled in turn by the conservative landed oligarchy, by an alliance of this oligarchy

TABLE 3

Occupational Distribution of the Jewish and Total Population of All Origins in Argentina (in per cent)

	Total population	Jewish population		
	1947	1942	1950	1954
Primary Activities Agriculture, forestry, fishing, etc.	26.4	13.0	21.0	10.7
Secondary Activities Construction, power sources, printing, metal, chemical, textile trades, etc.	28.6	19.5	10.0	22.1
Tertiary Activities Business, banking, securities, state bureaucracy, service activities, teaching, etc.	41.8	67.5	67.0	67.2
Indeterminate	3.2		2.0	
	100.0	100.0	100.0	100.0

SOURCES: *ORT Economic Review,* Volume 3 (April) New York, 1942; Jacob Shatzky, *Comunidades judías en Latinoamérica,* Buenos Aires, 1952; and Moisés Kostzer, "Problemas propios de la estadística relativa a los judíos en la Argentina," *Primera conferencia de investigadores y estudiosos judeo-argentinos en el campo de las ciencias sociales y la historia,* Buenos Aires: Universidad Hebrea de Jerusalén/Comunidad Israelita de Buenos Aires, 1961; Gino Germani, *Estructura social de la Argentina: análisis estadístico,* Buenos Aires: Editorial Raigal, 1955.

NOTE: The disproportionate percentage of Jews placed in the field of agriculture by Shatsky reflected his penchant for considering all Jews not living in the Litoral region as employed in the agrarian sector. In part, the shift registered between the 1942 and 1950 figures reflects the temporary post-war boom in Jewish colonization activities. Indeed, if the findings of Harari and Lewin (see Table 4) are correct, then even the figures of 13.0 per cent and 10.7 per cent are probably too high.

with the armed forces, by the military sector alone, by the military sector in conjunction with labor federations, and now obliquely by the military wearing a constitutional mask and civilian clothing. Insofar as the decisive political mainsprings have been military blocs, large-scale landowners, labor syndicates, and what there is of large-scale industry, the Jews have not been able to exercise an influence as *Jews*.[32] Such a phenomenon as exists in the United States of ethnic bloc voting plays little part in Argentina, where power is neither a consequence nor a derivative of this middle-class tradition of vox populi.[33]

The middle-class concern for education, health, welfare, insurance, and loan facilities displayed by Jewish voluntary associations is nonetheless indicative of high social (if not political) involvement in Argentine public affairs. While no exact statistics now exist for the Jews of Buenos Aires, we can take the figures in Table 3 as indicative.

What this table reveals is a preponderance of Jewish occupation in "tertiary activities." Even though Argentina has an extremely high percentage of its population in the middle sectors for Latin American, Jewish concentration, like the foreign-born population as a whole, is considerably larger than the norm. If we also take account of the 86 "banks" and 37 "loan offices" ministering primarily to Jewish needs, it is clear that a concentration of Jews in the middle classes is reflected in the high premium put on economic security. Since these economic associations are no less "voluntary" in character than hospitals and schools, it is correct to conclude that Jewish voluntary associations are strongly linked to middle-class social attitudes and ambitions.

More specific information about the middle-sector base of Jewish life in Argentina is forthcoming from the analysis of Harari and Lewin.[34]

Elsewhere they report that as of 1946 over 52 per cent of adult male Jews living in the *smaller urban centers* of Argen-

TABLE 4

Economic Structure of Jewish Communities in Argentina

City	Unclassified	Self-employed artisans	Industrial workers	Small business	White-collar employees	Professionals	Rentiers	Agricultural colonizers	Totals
Santa Fe	41	43	17	208	25	44	9	11	398
Córdoba	120	191	10	215	2	242	37	16	833
Lanús	11	18	15	125	65	15	3	—	252
Mendoza	9	27	2	93	16	12	1	—	160
San Juan	3	2	9	57	6	15	—	—	92
	184	281	53	698	114	328	50	27	1735

SOURCE: Iejiel Harari and Itzjak Lewin, "Resultado de la encuesta sobre profesiones, idiomas y crecimiento," *Nueva Sión,* February-July, 1950.

tina earned their livelihood through commercial and small business activities. Add to this the self-employed artisans (15 per cent) and professionals such as teachers, physicians, and lawyers (11.5 per cent), and you have more than 75 per cent in some sector of the middle class.[35] As is typical of middle-sector activities, a heavy premium is placed on education as the path to higher social mobility. Thus, in contrast to the national norm of 7.7 per cent of Argentine students in university attendance, the Jewish population shows a 22.5 per cent. Given the general isolation and non-participation of Jewish sectors of the Argentine population from political power, Jewish voluntary associations functioned to keep Jewish hegemony intact. But they proved singularly incapable of translating such hegemony into political pressure on the Argentine state as a whole.

VOLUNTARY ORGANIZATION:
FROM SURVIVAL TO IDENTITY

The most striking characteristic of Jewish group life in Buenos Aires is its completeness. The range of services is total, covering the entire spectrum of human necessities in a complex, highly mobile, urban environment. One is greeted not so much by a Jewish community as by a Jewish little society. The relative lack of involvement in political or military affairs is well explained by this near total absorption (especially by the first and second generation) in private, voluntary association as the basis of survival. While shifts in the national political scene are keenly observed and scrutinized, little participation in political party life at any level seems to occur. Rather, what is observable is that *within* the structure of Jewish organizational life one can find the entire political spectrum mimetically reproduced. There will be conservative, liberal, and radical shades of opinion as an outgrowth of policies formulated within the organizations of Jews as such.

A second prominent feature of these voluntary associations is their highly centralized and bureaucratic structure. The number of paid high echelon functionaries are few in number, since most of the leadership have as their main source of wealth independent businesses, small factories, or professional positions. However, a large staff of educators, religious counselors, social service workers, and lower echelon staff are paid and work on a full-time basis. Thus, the philanthropic character of these organizations is essentially intact, with the decision-making leadership also providing a large portion of the organizational funds. There is also considerable duplication and multiplication of organizational efforts, which tends to lessen the effectiveness of these associations. This duplication has nothing in common with the "national pastime" of wasting energies in fruitless directions and unprofitable undertakings. It is simply an outgrowth of Jewish stratification along older national lines (German Jews vs Russian Jews); religio-ethnic lines (Ashkenazim vs Sephardim); and regional lines (Galician Jews vs Lithuanian Jews). This internal fragmentation of Jewish life has been considerably modified with the maturation of a third generation Argentine Jew. The organizational apparatus nonetheless remains operative.

A third significant feature of Jewish associations, in contrast to specifically Catholic associations, for example, is the nearly complete domination of these associations by a lay body having either little or no substantive connection to the rabbinical councils. Indeed, the rabbi's authority is weaker in Argentina than in the United States, where the Protestantization of rabbinic functions has led to a view of the rabbi as spiritual leader and psychological counselor in contrast to the traditional function of the rabbi as teacher. These associations are able to involve a broad representation of Jewish sentiment, from the orthodox to the nonbeliever, without placing in the forefront those theological problems dividing Jews into conservative, orthodox, and reform camps. If intense social stratification is reflected in organizational multiplicity, this situation is somewhat alleviated by the fundamentally nonclerical character of these voluntary associations.

A fourth main feature is the tendency toward noninvolvement and insularity, not only from the broader society at large but also from each other. This fact deserves special consideration, since the tendency is to think of Jews en masse. This does not mean that an anarchic situation prevails. The welter of interconnecting organizational links from international to local levels is powerful evidence that a consensual basis does prevail. Nonetheless, the task of analysis is more complicated than it appears to be at first sight. Since we are dealing with a little society and not simply a little community, the ends of organization tend to become diversified if not diffuse. It is interesting to note that rebellious Jewish youths manifest their demands not so much by working in established associations as by setting up yet new organizations, often of paperweight strength.

Some indications of the intragroup divisions within Judaism are supplied by the state of Jewish parochial education. The battle between Hebraists and Yiddishists continues unabated. Unlike Jewish communities in North America, a rapprochement or an amalgam between the various ethnic branches of Judaism has not yet been achieved.[36] A reflection of its non-

TABLE 5

Linguistic Orientation of Jewish Education in Buenos Aires

Central School Agency	Sponsorship	Languages Taught
Vaad Ha-Hinnukh Ha-Roshi	German Jews	Hebrew and Yiddish
Adat Yerushalaim	Sephardic Jews	Hebrew
Yesod Hadat	Arabic Jews	Hebrew
Hafetz Hayyim	Eastern European Jews	Yiddish
La Organización Central de Escuelas Judías Laicas	Labor Zionists	Yiddish
Asociación de Escuelas Laicas ICUF	Socialists (Bundists)	Yiddish
Mendele Mocher Sefarim[a]	Communist	Yiddish

[a] Closed after two years in operation

SOURCE: Iejiel Harari and Itzjak Lewin, "Resultado de la encuesta sobre profesiones, idiomas y crecimiento," *Nueva Sión,* February-July 1950.

integrative character is the persistence of old-world cultural values which receive special attention in the Yiddish language. A reorientation toward Hebrew, while gaining momentum, continues in some quarters to be viewed as an acceptance of maximalist Judaism and/or Zionism. Hebraists, for their part, view Yiddish as a mark of the Diaspora and the ghetto and hence a permanent self-inflicted stamp of inferiority. Table 5 gives some indication of the split involved.[37]

Perhaps the most pointed commentary on this educational-organizational proliferation is that the Jews of Buenos Aires, after the initial immigrant generation, have tended uniformly to adopt Spanish rather than either Yiddish or Hebrew as their primary language. As a matter of fact, Yiddish-speaking parents tend to speak Spanish to their children.[38] To this degree, ethnicity has disintegrated under the pressures of the necessities of economic existence.

Regarding Jewish voluntary associations in Buenos Aires, we find that the single most powerful agency of Jewish life is the *Kehillah.* Organized in 1894 with 85 member families, it serviced no fewer than 50,000 households as of 1959. In point of authority and membership composition, it is of Russian and

Polish origin. Although it has various tenuous and amorphous connections with the German-Jewish community, its ethnic character remains basically intact. With an annual budget of about 60 million pesos (roughly $800,000 dollars), this is clearly the most potent organizational force. Nearly one-half of its budget is allocated to education of the young. Subventions for social welfare services, publishing, building additional centers throughout the city and country, colonization, religious activities, absorb the remainder of the funds.[39] The funds themselves are administered by a council of ninety members who are drawn from the specific organizations connected to the Buenos Aires *Kehillah*. These "parliamentary representatives" are elected every three years by the membership on the basis of proportional representation.[40]

Increasingly, the funds of the *Kehillah* are being used for educational purposes. Schools are in operation on all levels, from Kindergarten to Seminary. The struggle to create an intelligentsia out of a generation formed solely in Argentina has involved heavy investment of funds and energies. However, the actual increase in numbers of students at *Kehillah*-sponsored schools has increased only slightly over the years. It must be surmised that the "challenge" from Argentine society as a whole is growing, particularly in the relatively unimpeded post-Perón intellectual atmosphere. With the generational changeover, the "crisis" in Jewish associational life can be expected to show a marked increase.[41]

A sound index to the complexities of Jewish associational life in Buenos Aires is revealed by the German Jews who settled in Argentina during the Nazi period. Here we can observe in action some of the associational properties referred to above: organizational totality, multiplication, and bureaucracy. The powerful *Gemeinschaft* nature of German-Jewish life does little to support the conventional notions of the rootless, cosmopolitan Jew. It must be observed that their choice of *Gemeinde* is not synonymous with ghetto existence. A ghetto, at least as a segregated geographical area of Jewish housing, does not exist in Buenos Aires. There are no equivalents to the New York East Side of yesteryear.[42] Even Corrientes Avenue and its surrounding environs, where a higher proportion of Jews live than elsewhere in the city, does not show any decisive area characteristics. The Jews, in short, do not "flavor" the culture of Buenos Aires so much as they simply inhabit it.

This is particularly true of German Jewry, reared in the cultural and psychological traditions of *Aufklarung* and assimilation. Nonetheless, *Gemeinschaft* feelings, that Community of Fate in which hardships and sorrows as well as joys and achievements are shared in common, typifies the German-Jewish community of Buenos Aires. That fragmentation and condition of *Entfremdung,* which *Gesellschaft* life supposedly carries within itself, tends to be offset by common cultural factors of language, culture, and education, as well as more substantial identities of middle-class occupational roles and the cohesive effect of miraculous survival from the Hitlerian holocaust. The "hostile world" of Christian Argentina has its fanatical counterpart in total organization along *Gemeinschaft* lines.[43] It is a defense against outsiders as such, which may be defined by some German Jews as Christianity, by others as generated by the material inadequacies of Argentine society, and by still others as made inevitable by the encroachments and prestige seeking of "lower" types of Jews, especially those from Eastern Europe. The high level of organization achieved by German Jews often at the expense of larger-scale homogeneity within Judaism is a minute reproduction of East-West tensions. These reflect inherited animosities harbored by Germans against Russians (and vice versa) throughout recent history. That the Jew should be the symbolic bearer of these East-West differences may appear ironic in the light of his treatment at the hands of Nazism and to a lesser extent, Great Russian chauvinism. Even more ironic is the fact that the Jew reflects the same functional separations as does the Christian. In short, national and ethnic allegiances rather than religious credos have come to define modern social types in Argentina city life.

The powerful and long-standing divisions between Sephardic and Ashkenazic Jews along the religious axis and between German and Slavic Jews along the national axis show little abatement. Only the divisions between professional and lower-class Jewish economic interests may show signs of breaking down as a consequence of the "deproletarianization" of the Argentine Jew. There does seem to be an *absence* of what Handlin[44] has termed "competition for loyalty" between ethnic values and the larger values of the nation-state. Although the well-developed Argentine educational apparatus has advanced professionalization and, in some measure, has disaffiliated the Jews from their community ties, the Jewish community has resisted this with relative success by the firmness of its associational loyalties. Thus even among informants from second- and third-generation Russian Jews there remains a powerful residue of anti-German-Jewish feeling. Sephardic Jews, for their part, retain a distinctive associational apparatus, and the most recent survey, showing that "intermarriage" between Sephardic and Ashkenazic Jews is still somewhat of a rarity, is an index of these intra-Jewish separatist traits. The rise of a new postwar Jewish generation may alter the statistics somewhat, but the continued strength of old particularistic organizations makes the effect of such statistical shifts minimal in size and marginal in regard to the specific reference groups involved.

What can be observed is large-scale duplication and multiplication of effort in every sphere of Jewish voluntary associational life and a consequent weakening of the Jewish community as a whole. The Jewish collectivity of Buenos Aires tends to appear stronger than it actually is by virtue of its tendency to proliferate organizations and periodicals, each geared to preserve particularist trends in Judaism rather than to preserve Jewish life as a whole.[45] Functional specialization is indeed an integral part of community life. However, such specialized agencies as exist within Jewish community life may often be dysfunctional in relation to the social solidarity of the Jews as such.

A unique by-product of overspecialization has been a reinforcement of the fragmentation and atomization in present-day Jewish life. The generational changeover from the search for survival to the search for identity has tended to operate within a structural apparatus which is not necessarily prepared to cope with changing patterns. Organizations formed in the "age of survival" are not likely to be much concerned with those issues genuinely agitating the young Jew. As such, the new generation faces alternatives of *conforming* to the old institutional mores and folkways, *agitating* for increased power in Jewish agencies, or *abandoning* Jewish organizational life altogether. The fourth possibility, new organizational forms, has the effect of further fracturing Jewish life. Segments of the young intelligentsia have decided to pursue either this last possibility or have followed a policy of disaffiliation. The younger professional and business strata tend to identify more markedly with established organizational norms—either as conformists or as critics of the "old guard." It is fascinating to observe the degree to which Jewish associational life parallels developments in Argentine polity as such: the multiplication of organizational forms beyond their functional value, the rise of an entrenched bureaucratic stratum in policy-making positions, and a narrowing middle-class tendency to identify truth with wealth, learning with power.[46]

There are nonetheless powerful features which tend to establish a consensual base in Jewish life. There is first the unifying force of Israel, which has given Argentine Jews a rallying symbol in a form not subject to the fissures of internal criticism. This is not to say that they, any more than Jews in the United States, have any intention of leaving Argentina for Israel en bloc (although the most militant Zionist elements do have such ambitions). The maturation of Israel has, however, given them a sense of pride and achievement. The image of courage and constructive accomplishment projected by Israel has had a significant effect on broad sectors of the Jewish population. It has further given a *raison d'être* to many voluntary associations which were able to transfer activities from immigration from Europe to aid for Israel without undue organizational upheaval.

Another potent unifying agency has been the generational "retelling" in the form of the Nurenberg and Eichmann trials, in novels and essays, of the contemporary martyrdom of one-third of all Jewry, irrespective of particularistic affiliations or occupational ranking. This has reinforced the older survival ethos among the youth at a critical juncture.[47] The unity of Argentine Jews is seen as bound up with the lot of world Jewry —Morroccan and Ukrainian, Sephardic and Ashkenazic. This has served as a cohesive agency forestalling any mass disaffections or apostasies.

The largest unifying element in Jewish community life is what it has been traditionally: anti-Semitism. To discuss anti-Semitism in the same context with Jewish associational life is axiomatic. We have seen that from a physical, linguistic, and even psychological frame of reference the Jew is now well adapted to the life of Buenos Aires. And it must be said that this adaptation has been aided in no small part by the basic liberalism and cosmopolitan spirit of the city populace. Most Catholic men, for example, have no idea who among them is Jewish. The chauvinistic stereotype is to identify the Jew as a "Russian," but this is a stereotype with little operative value beyond the immigrant generation. The Buenos Aires resident or the *porteño,* especially the man, has a typically "Latin" attitude toward his Catholicism. He sees his church as a political agency, performing certain beneficial social rites "particularly for womenfolk." The lack of church attendance on the part of the Buenos Aires male population is a fact of life observable on any given Sunday morning. The core membership of the church is, outside of the hierarchy of the church itself, composed almost entirely of women parishioners. To use Fichter's pithy phrase, the *porteño* is a marginal Catholic. What this means is that role definitions and reference sets are basically defined by the "profane world," by one or a number of non-religious institutions.[48] The absence of expressions of religious superiority, or of a missionary attitude toward the non-Catholic population, accounts for the sizeable body of public opinion, both Christian and Jewish, which maintains that anti-Semitism is not manifest in Argentina.

If anti-Semitism were merely a matter of contrasting religious impulses or degrees of marginality or nuclearity, it would be true to say that relations between Catholics and Jews are harmonious.[49] However, other types of anti-Semitic syndromes are known to exist.[50] There is the psychological variant, in which stereotyping and negative attitudes toward Jews stem from feelings of frustration often connected with downward social mobility. Such manifestations are usually reserved for highly mobile societies heavily stressing pecuniary values. Then there is the more strictly psychosociological variety known as the "authoritarian personality" which, given a general proclivity to an oversensitized in-group/out-group approach, sees the Jews as a menacing out-group. While there are undoubtedly some variations on these patterns in Buenos Aires, the fundamental nature of anti-Semitism has not been found to be of such a type. The ordinary citizen of Buenos Aires, the *porteño*, makes few distinctions between Jews and Gentiles. Indeed, like the small-town citizen of the United States, he tends to have negative stereotypes of the Jew of such weak and amorphous nature that he neither wishes nor is able to act in response to them. This is particularly true with the linguistic identification of the second generation Jew with the Spanish language and the Argentine cultural-historical traditions.[51] Perhaps the most succinct expression of *porteño* feeling was the comment of a bookseller in reply to a query on whether he carried books on the Argentine Jew. The reply, although factually inaccurate, is significant: "No, there are no books on the Jews of Argentina, since the Jews here do not present any special problem." And as we have already observed, the church does not present that sort of reference group which could "key" non-Jewish reactions.

Anti-Semitism as a posture tends to be very sharply an upper-class phenomena. Neither blue-collar nor white-collar employees, nor the professional or business stratum as such, tend to include the Jewish community as a major source of irritation. These upper-class strata, recruited from wealthy landowners, professional militarists, and sectors of domestically controlled industry, are precisely the places where extreme right-wing nationalism feeds. The Jew is an object of attack in that he cannot be counted on as a celebrator of the myth of Argentine imperial power in Latin America. Where physical violence against Jews occurs, it is most often directed against those having strong Zionist feelings and some projected identification with Israel. A sector of the Delegación de Asociaciones Israelitas Argentinas (*Hajshara del Ijud Habonim*), which conducts workshops in the theory and practice of labor agriculture, simulating Kibbutz conditions in Israel and aiming at emigration to Israel, was on several occasions subject to anti-Semitic violence at the hands of a group known as Tacuara—a loosely knit organization of youths from upper-class Buenos Aires sections.[52] Their political slogan, "patriotism yes, Jews no," echoes most forcefully the fusion of this social sector to ultra-nationalistic aims of "moral" purification.

Organizationally, anti-Semitism is quite weak, despite (or because) of its exclusive upper-class setting. Fringe groups exist that disseminate anti-Semitic literature. None, however, are particularly potent. The educational system itself strongly supports democratic politics and is an area where intensive interaction of the Jew and non-Jew occurs; as a result, vehement forms of anti-Semitism take place only on the fringe areas of the school system. At the secondary school level, there is U.N.E.S. (Unión Nacionalista de Estudiantes Secundarios) and at the university level there is the S.U.A. (Sindicato Universitario Argentino). A large proportion of these student activities bear only indirectly on the Jewish question. The continuing struggle is between *Libre* and *Laica,* between Catholic and secular views of the correct relation of church and state. Anti-Semitism becomes a means for advocating a "morally sound educational system." The secularization of Argentine education is deemed wicked. The Jews are firm advocates of this separation. Therefore, the division between the world of learning and the world of theology is a Jewish plot to destroy the national integrity of Argentina. Such is the logic of anti-Semitism in this social sector. While this logic is basically an attempt to transform the basis of the Argentine educational system, it has had a particular effect on Jews, who felt themselves victims of discrimination, blocked entrance to particular university faculties, denied grants.

The overt political manifestations of anti-Semitic patterns generally derive from the same groups and have a clear *Falangist* character. Slogans of national liberation, national honor, anti-yankeeism, anti-capitalism, and anti-socialism tend to fuse into the myth of *patria* which is often directed against the Jew. The U.C.N. (Unión Cívica Nacionalista), composed of old-style corporativists, holds that the Jew stands in the path of national redemption, in much the same way as did such *fin-de-siècle* extremists as Drumont in *La France juive* and Toussenel in *Les Juifs rois de l'époque*.[53] The Jews are held the chief exploiters in commerce and merchandising, destroyers of the soil, corrupters of Christian virtue and, above all, alien by self-definition. And like the French anti-Semitism of the Dreyfus era, the U.C.N. presents an admixture of national redemption with utopian programs for an Argentine greatness.[54] The newest organization of this kind is the G.R.N. (Guardia Restauradora Nacionalista), which displays a parental affection for the

Tacuara movement and differs from the U.C.N. through its belief that redemption will come through the land rather than through industrialization. While it cannot be emphasized too strongly that these "political parties" are often of a paper-weight variety, more a matter of journalistic proclamation than numerical or organizational consequence, they still do reflect a sizeable body of upper-class Argentine opinion.

Overt hostility for the Jew represents a manifest reaction to more profound, if more latent, sentiments. The population explosion in the Litoral region, Buenos Aires and its surrounding environs, has made Argentina more from a rural to an urban slant. Coming after one hundred years of intense struggle between inland financial interests and Buenos Aires commercial interests, this shift marks a decisive conclusion to the conflict at the level of material culture. Ideologically, resistance to mass society remains.[55] The Jew, as a thoroughly urbanized creature, is seen as somehow accelerating, if not initiating, the demise of inland traditional agrarian interests. In addition, the real wealth created by agricultural and livestock products tends to be translated into the purchase of secondary consumer goods. The material needs of the large landowners are seemingly boundless, and the rationalization for these needs is the Jewish businessman who "robs" the innocent inlander of his wealth. The fact that many Jewish families are engaged in secondary sales and distribution of consumer items seems to reinforce this attitude. Argentine landowners have shown little interest in technological advancement and social reforms. The seller of goods absorbs the guilt for the buyer of the goods. As a recipient of sinful goods, the virtuous buyer becomes a fallen angel; as a seller of material goods, the artful Jew becomes the devil's advocate. The canon of pecuniary emulation becomes transformed into the canon of supernationalism.[56]

For the youthful, and generally more radical sociopolitical element, the Jew is pictured as the transmission agent for imperialist produce. Newspapers will refer to smugglers of contraband goods as "Jews" or as having "Jewish names." The Jew is linked in this way not only to a cosmopolitan plot against nationhood but, no less, against the urge to social reform felt by the younger generation of Argentine Jewry. In the realm of ideology similar stereotyping occurs. The myth of the land as the only true basis of national wealth has as its counterpart. The ultra-nationalists, of both right and left, see themselves as threatened by foreign music, foreign art, foreign languages, and the Jew again seems to be the chief culprit. His cosmopolitan image makes him the perfect scape-goat. Anti-Semitism has tended to increase, not decrease, as the middle class continues to lose ground politically to the "orienters" of policy—the military—and the "formulators" of policy—large-scale business and banking concerns.[57]

The Jewish community has reacted to these threats in various ways. First, the intellectual and professional groups have often denied that anti-Semitism exists at all. Second, the German-Jewish community in particular has recognized that anti-Semitism exists but has felt little else could be expected from such an underdeveloped Latin culture. Third, the Kehillah and the parent DAIA have made efforts to combat anti-Semitic outrages. These efforts, however, have rarely been directed at the specific phenomena of ethnicity and nationalism, cosmopolitanism and insularity, adaptation and integration, etc. Attacks of Tacuara upon Jewish institutions—theaters, agricultural cooperatives, synagogues, etc.—bring forth a flock of proclamations from church dignitaries opposing any manifestation of anti-Semitism, while Jewish organizational reaction is limited to consultations with police and articles on the "Christian Problem." The conversion of these outbursts into a religious issue tends to obscure the realities of either the Argentine Jew, fundamentally disengaged from the synagogue, or the Argentine Catholic, who likewise, shows no signs of mass conversion to a nuclear role in the church.

This question is, of course, particularly sensitive in a political context approximating Falangism. And the Jewish community has every right to be suspicious of "symbolic relations between socialism and nationalism." The last fusion of the words national and socialism produced Nazism, while the guarantee of "self-determination for all nations" has been a slogan more observed in the breach than in the execution by the Soviets. If the Argentine Jew is a political outsider, it is just as much a consequence of the general orientation of supernationalist politics in Argentina as it is a positive effort to guarantee some niche for the separate national flowering of the Jewish spirit. That the Jew is politically "deviant" in the context of Argentine nationalist "norms" is undoubtedly true. The exact composition of elements, positive and negative, remains a task for future research.

If these final pages have touched upon issues which are beyond the confines of organizational analysis of Jewish voluntary associations in Buenos Aires, it is because these larger social forces have been and remain significant in defining the content and roles of these associations. No sociologically sound definition of Jewish associational life in Buenos Aires can proceed without accounting for anti-Semitism since, in fact, the disequilibriated development of ethnicity and nationality has at its core the integrity of separate cultural forms and an obligation of the sovereign power to guarantee that organizational expression of these cultural forms are not tampered with. More effective participation of Jews in Argentine life is dependent upon a broadening of the social content and moral fibre of democracy in Argentina. The policy failures thus far—of Jewish *anti-politique* no less than of Argentine *pro-patria*—should not obscure the overriding fact that Argentina (and Buenos Aires in particular) has created generally favorable conditions for the settlement of Jews. The question of increasing moment for the Jewish community in Buenos Aires is thus no longer survival and shame, but identity and interaction. This transition period can be materially assisted by a firm policy decision by the Argentine government that ethnicity is not the mortal foe of nationality and that the paths of ethnic groups will be respected, honored, and defended.

SUMMARY AND CONCLUSIONS

1. Jewish voluntary associations were formed in the wake of various relatively independent and socially different immigration waves. As such, a duplication of institutions and agencies performing similar roles and fulfilling similar needs for the different sectors of the Jewish collectivity was created and maintained.

2. These voluntary associations have not dissolved despite the dissolution of distinctions between Jews of the second and third generation who have continued to live in Buenos Aires. The continued existence of such duplication leads to a situation in which numbers of associations are dysfunctional in the light of the total needs of the Jewish community. Duplication, reinforced by a bureaucratic apathy, perpetuates distinctions which are no longer important or valid and, latterly, prevents the establishment of organizations required to meet current, more vital challenges to the Jews of the city and the country.

3. The concentration of the Jews of Argentina in the capital city and its environs has made possible a rapid adjustment to urbanism as a Jewish way of life. As the "most Europeanized" city and as the city with the largest cluster of middle-class inhabitants in South America, Buenos Aires has contributed to shaping both the cosmopolitanism and commercialism of Jewish institutional life.

4. The urban character of Jewish life in Argentina and the poorly developed social services offered by the city are major factors in turning *Gemeinschaft* organization into voluntary associations. This totality, while it enables the Jewish community to maintain its compactness, nonetheless tends toward insularity, toward a minimum of participation in the larger affairs of polity.

5. Jewish voluntary associations in Buenos Aires are primarily social in character, with religious worship and instruction functioning as a subculture (often an insignificant part) within the total Jewish "community of fate."

6. The generational shift, the changeover from a transient Jew in search of a haven of rest to a birthright Argentine Jew, has changed the Jew's ideological moorings. While associational power continues to reside in the hands of the old world Jewish immigrant sector, the numerical and economic shift of power to the younger generation has created a disequilibrium between organization and ideology. The main issue has become the nature and value of Judaism rather than the organizational forms required to secure the continued survival of the Jewish community. Thus the chasm between generations is no less a conflict in social and intellectual aspirations.

7. The *place* of anti-Semitism in Buenos Aires is slight, of little organizational force, and remains mainly an upper-class phenomenon. The *character* of anti-Semitism is basically nationalistic and represents a demand for orthodoxy in matters of Argentine patriotism and manifest destiny. This accounts for the stress on the intrinsic outsider quality of the Jew, which is employed to rationalize the negative or nonparticipatory qualities found to exist in the Jewish community of the city.

8. Jewish organizational life, insofar as it offers positive responses to anti-Semitic patterns, attempts to show the anti-Christian as well as anti-human content of such attacks on the Jews which appear in print and in practice. However, for those generally disengaged from Jewish voluntary associations the response to anti-Semitism is one of detachment; whereas for those with powerful separatist inclinations in the Judaic fold there is a strong tendency to withdraw from Argentine realities altogether. In general, community *integration* is highest among the Slavic and Russian Jews, *isolation* is typical of the German and Austrian Jews, and *alienation* characterizes a wide sector of the Jewish intelligentsia.

POSTSCRIPT: A DECADE LATER—1969

A decade means less in terms of social changes in a nation such as Argentina than it does in the United States. There are buildings started at the beginning of the decade that still remain in a state of permanent disrepair. Yet, changes in the social and political system do occur including those which have affected the Jewish community of Buenos Aires.

The main changes which have taken place in the Jewish community can be listed under three categories: changes in the relationship between Jews and the political structure; changes which have taken place in the organization of Jewish religious and cultural life; and changes in the self-awareness of Jewish community and destiny which have occurred as a result of the impact of the social and behavioral sciences.

The coup d'etat that swept the regime of General Juan Carlos Onganía into power earlier in the decade clearly unnerved a good portion of the articulate middle-class Jewish community. The very real support General Onganía received for his initial bid for power in 1962 from the ultra-rightists of Argentina, coupled as it was with a program for moral redemption on conservative Catholic assumptions, had ominous overtones, reminiscent of European fascism. But what was not properly perceived, and what clearly emerged as central in the regime of Onganía, was the "military developmental" style of the new regime. Like the Kemalist regime of Turkey, the Onganía regime of Argentina perceived itself as the main catalyst for economic change within a Capitalist framework. And in this emphasis on development, the role of the Jewish community as a positive agency was recognized. Jewish corporate and commercial interests were given firm assurances that they would not be persecuted on religious and cultural grounds.

In point of fact, the Jews of Argentina suffered little from the military style of development, with the exception of the grotesque treatment of Jewish intellectuals who resisted the military intervention in university life. They were poorly represented and marginally involved in the basic political processes in the post-Perón epoch. The breakdown of political legitimacy in Argentina, a nation which seemed to have every major factor of modernization present, affected the Jews far less than the nation as a whole. Thus, the Jewish community today (again with the exception of the intelligentsia) finds itself in a relatively secure position, despite the strong conservative bias of the political-military apparatus.

It would be a mistake to assume that "liquidationist" and "assimilationist" tendencies described in my study no longer exist in Argentina. However, such tendencies seem to have been markedly arrested. The organizational base of Jewish life in Argentina has undergone a remarkable political and religious re-evaluation, largely as a result of a full-scale change in generational attitudes. Politically, the more left-oriented intellectuals have become prominent in Jewish circles. This has resulted in part from the militant attitudes instilled by the Israeli struggles and in part from the intimate involvement of the Jewish left with student left in general. This generational takeover has by no means been universal. Younger people, whether extremely orthodox or extremely radical have moved into what was in effect a cultural void.

Specifically, the younger people have provided efficient impetus to Jewish organizational life in Buenos Aires, pumping life back into the *Kehillah*. They have also provided a "confrontational" rather than an "accommodational" approach to the Argentine community in general. The fear and trembling of an earlier generation has subsided as a generation of Jews has emerged that is secure in its *argentinidad*. In addition, younger religious figures—rabbis trained and even reared in other countries and cultures, who in effect served as a missionary vanguard to the Jewish community of Buenos Aires—have exerted enormous influence. These younger religious leaders have been concerned with keeping the Jewish cultural tradi-

tions intact in the widest possible sense rather than with con-
versions or maintaining exclusivity.

Any estimate of the impact of Israel is speculative. Doubtless, the Arab-Israeli struggles have served notice upon the Argentine government that, even though all Jews are not Israelis, Israelis do remain Jews. And as the image of Jewish courage
replaces that of Jewish cowardice, the position of the Jew
seems to improve. At least equal in importance to the Israeli
regime has been the sobering effect of the United States, which
through its embassy and cultural offices has resisted openly and
vigorously any manifestations of anti-Semitism within the Argentine governing elite. And the American attitude has probably had more effect than the Israeli government in dampen-
ing anti-Semitic trends.

The rise of ecumenicalism has contributed not only to an
improvement in the "dialogue" between Christians and Jews
but also to an appreciation of the need for investigations into
the sociology of religion. The works of such outstanding Catholic scholars as Houtart, Vekemans, and Illich have been profoundly influenced by social science currents. Similarly, the
most advanced work on the Jewish community has been conducted by the Department of Social Studies and Statistics of
AMIA. It has pioneered in studying the demographic characteristics of the Argentine Jews, their ecological situation, and
the specific cultural features of Jewish community life. The efforts of Renata Kestelboim, Leonardo Rabinovich, and Jorge
Kaufman have been particularly noteworthy.

Unfortunately, scholarly research in the universities has not
kept pace with developments within the Jewish cultural and
religious organizational life. The same biases and fears which
inhibited such work a decade ago, still seem to hold. It is as if
"enlightened" attitudes prohibit the serious study by sociologists of religious activities. However, it seems likely that there
will soon be a burst of energy among Latin American social
scientists in religious research. The immense importance of the

sociology of religion in American and British sociology cannot help but have its effects, particularly since many of the leading younger social scientists of Argentina have been trained in United States centers such as the University of California at Berkeley and at Columbia University, where work in the sociology of religion has been stressed.

In conclusion, then, in Argentina the past decade has witnessed marked, if not spectacular, changes in Jewish organizational and cultural life. These changes have tended to stabilize the Jewish condition. Fears for Jewish survival have subsided; just as expectations of earlier generations for a new Zion had subsided. After all, Jews have survived several millennia as an identifiable group. The capacity to survive, rather than the quality of that survival, still characterizes the Jews of Buenos Aires and Argentina as a whole.

9 THE STUDENT AS JEW

Recently an article began circulating in the underground radical press entitled "The Student as Nigger." Needless to say, the article was written by a Jew. Whatever else might be said about this essay, written by Jerry Farber, it was provocative in form, and it raised by extension many issues that paralleled the historic condition of black people in America—everything from separate eating facilities and separate bathrooms to demands for deferential titles and differential treatment. While not accepting the soundness of the analogy, we can see that there are some similarities between the life style of the modern college student and the way of life of the modern black man.

But style is not substance. Superficial mannerisms should not be confused with significant behavioral consequences. The black condition stems from an American slave ancestry, the student condition from a European feudal ancestry. This is no small difference, since in slavery the master has all legal rights and is in fact the ultimate sovereign entity, whereas a slave has no legal rights and is not even a person, either in terms of law or custom. Under feudalism there is a definite relationship between lord and serf involving mutual recognition of *persona* and mutual responsibilities. These connections are formalized in a highly refined set of laws that, while clearly favoring the class of noblemen and priests, nonetheless articulate fundamental human rights beyond which exploitation cannot be sanctioned or tolerated. Not that the feudal system particularly epitomizes egalitarian relationships. Rather, universities still reflect their feudal origins in every part of the modern academic life, from graduation ceremonies conducted with the pomp of a French pre-Revolutionary court to deferential and often honorific titles that harken to days when sinecures were the normal rewards for men of breeding.

But it is risky to equate the student with the serf, for what is the role of the professor? Was he part of the ruling aristocracy or the powerless student body? It is not easy to answer this question either in the thirteenth or twentieth century. The modern university is part of the modern corporate structure. It is linked directly to industrial society at the level of economy, to national polity at the level of organization, and to the traditional cultivated elites at the level of religious and quasi-secular institutions and agencies such as private foundations and wealthy individual benefactors. The student is the raw recruit for this system of power, as well as the victim of it.

The student-as-black argument is provocative but not particularly penetrating. I propose that the condition of the student might better be equated with the condition of the Jew than with any other large racial or ethnic bloc in American society. Indeed, the overlap between Jews and students is probably greater than that between any other two independent groupings, while the relative sizes of the college and university population (seven million) and the Jewish population (five to six million) are also roughly analogous. Thus, even in crude statistical terms one can say there is a tighter link between students and Jews than between students and blacks. Further, if we refine our analysis, it is clear that the number of Jewish students who *finish* after enrolling in college is much higher than the norm.

The old canard that any argument by analogy is weak,

weaker by far than any other form of presentation of evidence, is impossible to avoid in methodological terms; the degree to which any two independent variables can serve to "explain" each other is highly dubious. Yet these arguments do have an attractiveness and appeal in that they sharpen our focus and illuminate areas which otherwise remain obscure and whispered about only in private company.

JEWS, STUDENTS, AND JEWISH STUDENTS

The historical grounds for discussing the student as Jew are that the Jew has a long legacy of faith in the efficacy of knowledge and in education as the basic instrument for survival and upward mobility into the world at large. There is no doubt that the post-World War II wave of college students had as its role model the Jews who inhabited the large urban colleges just prior to World War II and who returned to fill many of the teaching vacancies after the war. It became clear that postwar American society required just the kind of formal structure provided by the college degree. Further, what had once been true for Jews alone, namely, their need for special expertise in order to advance, became a general requisite for the more technological era that followed in the wake of the war. Thus the student as Jew precisely reflects this faith in the therapeutic powers of information and the economic powers of special service.

There are unattractive aspects to this historical analogue; namely, the Jewish working class was old and venerable, and still exists in mythic if not actual form in rural Israeli society; the fact is that the highly urbanized Jew emphasized intellectual work not only as a superior way of operating but also as an escape from the drabness and deadening sameness that physical labor implied. If the Jew was confronted with alienation as a cultural fact, he was a member of the first large group dedicated to the removal of alienation as an economic fact. It is no wonder that in his world the doctrine of alienation shifted from a Marxian emphasis on the special condition of labor to a Freudian emphasis on the general condition of man.

This emphasis on head over body complemented the status hierarchy that exists in American society, where high status occupations are generally connected with a low expenditure of physical effort—professors, judges, doctors—and low status is connected with high physical effort—the valuable garbage collectors and much maligned ditch diggers are special victims of this pecking order of man. But how does one determine the qualifications for intellectual labor rather than physical labor? Here the demanding society emerges to solve the dilemma. It introduces a world of professional specialization and occupational definitions that mark off various levels of what constitutes satisfactory or unsatisfactory work. The entire role of colleges and universities, particularly the liberal arts sector, comes to be linked with professions rather than with occupations. Gaining entrance into this world of intellectual effort (a world that seriously downgrades claims concerning the value of human physical activities) becomes the goal in itself rather than the instrument toward other goals.

The contrast of this situation with the life of the American black people is clear: if there is one property that characterizes the historic role of the blacks it is precisely an underestimation of the worth of intellectual pursuits and an overestimation of the worth of physical activity. It is probably not so much a matter of the blacks' overemphasis upon the worth of physical labor as the simple assignment by the status hierarchy of society of menial tasks to those who occupy the lowest rungs on the economic ladder. Given the fact that the blacks had neither the influence nor the instrumentalities to transform physical labor into intellectual activity, they became uniquely separated from, rather than integrated into, American higher learning. Even now, despite enormous pressures to the contrary, blacks are vastly underrepresented in college education in proportion to their number in the society. American society, even by modest census figures, is at least 10 per cent black; the university population is roughly 1.0 per cent black. This percentage does not include faculty, administrators, and professional staff. Indeed, among faculty and administrators the figure is closer to 0.01 per cent, rather than 1.0 per cent.

The simple mechanical equation of students to blacks overlooks some powerful statistics indicating an acute separation between the social clusters. But if one were to take the Jewish population and match it against the college and university population, one would find a statistical overrepresentation to at least the same degree as the blacks are underrepresented. This indicates that we are not simply dealing with the student as symbolic Jew but, more to the point, the student as a very real Jew. Add to this the fact mentioned before—that Jewish students tend to drop out less frequently than non-Jewish students—and the actual degree of overlap between the two groups can scarcely be reduced to a spurious or humorous analogue. We are dealing with an isomorphism where the Jew is often a model, and the student is in fact often a Jew.

LIKE THE JEW?

Like the Jew, the student is needed both for his competence and for his special knowledge. Yet he is despised for being different and presumptuous. The student is sent to college to learn the inner workings of society, and when he learns them and then the parts fail to fit together or make a perfect whole, he is attacked both for being a dupe of his professors and for having an ivory-tower image of the world.

Like the Jew, the student is denounced for opposite reasons by the same people simultaneously. He is declared to be middle class and opportunistic because he does not "work for a living" and because he sometimes sees college or university life as a way out of the selective service draft. Then at the same time he is attacked for being marginal to the class system, unconcerned about the future of the American economy or the importance of money, and for being moralistic. In the same connection, like the Jew, he becomes a sexually mysterious object: prudent, yet prurient; concerned with love, unconcerned with the institutions for lovemaking. In short, like the Jew, the student is in a can't-win moral situation with respect to the dominant sectors of society.

Like the Jews, students tend to be more politically leftist than American society in general, but not especially taken with economic utopias or political panaceas. The Jew is not only anti-Establishment, he is also anti-utopia, which makes him subject to severe assault by the political extremes. The extreme right sees the student as Jew because of the political disaffection from the leading canons of American society, and the extreme left sees the student as Jew for his cynicism with respect to the transforming qualities of apocalyptic revolution.

Like Jews, but quite unlike blacks, students can act according to roles other than those assigned them. Being a Jew and being a student are both achievement-oriented roles, while being a black is largely an ascribed status. The options of being a student are always there, but what exactly are the options of being a black man? It is the difference between volitional choice and a deterministic situation. While this point may seem quite obvious, it is nonetheless important enough to emphasize, particularly in light of the ambiguous status of the student subculture (perhaps the only subculture more ambiguous and amorphous than that of the Jew). Just as a Jew may be located on a continuum from someone who goes to Temple once a year (or never) all the way to the most devout or orthodox practitioner, the student too may be a hanger-on in a special no-credit course, or he may be someone taking five or six courses per semester for credit. In other words, role ambiguity no less than role shift is endemic as well as intrinsic to being both student and Jew. For the present at least, it is far simpler, by an act of negation or conversion, to cease being a student or even a Jew than a black man. The rejection of "passing" and the emergence of black pride, serves as a source of potential political strength for the black, while creating a kind of political vacuum for students and Jews alike.

There is the whole issue of Jewish marginality and student marginality in relation to the larger culture. Just as a Jew rarely finds himself fully integrated, whatever his wealth or social history, the student too rarely finds himself integrated into the university structure regardless of his grades. It sometimes seems as if marginality is a by-product of intellect, a consequence of learning, a phenomenon that separates both student and Jewish culture from the larger society and even from the administrative aspects of university life. This marginality is not simply one that is held in fear and trembling but is almost a built-in definition of the situation itself, of being Jewish itself, of being a student itself. It is as if marginality and the extent of it defines moral activism and moral politicking. If the whole society seems terribly concerned with what Digby Baltzell describes as the Protestant art of making money or the Catholic craft of making politics, the Jew in conjunction with the student seems dedicated to the reverse proposition, namely, the worth, the moral worth, of noneconomic and nonpolitical definitions of the higher learning and the higher realities. Indeed, many of the utterances of the student youth generation are remarkably similar to the positions taken by Jewish radicals and liberals of past ages.

Jews share with students a mistrust of (or at least nonparticipation in) the American working class and a concomitant distrust of the populist tradition. This is clearly a condition of the head-and-hand split spoken of earlier. Its existence can hardly be denied. The Jew is rarely seen as a factory-hand or a field-hand in the contemporary labor market. What the Jew is, almost abashedly, the student has raised to a level of ideology. Not only is he intrinsically suspicious of populist claims and mass appeals to working-class "racism" and "bigotry," but the student has often given up hope in the world and political propensities of the laboring classes. Not that all students have accepted this bias; the more politically conscious are aware that such a view is self-defeating. It simply remains a curious truism that, of all groups in American society which have strong aversion to the working class and its current role, the Jew is most closely aligned with the student in holding this animus.

The deproletarianization of the Jew has reached epic proportions. And from this occupational clustering into middle-class activities has flowed a typical middle-class faith in machines over man, capital-intensive over labor-intensive orientations. At the same time that the modern Jew celebrates the victory of mind over matter, techniques over tedium, he also decries the "alienation" intellectual activity creates. The student has brought this condition one step further. He has transformed a shamefaced attitude into a boastful ideology. The working class, particularly its "blue collar" members, is criticized for selling out to capitalism, of being an unworthy heir to the heroic labor struggles of previous epochs. Whether in fact there is such a widespread "working-class authoritarianism," or if it does exist, whether such attitudes are any more prevalent among blue collar workers than among middle-class doctors and lawyers, is not examined. The arrogance of students translates itself into unabashed animosity toward the working classes. Student alienation, while genuine enough, is often alienation from the laborer and the labor process, rather than alienation from the society in general, or from its oppressive elements in particular. Again, here the black students clearly remain closer in background and in aspiration to the labor process, although the fact that assaults by certain militant groups upon the black proletariat have become old-fashioned and outdated may signify that the black student at the white university now denies to himself the process of embourgeoisment he bitterly condemns in other religious and ethnic clusters.

IS IT GOOD FOR THE JEWS?

What characterizes both Jews and students is consciousness (sometimes to the point of collective autism). Neither is satisfied with observing the performance of an act, but both demand explanation of the rationale behind the act and what it means to themselves as well as to others. Historically no group has been more concerned with its self-reflection than the Jews, and currently no group seems to have assimilated and inculcated a self-critical set of reflections more keenly than the student radical movement. Both groups are invariably involved in identity crisis questions: "What am I?" "Who am I?" These are types of questions and issues for which the man of action or the man of pure zeal has neither time nor inclination. In part this may be a function of the transitional status of being a student and the marginal status of being a Jew. Yet, whatever its causes, this self-reflective quality is certainly special, a quality that characterizes both groups more keenly than any others in the society.

Like the Jews, too, American students are increasingly in search of social justice. They seek answers to their alienation, and they are concerned not with social problems but with social solutions. And quite unlike the blacks, they are interested not in capitalism either of the "black" or "white" variety nor in membership in the suburban yacht club, but in the positive value of new life styles that made the suburb such an interesting place in the beginning. It is not true that the Jew "ran away" from the blacks. It is rather, as Bennett Berger and Herbert Gans indicate, that they ran toward an alternative way of life, one that would be more feasible in the industrial society and one that would provide tranquility and security without giving up either the occupational or recreational aspects of the so-called inner city. In this sense the Jew has a self-definition of living in an oasis, not a ghetto. The students, too, in their deepest recesses, share with faculty and administration a belief that the college and university is an oasis in the midst of a political desert. This just as assuredly links Jews and students as it separates Jews from blacks, and students from nearly every major segment of our society.

It might well be that this present malaise among blacks, university administrations, and the population as a whole reflects the larger circumstance that the black is seeking to recreate a mini-ghetto in this oasis as a proud link and symbolic identification with the macro-ghetto which blacks occupy in American society. The black student is often torn between direct access to the higher echelons of legitimation and status in the larger society on the one side and the need to assist the "brothers" remaining in the ghettos on the other. The conversion of the campus "integrationist" atmosphere into a center of black power might be viewed as an appropriate response to this dilemma.

In the same connection students and Jews are involved in constant dialectical opposition to the rest of society. How they perceive themselves and how they are perceived by others remain at radical variance. What Jews see as a Jewish problem and what students see as a student problem is very different from what the larger world defines as their problems. While this is the classic interest-group condition, it is also a new experience for students in particular.

In these times of exacerbated Negro-Jewish tensions, it should be recollected how much these two minority groups resembled each other at the aspirational level in the past. Black people have traditionally respected Jewish mobility patterns constructed from education, the solidarity of Jewish home life, the general "soulfullness" of the way Jews live, and more recently, the transformation of a relatively docile, tranquilized people interested in survival at any price into a militant people capable of national self-defense and national liberation. It is so easy to think of black power as a special *aperçu* or aberration of black militants, forgetting that less than a quarter of a century ago Jewish power meant precisely the sort of guerrilla struggles, national consciousness, and ethnic pride that brought about the State of Israel and helped make the world Jewish community viable on the shoals of Hitlerism. This is so whatever one may think of the present tensions between Arabs and Jews in the Middle East or black identification with "colored" aspirations.

On the other side of the ledger, it is no less the case that Jews have played a special role in limiting the penetration of racial hatreds permeating America. Jews traditionally have been in the forefront of the struggle for black equality and black higher education; moreover, they have learned the most from black people. The world of acid rock groups, so deep into the black soul music, is populated by young Jewish musicians. The white hipster phenomenon Norman Mailer spoke of in the fifties is not just white but largely Jewish—and the model of cool behavior under pressure, the resurrection of sexual orgies, the renewed concern with labor and work as positive values, all aspects of black culture endemic to the Afro-American experience, have best been learned by the young Jewish people with whom blacks interact most.

This discussion of the student as Jew is not set up as an antithesis of black culture but rather as more nearly representative of how culture and education intersect and interpenetrate.

THE STUDENTS AND THE JEWISH PROBLEM

The analogy of student and Jew should not be considered as unqualified. There are serious differences between the two groups. Increasingly, the majority of Jewish people in the United States tends to celebrate this country and to have a vision of America not only as a good place but as the best place. Jewish radicalism increasingly tends to be diluted into a kind of stuffy liberalism that is more rhetorical than actual, more an electoral-day pilgrimage than an everyday involvement. The students, for their part, as noted by all polls and all survey researchers, are becoming deeply disaffiliated and disaffected from the larger American society. Student criticism oftentimes comes crashing in upon Jewish celebration. The increasingly abrasive contacts between students and Jewish officialdom, noted by many Jewish agencies, which have taken the form of disaffiliation of Jewish youth from various congregational and quasi-religious institutions, have become a major threat to Jewish solidarity.

Even here there is a peculiar phenomenon, because within the Jewish tradition there has always been strong emphasis on moral dissent in the larger Jewish matrix. Even now the proportion of Jews who are radicals is larger than the proportion of radicals to the general student population. Though the tendency of Jews may be growing toward an acceptance of the formal system of legitimacy, whereas student tendencies may be the reverse, they nonetheless share a common antipathy for a larger majority which is quite willing to accept the society on its own terms, and they move to assist the substantial minority which is unwilling or unable to participate.

Another crucial area in which Jews and students seem to be at odds is that of law, covenants, and normative restraints. The Jew has traditionally been not just law-giver but law-lover. He tends to have at least an unbounded fear, if not an unbounded admiration, for the law. For the Jew, historically, the law held all kinds of terrors, but it also held out a hope of manipulation of the power structure to gain his ends or at least to gain his survival. The law was universalism in practice. If the law was just, the Jew always was there to demand application of social justice to his brethren. The Jew, with his sacred covenant, carried over and sacerdotalized even profane covenants. As a tactic this has been historically brilliant. It has compelled institutions of law, order, and education to live up to their own rhetoric, since there would always be a Jew present to make sure that this rhetoric was widely promulgated and understood, even though implementation might be absent.

For the student, however, the acceptance of this legitimation has become sharply contested. The basis of law is viewed as a shield for authority and a sham behind which lurks unrestrained power. Coercion is faced by countercoercion or by a flat refusal to admit the legitimate claims of the courts of law, the police, or of any other agencies of law. If, for the Jew the phrase "moral law" has a veritable messianic force behind it, for the student the words "morality" and "legality" seem diametrically opposed to each other, with morality clearly being the superior concept if not always the operative term in student behavior.

This brings us to the confrontation of life and love. The Jew has historically been far more interested in the problems and processes of survival—and well he might be—than in the process and problems of love. It is not so much the figure of Jesus that separates Jew and Christian; it is rather the principles that are to guide the social behavior of men. The Jews willingly and consciously pay a high price for survival, and that price is. at times not less than love itself. It is not that Jews, any more than other people, are not interested in or do not need affection. It is only that the time and energy that one can dedicate to matters of the heart presuppose a social, political, and economic tranquility rarely allowed the Jew. The Jewish culture, after all, is a culture of necessity; not of violence, nor of philanthropy, but of sheer necessity. Even in the current condition of abundance, the phylogenetic memory of Jews tends to push them in the direction of easy mobility through education rather than the fixed status endowed by inherited wealth.

The meeting ground of the student culture and the Jewish culture is economics. Both are products of affluence and the consequences of a society that has promoted exactly the kind of open mobility in which Jews have best survived. And so it is no wonder that even from the "beat generation" and its poets to the present alienated generation the Jewish disaffiliate has been in the forefront of the student movement. Here again the Jew seems prominent in the heresy, in the break with tradition. The emphasis on Eastern religious cults, acid rock music, drug addiction, and all of the affairs of the private heart that are supposed to increase the quality of love and sexual freedom—these are surely characteristic of a love-oriented ethic. Nevertheless, the theme of self-destruction which appears in the youth culture and the self-sacrificing qualities of the young—whether they be viewed as foolish or heroic—are clearly gaps between the student culture and the Jewish culture that are not easily bridged and that sometimes go under the rubric of "generation gap." Again, it is not so much the formal words "life" and "love" but the contents of these terms, the radical difference between what Norman Podhoretz would call "making it" and Jerry Rubin would call "breaking it." A full circle is reached where the analogy, at least superficially, breaks down, and we are once more confronted with the unique claims of distinct groups.

The Jew has a final laugh, however, because within the Jewish tradition there has always been a place, a central place, for dialogue between reason and mysticism, radicalism and conservatism, self-examination and self-celebration. The Jew is a perennial seeker and very rarely the finder. Students too have opened up this world of sealed education once and for all, demanding dialogue and even confrontation. The renewed search for foundations is exactly the kind of "enterprise" that the Jew as an ideal-type has been promoting for six thousand years. The Jew can say to the student, "Welcome to the ranks." The students can say to the Jew, "We have arrived at the edge of marginality. We too are the new children of Zion."

10 THE JEW AS A TOTAL INSTITUTION: FROM JUDENRAT TO AKZIA

In a recent interview with Joseph Kraft,[1] Israel's foremost young novelist, Amos Oz, observed: "This is a country where times moves faster than elsewhere. See how many people talk to themselves as they walk by. Do you know why? They talk to themselves because there is a terrible gap between the day-time reality of a safe and prosperous country and the nocturnal memory of the holocaust. Every day we fight the Arabs and win. Every night we fight the Nazis and lose." But what Oz might have added is that the *Israelis* have the victories, while the *Jews* suffered the defeats.

Defeat is never beautiful, leastwise when it is accompanied by massive annihilation of a total people. Beyond that, defeat takes many forms, from the heroic to the hellish. And definitions of heroic defeat in Western culture generally involve struggle, armed or otherwise, in which to die fighting is the next best thing to fighting and winning. The Jewish culture, especially as it emerged under the adverse circumstances of late medieval and early Capitalist Europe, developed an ambiguous response to this vision of heroic death in the Christian Knighthood. While obeying scriptural messages of battles fought, won, and lost in uncompromising fashion, Jews also learned quickly that the law of life itself was to live—above all, to survive. And this instinct for survival soon became the guiding characteristic of Jews. Indeed, the barbaric impulses of the Nazis were undoubtedly inflamed by the belief that, unless Jews were physically destroyed, they would manage to find a way of multiplying and prospering. Of course, the huge number of impoverished, landless, homeless Jews spread throughout Europe was never allowed to interfere with this myth of Jewish prosperity.

However, survival as an ultimate goal comes into conflict with moral works as an ultimate goal. And the two locked horns and met in the Nazi occupied ghettos of Central Europe. For the most part, Jews behaved with incredible dignity as they identified with their Jewishness, bore the burdens of concentration camps, and went to their deaths knowingly, but with the conviction that their Lord and Maker would redeem the people of Israel and punish the despoilers of the Jewish dream. One cannot help but be impressed by the dignity of Jews sewing their yellow armbands with the Star of David and publicly announcing an identity with a Jewishness that many had forgotten and even abandoned. In this supreme moment, Jewish secularists and Jewish pietists became united in a shared fate of programmed death.

Not all Jews reacted in this way. For some, survival under the Nazis became simply one more round in the struggle for survival as such. What after all was so different between Nazis and other species of Jew-haters? This question was soon to be answered: the shared belief in the invincibility of the Jews, the Jews as a chosen people—as long as the chosen ones lived. And that was the difference: the Nazis understood the "shrewd" Jewish instinct for survival. And the oppressor this time programmed the oppressed for death and not simply deprivation. This was a difference with a vengeance, one hardly understood by the "survivalists" in the ghettos. And so opened a chapter as mortifying and saddening as any in the previous history of Jewish people: the formation under Nazi sponsorship of the Jewish Councils of Central Europe.

The key to so much Jewish history between the seizure of power by Nazism in 1933 and the establishment of the State of Israel in 1948, a remarkably short fifteen years, but a millenium in terms of emotional history, is the word *survival*. That word has been the curse and the cure, that which unites and divides the Jewish people. Survival seems noble when confined to functional explanations of what makes a people cohere over time. And yet, survival is something less than noble when it means a choice between Jews rather than of Jews as an entity and a wholeness. In a fearsome chapter in Jewish history the Jewish Councils of Eastern Europe shared in the ultimate act of self-immolation under the threat of immediate decimation by the Nazi armed forces and Gestapo.

In his staggering and still unsurpassed masterpiece, *The Destruction of the European Jews*[2], Raul Hilberg notes in his Postscript, that "one of our difficult problems is to understand how the German bureaucracy started its work, how its very first moves were made." Isaiah Trunk's work can be viewed as one effort to comprehend the nature of the holocaust by examining how the Nazi bureaucratic apparatus enlisted the support of a portion of the Jewish community to do its bidding within ghetto walls. The actual decree of Adolph Hitler and Governor General Hans Frank concerning the establishment of Jewish Councils was issued on October 12, 1939, and read in part as follows:

In every community a representative body of the Jews is to be formed. In communities of over 10,000 inhabitants this representative body, the Jewish Council (*Judenrat*) is to consist of 24 Jews from the local population. The Jewish Council is to be elected by the Jews in the community. If a member of the Council leaves, a new member is to be elected at once. From among its members the Jewish Council will elect a chairman and his deputy. . . . The Jewish Council is obliged to receive, through its chairman and his deputy, the orders of German official agencies. Its responsibility will be to see to it that the orders are carried out completely and accurately. The directives which the Council may issue in the execution of German orders must be obeyed by all Jews and Jewesses.

It is necessary to constantly remind oneself that the *Judenrat* at no point behaved in an autonomous way; that behind its every major decision, strategy, and tactic, was the Nazi war machine and the Hitler regime's commitment to make the destruction of all Jews a primary goal—even at the cost of possible military defeats.

To describe the work of Isaiah Trunk[3] as a labor of love would be wild irony, but it is not a labor of hate, either. Too much care, patience, and even apologia has gone into this work for it to be described as a product of animus. The key chapter is called "The Strategy and Tactics of the Councils." Here we see, hidden beneath a veil of tears, their "rescue strategy" in which the majority of Jews would be saved and the minority of Jews would be sacrificed. As the author notes, "it is hard to judge now how much of these sickly fantasies about historic missions was pathological *mania grandiosa,* encouraged by the German stratagem of granting deceptive 'authority' over large Jewish communities to individuals whom they kept firmly on a leash, or how much was simply rationalization of an urge for personal prestige and power dominating ghetto heads." Suffice to call this a labor of historical record, an effort to move beyond the mistaken assumption of total ghetto rebellion and beyond the shallow Israeli militants who consider the entire history of European Jewry as bathed in weakness, cowardice, and treachery.

Trunk attempts to show that the *Judenrat* was of one piece with the *Kehillah,* a Jewish communal organization which persisted throughout the Diaspora, pre-dating the Nazis by hundreds of years. Indeed, he demonstrates a continuity of *leadership* between Jewish communal life before and during the Nazi period. Yet, for all the careful intellectual maneuvering between sentiment and sense on the fine line between Jewish cooperation and collaboration with the Nazis, the conclusion of the book is more than a disappointment; it is something of a failure. For the author's retreat to simpleminded organizational theory, to a *sociologie manquée* claim that the *Judenrat* were historically derived from the *Kehillah* and that a distinction has to be made between collaboration with the State in general and with an ideology in particular, is ingenuous. No State ever existed "in general." And the Nazi State was no ordinary event, nor a simple continuum with the Weimar Republic.

The belated participation by Jews in the European liberal tradition was a failure, because European liberalism collapsed in the face of fascism. A central tragedy of the Nazi epoch is that the Jewish converts to enlightenment retained their fervor long after the contents of European liberalism had been emptied into the bloodstreams of extremist movements overtly hostile to Jewish survival. What has still to be understood is that the survival ethic itself had been destroyed by the holocaust and by Jewish collaborationist efforts. The rise of Israel along fundamentalist lines, with a re-establishment of neo-orthodoxy, cannot be understood simply as a return to tradition or a consequence of Zionist predisposition to religious orthodoxy. If anything, Zionism shared the European values of enlightenment; present battles with religious orthodoxy in Israel attest to this. Religious neo-orthodoxy emerged with renewed vigor from the ashes of war and concentration camps because of the ineffectiveness of a survivalist ethic that had displaced ethnicity with ethics; that had forgotten the fundamentals of Judaism as an ethical and historical religion. The conversion of Judaism into a pragmatic code of clever secular concepts counted for little against the Wehrmacht, the Gestapo, and the gas chambers. All cleverness crumbled before the Nazis, and total destruction became the order of the day, every day.

How diabolically clever it was of the Nazis to capitalize on the almost innate Jewish responsiveness to the theme of law, order, and self-regulation. We are confronted with the supreme irony that the Jewish Councils carried more authority than any other Jewish body since the Middle Ages. This alone weighs heavily *against* the author's idea of continuity with the *Kehillah,* which, after all, had little legal or political weight by contrast. That this bestowal of authority should have been extended by their executioners led the survivors to a total moral nihilism. But this positivist nihilism stemmed not just from the Nazi experience, but from the enlightenment experience. This later was to cleave into the Socialist experience (in which Jews suppressed their names and their identities to the larger tasks of Bolshevism) and the Bourgeois experience (in which Jews suppressed their names and their identities to the larger tasks of capitalism). What we had in the *Judenrat* was the Jew as a "national question," the Jew as a "cultural question," the Jew as an "economic question"—always a question, never a person. Everything but the Jew as Jew. The absence of this seemingly tautological dimension compromised the European Jew. The ferocious reminder of the prophet Isaiah to his people, when their pride and arrogance brought them close to disaster, is apt: "For you forgot the God who delivered you, and did not remember the rock, your stronghold." The promise of redemption in Judaism is delivered only through struggle. That is the message of the prophets; and that is what the simple theory of group survival at any spiritual or material cost fails to heed.

Social science comes upon the limits of imagination in the matter of holocaust, survival, and transcendence. Perhaps there are sociological lessons in not exaggerating even the significance of the religious factor: Jewish policemen of Lodz, Vilna, and Warsaw were, after all, still policemen. They functioned as repressive mechanisms of *Leviathan* not as members of God's *Commonweal*. One might ask those who argue the case for community control, for the displacement of white policemen with black policemen, for example, whether this is, after all, an entirely satisfactory victory or one more degradation ritual. There is a sense in which Jews being clubbed by non-Jewish police made a more meaningful, if not a more appealing, sight than Jews committing Jews to their deaths. At least the capacity for moral outrage remains intact. Indeed, I have rarely felt the obscenity of Nazism more acutely than when looking at a picture of Jewish police officers, the only efficient sector of the ghetto! Perhaps, I now better understand black radicals and their own sense of shame toward black officers— agents of laws they do not make, victims of ideological egalitarianism without the substance of true economic and political equity.

As a work of social analysis, replete with the accouterments of survey questionnaires of Council members and ghetto police, plus tabular materials on the fiscal and demographic characteristics of ghetto life, the book succeeds admirably. As a work of history, it is less successful, not really putting into adequate perspective the indifference and ennui of Christian Europe to the plight of the Jews, an indifference that clearly must have enhanced the "pragmatist" insistence upon cooperation through the *Judenrat*. As a work of Jewish analysis, i.e., of the analysis of the Jewish character, the work is a tragic failure. This is illustrated in the introduction by Jacob Robinson: "The Warsaw Ghetto Revolt of April 1943 was the first direct armed confrontation of local forces with the Nazis. The revolts of the ghettos were attempts 'to save the Jewish honor.' In view of the high price paid in human lives it proved to be no alternative to 'rescue through work,' however ineffective." Apparently, we are to infer that the quality of death means nothing, as this hideous equation of death in rebellion and death in acquiescence reveals.

The conclusions of both the author and his sponsor are that, when all factors are considered, Jewish participation or nonparticipation in the deportations had no substantial influence, one way or the other, on the final outcome of the holocaust. This sort of ex post facto reasoning is precisely what the author cautions against throughout the book; and yet, it is indulged in freely in the Introduction. Indeed, we are given a typical apology for the *Judenrat* in the claim that "it is only by accident of military history that a considerable portion of the

Lodz Jews did not survive." The claim is made that if only the Red Army had continued its July 1944 advance into Lodz, the 68,000 remaining Jews might not have been "resettled" (read annihilated). But, of course, resistance might have made the tasks of the Red Army simpler and its military advances swifter. Resistance at an earlier stage might also have encouraged the Nazis to abandon their plans for the depopulation of Lodz. In the world of might-have-beens, resistance and rebellion certainly deserve no less praise, and much less scorn, than accommodation and acquiescence.

Maimonides, whom Mr. Robinson cites, said it all—not just from the viewpoint of the traditional Jews (who constituted a minority in the Councils) but from the viewpoint of Judaism— "If pagans should tell them [Jews], 'Give us one of yours and we shall kill him, otherwise we shall kill all of you,' they all should be killed and not a single Jewish soul should be delivered." And who is to say that Maimonides was wrong, and the small portion of enlightened, secular bourgeois Jews serving Hitlerism were right? At least Jewish *souls* would survive, even if their bodies would not. Under the *Judenrat* policy, precious few bodies made it through the holocaust, and even those were bequeathed a legacy of moral compromise.

Whatever the moral culpability of the *Judenrat*, the political realities were constant: the Nazi policy of total extermination of the Jewish ghetto population. At first the directive to the *Judenrat* for the deportation of 6,000 people daily was simply ignored, and 10,000 Jews were sent to the concentration camps. After a while, by mid-1942, blocks were sealed off by the German secret service and their inhabitants deported en masse[4]:

A whole community with an ancient tradition, one that with all its faults was the very backbone of world Jewry, is going to destruction. First they took away its means of livelihood, then they stole its wares, then its houses and factories, and above all, its human rights. It was left fair prey to every evildoer and sinner. It was locked into a ghetto. Food and drink was withheld from it; its fallen multiplied on every hand; and even after all this they were not content to let it dwell forever within its narrow, rotten ghetto, surrounded with its wall through which even bread could be brought in only by dangerous smuggling. Nor was this a ghetto of people who consume without producing, of speculators and profiteers. Most of its members were devoted to labor, so that it became a productive legion. All that it produced, it produced for the benefit of those same soldiers who multiplied its fallen. Yet all this was to no avail. There was only one decree—death. They came and divided the Warsaw Ghetto into two halves; one half for sword, pestilence, and destruction; the other half for famine and slavery. The vigorous youth, the healthy and productive ones, were taken to work in the factories. The old people, the women, the children all were sent into exile.

The movement from *Judenrat* acquiescence to *Akzia* (action) resistance to tyranny has often been viewed as the final act of heroic desperation; and it certainly was that. Akzia represented the clear understanding that death to the ghetto Jews was inevitable and that the only remaining question was the tactics and strategy of dying. The two wings of Jewish resistance—The Jewish Military Union and the Jewish Fighting Organization—set about the task of preparing for guerrilla war. The first task was to weaken, if not snap the bonds linking the Judenrat to the Storm Troopers and Gestapo. This was achieved by intimidating and even killing Judenrat members and the Jewish Ghetto police. The second task was developing clear lines of organization that could not be infiltrated by secret agents of the Gestapo. The final task was armed struggle with the German occupying military.[5]

The conflict period itself lasted ten months—from August 1942 to May 1943. The outcome was pre-ordained—the slaughter of the final vestiges of a once-great Jewish community in Central Europe. But in a strange way the Warsaw Ghetto uprisings presaged the post-war world as much as drew the final curtain down on pre-war Jewry. The Jewish Military Union was comprised of Socialists, Communists, youth groups, and generally secularized Jews, whereas the larger Jewish Fighting Organization was generally comprised of Zionists. Their capacity to work together for a Jewish purpose broke the class and caste barriers that marked the European Diaspora.[6] But quite beyond that, the formation of military units within Jewish life shattered both the myth of survivalism as an ideology and established a pattern of guerrilla behavior that became crucial in the pre-State struggles in Palestine between 1945 and 1948. The price of national consciousness came exceedingly high—six million deaths; but the emergence of the national State without such an altered mode of action is inconceivable.

It is simply not possible to speak of Jewish guilt and redemption without a comment on Gentile guilt and redemption, and in inverse proportions—the small numbers of Jewish traitors and large numbers of Jewish martyrs and the small number of "Aryan" martyrs amidst a world of silence. True, Polish Socialists, Dutch entrepreneurs, Danish workingmen, all performed acts of courage that in retrospect appear all the more remarkable in the light of Nazi barbarism. Yet, the net result was the emergence of Jewish self-reliance that shattered the dream of European enlightenment. The ideals of enlightenment remain intact, but its cultivated bearers had disappointed Jews for the last time. Nationhood became the last gasp of a shattered European Diaspora. Israeli exaggerations, mannerisms, and conceits, relate back to a period of defeat that no amount of macho militarism can erase. The Jew after all stands as person, not as legend: exploiter and exploited, agent of the oppressor and instrument of immolated opposition, maker of a new nation, breaker of old internationalist dreams. The Jewish people in their sensuous totality represent dialectics, the polarized representation of evil and good so tragically expressed in the Warsaw ghetto by the words *Judenrat* and *Akzia*.

11 LIQUIDATION OR LIBERATION: THE JEWISH QUESTION AS LIBERAL CATHARSIS

When the persecution of the Jews ceases, there will no longer be any need to make portentous inquiries into what it means to be a Jew. But until that long-awaited, but probably never to be realized, Day of Judgment, Jewish self-definition will continue, if only as a survival mechanism. This impulse toward self-definition is particularly apparent among Jewish radicals, since historically at least, the tenets and canons of a well articulated Judaism, like those of a well defined radicalism, are not just universalist in their appeal, but tend to be exclusivist as well.[1] It is this aspect of the Israeli imperative and Jewish agony that I want to herein explore—with special reference to two major figures who could claim with considerable justification to have attempted to bridge the unique demands of both modern radicalism and present day Judaism.

One of the high ironies of fate is that the perfect anti-Semite, the Nazi, has a thoroughly cosmic view of what defines a Jew. It extended from anyone whose first cousin is Jewish to anyone who identifies himself as a Jew. On the other hand, the perfect Jew, the ultra-orthodox, Talmud-citing Jew, sees the size of Jewry shrunken to like-minded Orthodox adherents (and even some of those cannot really be trusted). But this only means that the nastiest of oppressors and the noisiest of oppressed "play the game" of Jew and anti-Jew unambiguously. Everyone else—and that includes the overwhelming portion of the non-Jewish world, no less than an equally large majority of the Jewish tribes—must live in a world of paradox tinged with purpose, doubted lined with duty. The works of Isaac Deutscher[2] and Albert Memmi[3] are addressed to this vast majority.

Let it be said at the outset that both volumes display an intensity of feeling and a sincerity of purpose that characterizes the works of Deutscher and Memmi in general. They are, after all, not ordinary Jewish propagandists of the word. They both live with their left-wing ideology in far greater comfort than they do with their theology. Deutscher was, until his recent death, one of the ablest Marxists in Europe. A prolific writer, he is best known for his biographies of Stalin and Trotsky; at the time of his death he was working on Lenin. (When we met in 1962, while I was Visiting Lecturer at the London School of Economics, he even suggested a work on Plekhanov if his health and life held out long enough.) In addition, Deutscher wrote a brilliant series of essays on political themes, which, during the Cold War period, served as a beacon of good sense and political decency in the face of half-crazed critics on both the left and the right. Deutscher's political activities reached a high point in the 20's and early 30's, when he was involved in the affairs of the Polish Communist Party. After his self-imposed exile to England he continued to serve as informal advisor to various left-wing Laborite causes.

The case of Memmi is somewhat distinct. Cosmopolitan in a different way, Memmi spent his entire youth in Tunisia. During World War II as a young man, he was arrested and sent to a forced labor camp from which he escaped. After the war he returned for a brief period to Algiers and then went to the Sorbonne, where he studied philosophy and stayed on to teach. His book on *The Colonizer and the Colonized* ranks with Fanon's *The Damned of the Earth* as a masterpiece in the social psychology of oppression and the special forms it manifests in the Third World. I found Memmi's book superior to Fanon's precisely to the degree that the philosophical tradition provides a richer background than the narrowly focused psychoanalytic constraints within which Fanon operated.

The backgrounds of these two men are important, not so much to announce their respective *bona fides*—they hardly need such expressions of support. Rather, they reflect the special left-wing proclivities that dominate their respective works and the deep seriousness with which they, as left-wing partisans, approach the tragedy of the Jew. That they come up with different diagnoses and hence different conclusions is important, but perhaps less important than the simple fact that two such sterling figures of the European left dared make an attempt at reconciliation of political ideology and national identity.

It would be a profound mistake to draw the conclusion that Memmi and Deutscher represent the same point of view on the Jewish question as a consequence of their shared faith in the ultimate worth of socialism. On all the political questions of current importance they stand at opposite poles. Memmi has become increasingly convinced of the necessity for a solution, indeed a liberation, of the Jew on the basis of Israel. Deutscher grew increasingly hostile to Israel, until he reached a near complete condemnation of Israel's Six-Day War against the Arab states.

Before getting into specific contrasts, we must understand the source of these differences. They clearly are to be found in the difference between Marx and the materialist tradition represented by Deutscher on the one hand and Hegel and the dialectical tradition represented by Memmi on the other. It requires no great acumen to appreciate the degree to which dialectical materialism was always an uncomfortable and at times disquieting resolution of nineteenth century German romanticism. Like its *Sturm und Drang* predecessors, it neatly resolved in theory all the problems that remained to be solved in practice. Perhaps for this reason, Marx abandoned any intimate interest in expanding the philosophic horizons of his thought and left such mundane matters to his co-worker Engels, who proceeded to botch things, albeit brilliantly, by going off into the deep murky waters of a "dialectics of nature."

Like all resolutions that leave the problems intact, the doctrine of dialectical materialism had a stormy career, particularly in the Soviet Union during the late 20's and early 30's, where first the "mechanists" and then the "dialectical idealists" were made to pay the price for their improper emphasis. But perhaps the Russians perceived politically what they were unable to respond to philosophically, namely, the untenable nature of the theoretical "synthesis" to begin with. This is certainly apparent if we contrast the work of Deutscher and Memmi, who in their own ways exhibit the strains within the system of thought in which they worked. Deutscher the mechanist can hardly accept the idea of historically unsanctioned events, while Memmi the dialectician must structure his book in triads, his chapters in three parts, and even his paragraphs in three sentences.

Deutscher's book is that of "an unrepentant Marxist, an atheist, an internationalist." His vision of Judaism is shaped by a theory of marginality called the "negative community." In this universe, anti-Semitism is an unspent force. Since the Jew is historically the enemy of racialism, nationalism, and xenophobia and since he is the incarnation of the alien man from within, he becomes for Deutscher a prototype of radicalism, whether the Jew wills it or not. But precisely such a definition of Judaism causes Deutscher great grief in response to the current Israeli-Arab situation. He sees the Israelis "in the role of the Prussians of the Middle East"—a definition not far removed from the Soviet denunciation of Israel as the neo-Nazis of the Middle East. So far removed are the Israelis from Deutscher's prototype of the marginal Jew that they "now appear in the Middle East once again in the invidious role of agents not so much of their own, relatively feeble capitalism, but of powerful Western vested interests and as *protégés* of neo-colonialism. This is how the Arab world sees them, not without reason. Once again they arouse bitter emotions and hatred in their neighbors, in all those who have ever been or still are victims of imperialism." Thus it is that Deutscher's Marxism triumphs over his Judaism. What is important to him is not victory but purity, not the social system but the correct values.

But this Marxism does more than shape Deutscher's vision of the Jews; it also distorts his statements on actual political history. In the conclusion to his essay on the "non-Jewish Jew," he notes that "the decay of bourgeois Europe has compelled the Jew to embrace the nation-state. This is the paradoxical consummation of the Jewish tragedy. It is paradoxical because we live in an age when the nation-state is fast becoming an anachronism, an archaism." This must surely represent the ultimate triumph of Deutscher's purified Marxism over common sense. For the simple question is: where are there signs of "anachronism" to be found? Where is the nation-state crumbling? Certainly not in Africa, the Middle East, Southeast Asia, South America. Obviously the nation-state is the very alpha and omega of modern developmentalism. Even revolutions made in the name of Marxism must assert the full authority of nationalism to achieve even a modest degree of mass mobilization. Deutscher's further comment that the nation-state is an anachronism even in the United States, Great Britain, France, Germany, and Russia also rates a raised eyebrow. Here too, is the substitution of internationalist rhetoric for nationalist reality. Has Deutscher forgotten that in two world wars, with the votes and then ultimately the blood of the working classes of all of these nations, "the people" demonstrated an overriding faith in their nations and a complete lack of faith in class solidarity across national lines? In short, the Marxism of Deutscher serves to falsify the historical epoch itself and thus makes a caricature of Jewish demands for a state called Israel.

In a sense, Memmi picks up where Deutscher leaves off:

Why the concern with "blame" of which Deutscher always speaks? Does Marxism come down to a statement of moral perfections and imperfections?

In what could well stand as a Third World rebuke to the Orthodox European Communist, Memmi writes in a particularly impressive passage that for him, "The dignity of the oppressed begins, first, the moment he becomes conscious of his burden; second, when he denies himself all camouflage and all consolation for his misery; third, and above all, when he makes an effective decision to put an end to it. May all the victims of history forgive me. I know only too well how a victim becomes a victim. I understand the subterfuges which enable him to survive. I pity his inner ruin, but I do not admire his grimaces of pain or his scars. I do not find his suffering face the most beautiful in the world nor do I consider the plight of the victim to be very admirable." Memmi recalls the Eichmann trial, particularly the "irritated and slightly scornful astonishment of the young Israelis at the Jews of the Diaspora who allowed themselves to be slaughtered, too often without the slightest gesture—even of despair. I must admit that whatever the naïveté, the ignorance, the insolent thoughtlessness of these young men so freshly minted, I am in the end more on their side than on that of these perpetual victims, complaisant towards their pitiable fate, which the immense majority of us were." And, indeed, in Deutscher there is the spectacle of the left-wing man celebrating precisely the sort of alienation that led the oppressed Jews of European charnel houses to defend their own misfortunes.

And for the cosmopolitan left, as for the nativistic right, the issue comes down to the claims of Israel of Statehood and Nationhood. That nation, which has become the fulcrum of the Middle East crisis, has just as assuredly become the core of the Jewish identity crisis. For just as Deutscher sees in Israel the Middle East phalanx of imperialism, Memmi sees Israel as the vanguard of Jewish liberation, a "specific liberation" in which the "oppressed person must take his destiny into his own hands." The life of the Jew "must no longer depend on any treaty, often signed with other ends in mind, by anyone with anyone." If the Jewish condition reveals a "total misfortune," so, too, for Memmi the Jewish destiny must find a "total solution."

Following Hegel's *Philosophy of Law* rather than Kant's Essay on *Perpetual Peace,* Memmi rests his case for the Jews on nationalism, not on internationalism, either of a pacifist or Marxist variety. "In short, the specific liberation of the Jews is a national liberation and for the last years this national liberation has been the state of Israel." It is not that Memmi fails to see the nationalist excesses that Deutscher speaks of, only that he fails to understand what options exist. For Memmi, "the national solution is not one of several; it is the only definitive solution, because it is the specific solution to the Jewish problem. Israel is not a supplementary contribution, a possible insurance in case of difficulties in the Diaspora; it must be the frame of reference for the Diaspora which must in the future redefine itself in relation to it." Ultimately, the question for Memmi is how to be a *Jewish non-Jew*—the very reverse of Deutscher's question of how to be a *non-Jewish Jew.* For Memmi all answers are wrapped up in the national question: "The Jew must be liberated from oppression, and Jewish culture must be liberated from religion. This double liberation can be found in the same course of action—the fight for Israel." Clearly, for Deutscher the same survival needs dictate a reverse answer: the fight against Israel, or at least, against the imperialist forces Israel has come to represent.

I do not wish to reduce the writings of either Deutscher or Memmi to this one issue. Indeed, some of the most incisive and interesting comments in their books are ones on subjects unrelated to ultimate issues. Deutscher's best writing, for example, is on the kibbutzim and their limitations in Israeli political life, while his text on the Russian Revolution and the Jewish

problem is certainly a corrective to the often exaggerated asser-
tions concerning Soviet anti-Semitism and the equally outrageous statements that Jews never had it so good as under
Soviet rule. It is a masterful and balanced statement. Memmi's
volume contains sparkling chapters on everything from mixed
marriages to the art and culture of the Jew. He is both knowing and generous in his appraisals, and, if the polarities drawn
are sometimes caricatures, they nonetheless draw sharp attention to the major and minor irritants of secular Jews trying to
reconcile their leftism and their Judaism.

In both volumes there is a personal touch that borders on
self-congratulation. Memmi sometimes writes as if he had in-
vented the Jewish question rather than serving as its commentator. And Deutscher's widow prepared both the Foreword and
the Introduction on "The Education of a Jewish Child."

The uncontaminated egotism of both authors, however, is
stifling, since both write as if to be a Jew is equivalent to knowing everything of value about all Jews, past and present. In
contrast, the writings of even a generalist historian such as
Arnold Toynbee are refreshingly free of such self-advertisement
and personal promotion in the name of "total peoples" and
"total solutions." (What an eerie phrase Memmi uses to describe the Jewish fate, in the light of Hitlerism and the
Holocaust!)

These are books in the European manner—the historian
writing as philosopher; and the philosopher writing as a Guide
for the Perplexed. Qualifications are few in number; possible
admissions of analytic shortcomings nonexistent; and polemics
against unmentioned enemies abundant. Under such circumstances to ask for references to other European works of scholarship, not to mention works by social scientists on the Jews,
would be somehow unclean. The dialogue goes on at a level of
brilliance far above the level of competence most analysts in
the United States have come to expect or at least desire. In
this sense, Hegel and Marx are reproduced by Memmi and

200 ISRAELI ECSTASIES | JEWISH AGONIES

Deutscher, rather than transcended. How strange it is that scholars who can be quite fastidious—indeed, the Trotsky trilogy is breathtakingly rooted in all available archive data, and Memmi's writings on the *Colonizer and Colonized* quite free of empty assumptions—become so freewheeling on the Jewish question. One may take this as a measure of the personal and internalized nature of their respective visions of Judaism, or simply as a measure of their unstated conviction that certain things require no evidence, only insight.

Both works set for themselves the same task: to place Judaism in the radical movement, and the corollary, to place radicalism in the Jewish tradition. Curiously, both works devote relatively little time to this latter tough nut, preferring a rhetoric that will either be pleasing to the Zionists (as in the case of Memmi) or to the cause of the Marxists (as in the case of Deutscher). Just what the interrelationship is, or should be, remains curiously unanswered. And it becomes apparent that perhaps the question posed in such a way does not admit of any ready answer. The choice of Israel may be in fact a choice against Middle East socialism, whereas a choice in favor of Middle Eastern development may entail nothing less than the destruction of the Israeli nation—a formulation that Deutscher comes perilously close to accepting. Under such circumstances, these books will perhaps leave the reader with at least as much anxiety at the conclusion as at the beginning. I would suggest that the reason for this stems from a misanthropic view of the Jewish question to begin with—a view which shapes a Procrustean bed that no Jew could seriously be comfortable in for a single instant; and one that no radical would spend time fashioning to start with.

I cannot help but wonder whether these essentially nineteenth century dialogues between Deutscher and the ghost of Marx and Memmi and the ghost of Hegel, is not itself largely the reason for my essential dissatisfaction with their books. For the ideological view of the Jews translates itself into a Jewish ideological view of the world. Both men present a totalistic picture of the Jewish condition, and both present an essentially totalistic response: in the case of Deutscher it is marginality; in the case of Memmi it is nationality. But for both the European experience—rather than the two major forces in twentieth century Jewry, the rise of a powerful American Jewry and the post-war maturation of an Israeli Jewry—remains dominant. They are men who reflect upon, respond to, ruminate about these new factors, but always as outsiders. Deutscher's marginality is only the pale afterglow of a first generation liberated Jew, while Memmi's powerful support of Israel as the ultimate resting home for liberated Jews comes upon the hard fact of the dust jacket announcement that he and his family live in a Parisian suburb. The fact is that neither London nor Paris ranks with New York or Tel Aviv as centers of Jewish activity.

Not that either man should necessarily have migrated elsewhere. Indeed, what they say derives a great deal from the spiritual richness of their cosmopolitan contexts. But these contexts are themselves limiting—a recognition that I fail to detect in their writings. It is true, as Deutscher points out, that many Jews in the United States, particularly, have joined the celebration of a decadent system. But it is equally true that the Jews continue to form the vanguard of the critics of that system. And this has proven a neat trick, since Jews must become radicals despite the vicious prejudices against them by their "friends and allies" among the blacks and the Third Worlders. To support the Cuban Revolution means to do so despite Fidel's critiques of the Israeli Six-Day War. To support Egyptian socialism is to do so despite the woeful inadequacies of the Nasserist military vision of social change. To support the black student movement is to do so despite some of the crudest and cruelest assaults on Jews ever heard in the United States.

In short, it is not that some Jews have become part of the Establishment, politically as well as economically, that is interesting, but how few have done so. Many Jews, especially the young, have remained loyal to the principles of radicalism despite incongruities and anomalies. Jews have always lived well with paradox. And that is because, in the main, they are neither Hegelians nor Marxians, but rather the original Jamesians. They live well in a partial world, because a total world spells their doom. They function well in the marginal interstices of society because a society which fails to provide such margins spells disaster for the Jews, Socialist or Capitalist. To be a Jew means to operate within a framework of survival codes as defined by alien cultures: Christian principles of love, Capitalist principles of weath, or Socialist principles of harmony. And to accept survival as an operational codebook means to absorb the Deutschers and the Memmis into a larger frame of reference which they themselves might refuse to acknowledge, but which, nonetheless, does exist for Jews *sui generis*. In short, Judaism has the capacity for universalism without demanding an exclusivism in ideology.

Some years ago, when my oldest son was attending Hebrew Sunday School, his skills in reading and reciting Hebrew were brought to the attention of the local rabbi. He, in turn, contacted me, informing me of the Sunday School teacher's appraisal. He then said, "Your son should become a rabbi." At which point I simply scoffed, and replied, "His interests are in pure science, not theology." The unexpected, but I-should-have-known inevitable, retort shot back, "So what! He can become a scientific rabbi." I wonder whether this weird sense of accommodation, this poor man's pragmatism, does not operate as an unwritten handbook for keeping Jews in the fold. "Dialogue" is a fanciful word, behind which lurks the constant demands, rigorous demands at that, which compel Jewish atheists to speak to Jewish theists, Jewish Zionists to deal seriously with Jewish Communists, Jewish bakers to demand equality with Jewish bankers. For, however unequal the struggle between Jew and Gentile, the struggle between Jew and Jew is always between equals—between men who recognize that the Diaspora of men has created a pragmatism of mind.

If Jewishness is to be "defeated," it will be done precisely by the same forces of fanaticism assaulting liberalism. For Judaism has become, perhaps against its own theological predilections, a cardinal expression of liberalism. And for the liberal society, the attitude toward Jews has become a test case of whether liberalism is possible. Insofar as Nazism, communism, or any totalist system is unqualifiedly victorious, Judaism will be finished. For Jews live not only in an adoptive context of Christians, Capitalists, and Communists, but in a context of other Jews. And it is precisely this double life which modern industrialism has provided, precisely because it has made possible the separation of economic and political power and has placed limits upon each aspect within the industrial system. Lurking behind Deutscher is not so much Marx as Sombart: the Jew as Capitalist. The fact is that Jews as Capitalists have been few in number; the Jew as petit-bourgeois is more to the point. The world of middlemen, intermediaries, the unconvinced, of those who view self-reliance as a form of group survival, is more easily compatible with the liberalist spirit found under Capitalist democracy than under other systems. It might even be that socialism, the mild anti-Capitalist bias found in Israel, does more to explain the differences in character traits between Diaspora Jews and Sabras than does nationalism.

In short, the liberal society has historically been best for Jewish subculture, whether in medieval Spain, Reformation Holland, Enlightened Germany, industrial United States, etc. And it is always the illiberal turn of these societies that has been worst for the Jews: these same countries in the posthalcyon days of their growth have been holy hell for Jews and liberals alike. Thus, as an attempt to my own question—what is the Jew?—I should note the following: He is the man who provides global society with an operational set of liberal values; and who in turn fares best in a global society that has a vested, legitimated interest in precisely fostering open-ended values for its own thoroughly non-Jewish reasons. And if Israel seems so hopelessly out of favor with the Third World, or with the developing nations, it may well be because it uniquely combines a political framework of liberalism and a Jewish culture which accentuates and reinforces an industrial system and developmental ideology.

We may not like liberalism; we may consider it a profound anachronism. We may claim that the costs of liberalism are too great and affect too few people; we may claim that it cannot produce an accelerated developmental pattern in backwoods areas; but we cannot deny the historic and contemporary connection between Judaism and liberalism. I think we cannot either deny that whither goes liberalism, so goes the destiny of the Jewish people. For this reason, Deutscher's non-Jewish Jew and Memmi's Jewish non-Jew must both remain locked into the larger struggles for democracy—both its mass and bourgeois forms—in the twentieth century.

12 POLITICAL TERRORISM AND STATE POWER: SOME ULTIMATE CONSIDERATIONS

The human world is an open or unfinished system and the same
radical contingency which threatens it with discord also rescues it
from the inevitability of disorder and prevents us from despairing
of it, providing only that one remembers its various machineries are
actually men and tries to maintain and expand man's relations
to man.[1]

The question of terrorism is new to the docket of the United
Nations General Assembly, if not exactly new to the life of society. The fact that the scale of violence and death resulting
from terrorist activities has reached such international proportions as to persuade the United Nations to consider the problem and possible remedies is indicative of a growing awareness
that the question of terror must be answered by all social systems, that neither capitalism nor socialism, democracy nor totalitarianism, market economies nor collective economies can
remain aloof from it.

The minute one attempts to profile the terrorist, enormous
problems of definition arise that inhibit possible remedial action. Can the IRA (Irish Republican Army) operating in Northern Ireland really be compared to the PFLP (Popular Front
for the Liberation of Palestine)? And if so, on what bases?
Membership in the former is large scale, with the support of
wide numbers, operating on a well-defined home terrain. Membership in the latter is extremely small, with more covert than

overt support in the Middle East. Yet, there are similarities: the militant Palestinians believe that the destruction of Israel is a prerequisite for a general peace settlement, while the leaders of the IRA, for the most part, believe that the defeat of Protestant Northern Ireland and its reunification with the rest of Ireland are necessary for peace.

In other words, a large factor in ascertaining the differences between guerrilla warfare and terrorist activities is linked to the size of the movements, their organizational efficacy, and geographical locale. And even when ideological predispositions are similar, one may still claim a difference between guerrilla organizations and terrorist operations.

The essential difference seems to be that the Irish Catholic militants are involved in an internal struggle for political control, whereas the Arab Palestinians are involved in an external struggle for geographical control. It is precisely this gulf between national liberation efforts and international symbolic acts that seems most emphatically to distinguish guerrilla warfare from terrorist activity. Rather than emphasize the points of similarity between terrorists and guerrillas, it would appear more worthwhile to draw a profile that makes plain the differences. This is not always easy; for example, the psychological characteristics that lead some to guerrilla movements may be similar, if not entirely identical, to the psychological characteristics of members of a terrorist group. Nonetheless, despite the difficulties a tentative evaluation of the essential nature of the terrorist threat is required.

PROFILE OF THE TERRORIST: SOME PROPOSITIONS

1. A terrorist is a person engaged in politics who makes little if any distinction between strategy and tactics on one hand, and principles on the other. For him (and for the most part terrorism is a male activity), all politics is a matter of principle, and hence, nothing beyond the decision to commit a revolu-

207 POLITICAL TERRORISM AND STATE POWER

tionary deed of death and personal commitment requires examination, planning, and forethought.

2. A terrorist is a person prepared to surrender his own life for a cause considered transcendent in value. A terrorist assumes not only that taking the lives of others will lead to desired political goals, but that the loss of one's own life is a warranty that such a cause or political position is correct and obtainable.

3. A terrorist is a person who possesses both a self-fulfilling prophetic element and a self-destructive element. The act of destruction of another person or group of persons itself becomes the basis upon which future politics can be determined and decided, and the absence of terror is hence held to signify the absence of meaningful events. The self-destructive element is coincidental with the previous point, namely, that one's own death is the highest form of the politics of the deed: the only perfect expression of political correctness.

4. A terrorist is a person for whom all events are volitional and none are determined. The terrorist, in contrast to the revolutionary, perceives of the world pragmatically as a place to be shaped and reshaped in accord with the human will or the will of the immediate collective group. Beyond that, there is no historical or sociological force of a hidden or covert nature that can really alter human relationships, geographic boundaries, and so on.

5. A terrorist is a person who is young, most often of middle-class family background, usually male, and economically marginal. Collectively, persons caught as terrorists, whether highjackers, assassins, or guerrillas, are remarkably similar: aged twenty to thirty-five, relatively well educated, with some college or university training, but rarely of the uppermost achievement levels, and clearly not of peasant or working-class stock.

6. A terrorist performs his duties as an avocation. That is to say, he may hold a position in the larger society quite unrelated to his terrorist actions. This anonymity provides an es-

sential cover for his activities. It also makes the contest between police power and political terror far more problematic, since sophisticated weaponry is relatively useless without adequate methods of detection and prevention.

7. The terrorist defines himself differently from the casual homicide in several crucial respects: he murders systematically rather than at random; he is symbolic rather than passionate, that is, concerned with scoring political points rather than responding to personal provocation; and his actions are usually well planned rather than spontaneous. Terrorism is thus primarily a sociological phenomenon, whereas homicide can more easily be interpreted in psychological terms. Terrorism essentially has a group nature rather than a personal nature.

8. The terrorist by definition is a person who does not distinguish between coercion and terrorism because he lacks access to the coercive mechanisms of the State. The essential polarity is not between pacifism and terrorism, which is mechanistic. The essential choice that those responding to terror can make is either coercive mechanisms—which may range from the mild presence of police or the military in the body politic to imprisonment and limitation of the rights of oppositionist groups—or outright counterterrorism—which goes far beyond coercion, since it violates the sanctity of life itself as an overriding perspective. The believer in coercion must also assume that the victims of coercion can be rehabilitated; the terrorist denies the possibility of rehabilitation for the victim.

9. A terrorist is a person who, through the act of violence, advertises and dramatizes a wider discontent. The advertising function does more than make evident public displeasure with a regime. It provides instantaneous recognition of the person performing terrorist acts through mass communications. Terrorism becomes a fundamental way of defining heroism and leadership.

10. A terrorist believes that the act of violence will encourage the uncommitted public to withdraw support from a re-

gime or an institution, and hence make wider revolutionary acts possible by weakening the resolve of the opposition. Practically, however, such acts often work to lend greater support to the regime, by drying up fissures and contradictions in the name of opposing a common enemy, the terrorist.

11. A terrorist may direct his activities against the leadership of the opposition by assassinating presidents and political leaders; such terrorists usually tend to function alone and in the service of an often poorly defined ideology rather than a political movement. Other terrorists may direct their activities against the symbols of establishments and agencies; such forms of terror are less concerned with the individuals against whom terror is performed than with the organizations and agencies of which they are a part. For example, the Munich massacre of Israeli athletes was directed at the State of Israel: the specific people eliminated were not an issue. This kind of terrorist is usually himself under a strict political regimen and is responsible to counterorganizations or guerrilla groupings that define and determine the extent and types of terrorism.

12. A terrorist does not have a particularly well-defined ideological persuasion. He may work for the State or against the State, for an established order or in an effort to overthrow one. The level of his ideological formation is generally poor and half-digested, reflecting a greater concern for the act than for alternative systems that may flow from the act. It is important in a morphology of the terrorist not to confuse such rhetorical features with the generic nature of terror, which transcends personality and even social structural characteristics.

THE UBIQUITOUS NATURE OF TERROR

These twelve items stated, we must now turn to a consideration about the generic nature of terror and not just the biographic nature of the terrorist. The definition of someone as a terrorist is a labeling device. The act of homicide, or at rare times even ter-

rorist suicide, cannot disguise the moral aspects of such definitions. What is usually referred to as terrorism is unsponsored
and unsanctioned violence against the body or bodies of others.
However, whether violence performed with official sanction,
against the leadership or the membership of other groups and
institutions is nonterrorist in character, it is part of a continuous process of definition and redefinition in political life. And in
the current ambiguous and even ubiquitous conditions, performing a terrorist act does not uniquely make one a terrorist,
any more than random nonviolence alone defines the pacifist.

This raises the entire matter of legitimation and labeling,
since terrorism is not uniquely an act but a response to an act;
and, further, since terrorism is a set of punitive measures taken
against those so defined, the problem of definition is com-
pounded by the existence of subjective factors in the body
politic—factors, which in some measure, help define and even
determine the treatment, punishment, and reception of acts of
political violence.

When terrorism is an "internal matter" and not a mini-
group invasion of a nation by foreign citizens and alien subjects, the approach must be more sensitive to the ills in the society being addressed. The armed forces and police have a
much easier time dealing with foreign nationals, such as the
Japanese in the Lod Airport raid in Tel Aviv, or Arabs in the
Munich Olympic encampment. The difficult chore comes in
handling native populations. Here we must make a fundamental distinction between guerrillas and terrorists. The distinction must be made on the basis of whether the participants
in assassination attempts, bombing of buildings, and so on, are
nationals or foreigners. In the case of the latter, true terrorists,
it is possible to employ the police and the armed forces to defeat and destroy them. In the case of nationals or guerrillas, the
aim of the State must always be to contain, restrain, and finally
reconcile. This distinction between guerrillas and terrorists is
significant not simply as a typology but in terms of operational

responses to terror as distinct from national guerrilla movements, which frequently are a response to long smoldering in-
equities.

MARXISM AND TERRORISM

In a special sense the question of terrorism, quite apart from
the characteristics of the terrorists, is an "internal concern" of
Marxism and the Socialist tradition. Within Western liberal
democratic thought, from Locke to Montesquieu to Mill and
Dewey, there has never been any doubt that terrorism is largely
counterproductive of real social change and that excessive use
of terror to put down terrorism is even more counterproductive, since it calls into question the legitimacy of the entire
body politic. Of course, there have been bourgeois and populist traditions of romantic violence. Theories of the Will em-
anated from the bowels of European irrational and mystical
traditions. Yet, overall, and especially in the Anglo-American
framework, terror has been declared outside the purview of the
legitimate exercise of protest and opposition.

The Socialist and Marxian traditions are quite different.
From the outset, Marx contested Proudhon, and Lenin and
Stalin argued with the Russian Narodniki and Anarchists. In
general, the organizational tradition has been dominant. The
argument against "spontaneity" rests at its core on a disbelief
in the efficacy of violence. Even the Chinese representative, before the United Nations debates on whether the discussion of
terror should be on the agenda of the General Assembly, ad-
mitted to a parting of the ways with the Arabs on the question
of the political payoffs of terrorist tactics.

That is to say, the Chinese, insofar as they respond as Marxists and also insofar as the whole Maoist notion of the revolution involves armed military struggle, react negatively to the
current wave of Arab "petit-bourgeois violence" associated
with leaders like Yasir Arafat, not on the basis of long-range

goals but on the basis of belief in slow paced military operations, performed in conjunction with the support of a mass peasant people, in contrast to the *foco* belief that one can have hit-and-run military operations that are successful. In other words, the Chinese position, if anything, demands even greater adherence to organizational constraint than the Soviet position does, since Russian Bolshevism was based on party organization, whereas the Chinese Party position is based on military organization. Both in the past and the present, the Orthodox Marxist vision has been one of high organization, disciplined assaults on class enemies, and a strong sense of leadership to reduce random acts in politics. A belief in history rather than in human volition dominates this tradition: faith in violence is tempered by a belief that the laws of history are inexorable, only the timing of such historical inevitabilities remains to be ironed out by human action.

A minor motif has run through the Socialist-Marxist tradition. It extends from Sorel's vision of the general strike that spontaneously brings down the system to Régis Debray and the theory of the *foco*. It is based upon the idea of the unattached group affecting revolutionary change. Given the current political behavior and posture of China and Cuba, no less than that of the Soviet Union and Eastern Europe, it seems unlikely this approach has much appeal to the Marxist world of this day.

The reasons the debates within the Western world seem so much beside the point is the assumption that the existing order of things can somehow either survive or only be changed through parliamentary mechanisms. As a result, one finds a lumping together of quite distinctive phenomena, class conflict such as mass guerrilla warfare with minoritarian phenomena such as urban terror. They all seem to be linked as one of various pieces in the same red garment of rebellion; and hence, so much discussion on terrorism in the West is a surrogate for discussions on social change of any sort.

The new wave of terror is both menacing to those singled

out for assault, and novel in the random internationalization of victims as well as terrorists. The use of Japanese terrorists to perform essentially Arab actions is but the most refined aspect of this randomization of violence. The question of terror, however, is not going to be significantly altered by finely worded judicial statements calculated to appease the intended victims of random terror. It can be altered by a recognition within the Socialist camp that gains of a substantial sort have been made without terror, for example, in Allende's Chile; and that the resort to terror may have become counterproductive to the maintenance and growth of socialism in the Third World. Of course, if there were a collapse of this phase (of what once was referred to as "legal socialism" in pre-Bolshevik Russia) the question of terror might well create an East-West confrontation all over again. But again, this seems unlikely given the present era of good feelings between the big powers—East and West, Communist and Capitalist, authoritarian and democratic. And with so much at stake in terms of a broad-ranging Metternichean settlement now under way between the Great Powers, it is extremely doubtful that random terrorism will be countenanced in the Communist bloc nations, any more than it is within the Western bloc. This international rapprochement of power, rather than the cries of anguish by the powerless, will probably lead to an early end to the current terrorist wave.

ALTERNATIVE RESPONSES TO TERRORISM

Resolutions or recommendations for controlling terrorist activities, no matter from which quarters they emanate, are scarcely going to be enacted if the leadership of a nation feels that its interests are served by a particular form of terrorist engagement. But certain frameworks can be devised in the international community that might delegitimize, if not entirely curb, acts of terrorism.

Terrorism as a primary tactic, as we have indicated, will tend to be viewed negatively by "Socialist" States as well as by "Democratic" States. Hence, it should be possible to draw up a bill of human rights under United Nations sponsorship, indicating a universal belief in the right of the citizen to life, including the rights of people to free international travel and communication. Such a bill, to have teeth, must be built into legislation concerning postal regulations and international sea and flight rules. Random populations cannot become the objects of political actions without all norms of international association becoming dismantled and unhinged.

Insofar as possible, a statement of what measures a nation will employ in responding to terrorism should be outlined in advance, so that those engaging in terrorist activities of a specific or random variety will at least be aware of the consequences of their acts. At present, every situation involving terrorists, from kidnapping embassy officials to bombing department stores in crowded neighborhoods, becomes a dramatic confrontation treated *sui generis,* without a uniform standard of response.

Since the state is the repository of authority and of the mechanisms of coercion, it cannot only refuse employment to terrorists but can also punish the random use of violence. This it must do, for national polity and national survival depends in part on maintaining a monopoly of the means of violence. Indeed, when the state can no longer do so, its very survival becomes conjectural. The inability of the United States Congress to enact tough gun-control legislation may thus be viewed as a limitation of the American State to control its citizenry.

Through such mechanisms as Interpol, a file and fact sheet should be maintained on terrorists who cross national boundaries. Just as those who cross state boundaries to perform illegal actions within a nation such as the United States are subject to heavy penalties, so, too, should this principle be applied to terrorist movement across national boundaries. In that way, legitimate national liberation movements will be able to survive and grow insofar as they actually reflect a national consensus or dissensus, while the use of terrorism abroad, precisely because of an absence of true national support, would be profoundly curbed, if not entirely thwarted. The problem here is that legislation that would reinstate the death penalty, for example, might be considered retrogressive rather than ameliorative.

It must always be added that the actual lines of distinction between guerrillas and terrorists are hard to establish, just as the definition of legitimate geo-political boundaries may vary. For example, if the Cubans define their activities as the liberation of Latin America as a whole, can the incursion of Che Guevara into Bolivia be considered a terrorist invasion of foreign terrain? The point here is that the Cuban government, and not a small band of uncoordinated terrorists, made this decision. Similarly, the Egyptian government has recently urged upon the Palestinians that they form a government in exile. This suggestion was rejected, and in a sense, the idea of national legitimacy and responsibility was repudiated. So what one witnesses in the Arab context, in contrast to the Cuban context, is precisely a continuing reliance upon terrorism as a method of political pressure and a rejection of government legitimacy as a means for realizing such demands. Such problems are real and must be presented fairly. However, the problem of terror is also real and must be faced.

Ultimately, terror is a disruption in the modern technological order. The number of people involved can be exceedingly low and the amount of damage created exceedingly high—that is in the nature of a high velocity military and weapons technology. But in another larger societal sense terrorism has always been with us and always will be, as long as a monopoly of terror is reserved for a small fraction of society called the state and as long as people are divided into units called the nation. Perhaps in that sense, the very existence of terrorist groups is a warrant to the health of a particular nation-state: if it can survive terrorism, if in the face of personal tragedy it can forge public solidarity, terrorist acts will be proven counterproductive. But if such terrorism forges links with the broad masses, if it articulates the feelings and beliefs of large numbers, and if the states involved are indecisive and insecure in the face of such unsanctioned violence, then the state is doomed to perish; and here the purposes of terrorism will be proven quite productive.

I had occasion to write several years ago in my report before the National Commission on the Causes and Prevention of Violence that no one should ever doubt that a society of law and order can be built. The historical evidence is clear that Germany under Adolf Hitler and the Soviet Union under Joseph Stalin had less "crime in the streets" than did the Weimar Republic or Russia under the Constitutional Duma. The real question is: Does the price of gaining law and order exceed the social value received, if that price produces the further militarization of the civilized world?[2]

What one must say therefore, in conclusion, is that terrorism can indeed be stamped out—or at least drastically limited—but that, in so doing, society does not necessarily offer a demonstration of its health but perhaps a reflection of its weakness. That is to say, if the capacity for totalitarianism is completely exhausted in an effort to combat random terrorism, the social costs and political consequences alike become so grave that the very foundations of the system become more menaced than they could possibly be by any set of random terrorist activities. Indeed, if it is correct to point out that such random terrorism has a highly mobilizing effect on the masses of the population, rallying that population to the political commonweal, then one might also reasonably infer that the total repression of terrorism could have a demobilizing, and even worse, a demoralizing effect on these same masses, and would ultimately serve as a catalyst for a new round of social revolutionary actions that ironically serve the purpose of terrorists more nearly than they do established authority. Such then is the dialectic of terrorism: its existence may prove the health of a society, and its absence may be a demonstration of the stagnation of a society.

The specific problem of Arab terrorism links up directly with the absence of legitimacy and territoriality within the boundaries of Israel. The various factions of the Palestinian Liberation Movement face a common dilemma: the need to fight a guerrilla form of warfare without having the core advantages of guerrillas elsewhere. Those advantages are clearly articulated in the literature from Mao Tse Tung to Che Guevara: blending into the natural terrain, cover support or at least the positive neutrality of the local inhabitants, a corrupt regime that invites popular discontent, and a program and/or ideology that offers positive, sensible options to vast numbers of oppressed peoples. The plain truth is that scarcely any of these factors exist in relation to the Palestinian Arab campaigns against the Israelis.

The vast majority of the Israeli population is Jewish, or if Arabic, clearly identified with the tasks of construction and active participation. Thus, the guerrillas appear to the populace as terrorists precisely because they remain extrinsic to the nation as a whole. While the guerrillas have gained limited access and support in the Arab settlements of Israel, more often than not, the guerrillas cannot count on any sort of cover or support over long periods of time; and as the Arab communities of Israel become more deeply involved in the overall Israeli economy and in political self-management through local elections, even such limited support as existed in the past is unlikely to continue. Whatever else might be said of the Israeli political structure, no serious charge of basic corruption has yet been lodged. True enough, there have been political scandals that have shaken up and shaken out the political processes, but the level of political participation of the populace and personal integrity of politicians is probably as high, if not higher than that found elsewhere in the democratic world; and certainly within a Middle East context, the Israeli political culture presents a veritable model of integrity that begs comparison. Finally, the guerrilla movement is cleverly aimed at the destruction of the Jewish population, or at least the perception of such destruction through the liquidation of the Jewish State as such. Under such circumstances, the guerrilla movement can only offer the prospect of a "multinational and multireligious" State or a return precisely to the conditions which existed in the area prior to the formation of the State of Israel. And without hope for the tranquilization of the area, the guerrillas remain isolated and fragmented—with scant hope of success.

Then the issue becomes transformed from success as political power to success as simple terrorism, that is to the variables listed as defining the terrorist phenomenon. In this connection, Segre and Adler have understood how the minimum critical mass necessary to be effective has been reduced with the evolution of an advanced military hardware. "Modern technology has increased the magnitude of the means in the equation, making it possible for extremely small groups to achieve the minimal critical mass necessary for the perpetuation of operational terrorism."[3] This technological complexity permits not simply small numbers, but simpleminded generalizations of apocalyptic dimensions concerning world revolution, racial brotherhood, religious *jihad,* and so on. Indeed, the smaller the terroristic group, the larger the ideological claims—precisely because such grandiose claims cannot be checked by the normal point and counterpoint of legitimate organizational life or by the organizational life of the revolutionary parties. The simpleminded anti-intellectualism of most terrorist operations is derived not only from sheer religious impulses but from the absence of secular political processes that all party life, radical and conservative alike, is subjected to as well.

The Palestinian terrorist organizations, such as the Black September movement, illustrate this tendency very well. The extreme pressure which the Israeli military has placed on the Arab guerrillas has compelled them to avoid any major operations within Israel, and, indeed, to curb most serious operations in the surrounding Arab nations. By applying selective pressure on Jordan in 1971 and Lebanon in 1973, the Israelis have compelled the Arab guerrilla movement to seek refuge within the Palestinian settlements that are the remnants of the United Nations Relief Organization effort from the late 1940's. Whatever else can be said of such encampments, they do not form a nation; and any effort to develop national aspirations, even within militarily weak nations such as Lebanon or Jordan, have met with firm rebuke and a veritable collapse of the Palestinian effort entirely. Indeed, what commenced as an Arab effort has not been reduced to a Palestinian refugee effort; and whatever one might claim about the moral soundness of the Palestinian position, the military implausibilities of their position are beyond dispute.

In this removal from the area, much less from Israel, of the guerrilla effort, the terrorist nature of Arab operations has only been emphasized. Unable to infiltrate effectively the Israeli borders or to spark a popular war of resistance among the Arabs living within Israel, and, even more fatal, incapacitated with respect to their fellow Arabs living in surrounding nations, the terrorist factor has increased as the guerrilla factor has decreased. This is made especially pointed by the basic regrouping of the terrorist activities in Europe rather than in the Middle East. For this has only enhanced the random character of the assaults on Israelis, and in fact, has led to a generalized assault on Jewish diplomats and all sorts of nondescript personnel, which serves only to weaken the Arab posture before the world: namely, that they do indeed distinguish between Zionism and Judaism. They may like to make such a distinction, but the very awkwardness of their military and political position makes such a distinction a nicety rather than a necessity.

The logistics of this latest phase in the transformation of guerrilla insurgency to random terrorism is underscored by the size and peculiar student nature of the Arab population living on the European mainland:

With the active sympathy of tens of thousands of expatriate Arabs and the ideological, moral, and occasional logistical support of leftist political groups, the fedayeen enjoy great mobility across the face of Western Europe, Denmark, with almost 5000 Arabs and a tolerant government, is a convenient place for banking fedayeen funds. So is Switzerland, where the Poplar Front for the Liberation of Palestine has an office. Italy, center of Egypt's European espionage network, has 4000 Arab students; in the university town of Perugia almost 1000 Palestinian students, many of them fedayeen sympathizers, actively recruit and propagandize for Black September while receiving subsidies from Fatah.

Germany has more than 55,000 Arabs who have moved there for jobs, plus 4000 Arab students. Extreme leftist students in Sweden help Fatah to function there, and in England 6000 Palestinian students raise funds and print fedayeen newspapers. Belgium, Austria, and Holland all have sizable Arab "diasporas." They have been used unwittingly as transfer points for fedayeen personnel and arms, as well as dispatch stations for the posting of letter bombs. Yugoslavia provides an officially sanctioned refuge and operations base, believed to be in Ljubljana, for the Palestinians.[4]

It would, however, be dangerous to assume that every Arab living in West Germany, or every Arab student in Denmark, is actively supporting the cause of the fedayeen. Nothing could be further from the truth. In fact, one could just as well surmise that the West European experience, and even the East European experience, has a highly qualifying effect on active participation in the terrorist organization. For the most part, the impact of Western culture is to lessen fanaticism and zealotry, and increase an awareness of other peoples, other concepts, and basic scientific technological needs of the Middle East as seen from a European perspective. In that sense, the sheer existence of Arabs in Europe or North America can by no means be taken as a measure of terrorist strength.

The Israeli exercise in counterterrorism is both sizeable and equal to the task. In part, the extensive use of counterterror rests on a strong Israeli military persuasion, that only terror is an adequate response to the Arab cause; and in fact, among certain circles, it is clear that the position is not simply measure for measure, but overkill for kill. And this in part contributes to the continued escalation of the tension and crisis between Arabs and Jews. The very internationalization of terrorism serves to make the problem acute not just for the Israeli citizen but for Jews the world over—and indeed, for Arabs the world over. One unique factor in this form of terrorism and counterterrorism is that boundaries mean so little and ideological considerations mean so much. In this sense, therefore, the need for pacification of the Middle East is not merely a regional matter or just a humanitarian concern, but it represents a major link in the pacification of the world as a whole. It is vital that mankind and its unique agency, the United Nations, find a way of resolving this terrorism as soon as possible.[5]

NOTES

2 ISRAEL: A SOCIAL AND POLITICAL OVERVIEW

1. Werner Sombart, *The Jews and Modern Capitalism,* M. Epstein, trans., Glencoe: The Free Press, 1951, pp. 192-95.
2. Jacob Talmon, *The Unique and the Universal: Some Historical Reflections,* New York: George Braziller, 1965, pp. 64-90.
3. S. M. Eisenstadt, *Israeli Society,* New York: Basic Books, 1967, pp. 372-81.
4. Alan Arian, *The Elections in Israel—1969,* Jerusalem: Jerusalem Academic Press, 1972, pp. 11-18.
5. Leonard J. Fein, *Israel: Politics and People,* 2nd ed., Boston: Little, Brown, 1968, pp. 87-138.
6. Oleg Smolansky, "Quasim and the Iraqi Communist Party: A Study in Arab Politics," *Il Politico,* Vol. 32, No. 2, 1967, pp. 292-307; No. 3, 1967, pp. 530-47.
7. Amos Perlmutter, *Anatomy of Political Institutionalization: The Case of Israel and Some Comparative Analyses,* Cambridge: Harvard University Center for International Affairs, 1970, pp. 50-51.
8. Nora Levin, "Israel in Africa," *Reconstructionist,* Vol. 39, No. 2, March 1973, p. 18.
9. Dan V. Segre, "Israel and the Third World," *Middle East Information Series,* American Academic Association for Peace in the Middle East, Vol. 22, February 1973, pp. 10-12.
10. Ovadia Shapiro, "Political Parties in Transition," mimeographed. Presented before the International Political Science Association, Eighth World Congress, Munich, September 1970, p. 44.
11. Arie Eliav, "We and the Arabs," *Foreign Policy,* Whole No. 10, Spring 1973, p. 62.

3 THE ARAB NATION AND THE JEWISH STATE

1. Don Peretz, *The Middle East Today*, 2nd ed., New York: Holt, Rinehart and Winston, 1971, p. 455.
2. J. C. Hurewitz, "Nationalist Rivalry in Palestine," in Benjamin Rivlin and Joseph Szyliowicz, eds., *The Contemporary Middle East: Tradition and Innovation*, New York: Random House, 1965, p. 265.
3. Muhammed Asad, "For an Islamic Polity Today," in Rivlin and Szyliowicz, eds., *The Contemporary Middle East*, pp. 179-87.
4. Norman L. Zucker, *The Coming Crisis in Israel: Private Faith and Public Policy*, Cambridge: MIT Press, 1973, esp. pp. 37-60.
5. Musa Alami, "The Lesson of Palestine," *The Middle East Journal*, Vol. 3, No. 4, 1949, pp. 373-405.
6. Abd Al-Rahman Al-Bazzaz, "This Is Our Nationalism," in Jacob M. Landau, ed., *Man, State, and Society in the Contemporary Middle East*, New York: Praeger, pp. 22-23, 29-30.
7. Abdul A. Said, "Arab Nationalism," in Michael Curtis, ed., *People and Politics in the Middle East*, New Brunswick: Transaction, E. P. Dutton, pp. 278-92.
8. P. J. Vatikiotis, *Conflict in the Middle East*, London: George Allen & Unwin Ltd., 1971, pp. 214-15.
9. Ronald Segal, "The Palestinians and the Dead End of 'Arab Zionism,'" *Center Report*, Vol. 6, No. 2, April 1973, pp. 22-23.
10. William B. Quandt, Fuad Jabber and Ann Mosely Lesch, *The Politics of Palestinian Nationalism*, Berkeley and Los Angeles: The University of California Press, 1973, p. 214.
11. Atallah Mansour, "The Future Is the Son of the Past," in Irene L. Gendzier, ed., *A Middle East Reader*, New York: Pegasus-Western Publishing Co., 1969, pp. 441-53.
12. The best renderings of the "unity" represented by the phrase "Middle East" are to be found in two survey volumes. For a quantitative orientation, see Peter Mansfield, *The Middle East: A Political and Economic Survey*, 4th ed., London: Oxford University Press, 1973; and for a qualitative orientation, see Benjamin Rivlin and Joseph S. Szyliowicz, *The Contemporary Middle East: Tradition and Innovation*, New York: Random House, 1965.
13. Yehuda Karmon, "Water: A Lever for Development in the Middle East," in M. Eisenstaedt, ed., *Middle East Development:*

Some Current Economic Problems, Jerusalem: The Hebrew University, 1968, pp. 64-78.

14. Howard M. Sachar, *Europe Leaves the Middle East, 1936-1954,* New York: Alfred A. Knopf, 1972, pp. xi-xvii.

15. Nissim Rejwan, "Israeli Attitudes to the Arab World," in Irene L. Gendzier, ed., *A Middle East Reader,* New York: Pegasus-Western Publishing Co., 1969, p. 247.

5 FORCED COEXISTENCE

1. Jacob L. Talmon, *The Unique and the Universal: Some Historical Reflections,* New York: George Braziller, p. 68.

2. Nathan Glazer, Moshe Decter, William Korey et al., *Perspectives on Soviet Jewry,* New York: KTAV Publishing House for the Anti-Defamation League of B'nai B'rith, 1971.

3. Zvi Yavetz, "Youth Movements in Czernowitz," in Gerd Korman, ed., *Hunter and Hunted: Human History of the Holocaust,* New York: The Viking Press, 1973, pp. 138-39.

4. Julius Jacobson, *Soviet Communism and the Socialist Vision,* New Brunswick: Transaction Books/E. P. Dutton, 1972, pp. 163-205.

5. For two contrasting analyses of this, see Solomon M. Schwarz, *The Jews in the Soviet Union,* Syracuse: Syracuse University Press, 1951; and for a more recent survey of the earlier period in Russian Jewish life, Louis Greenberg, *The Jews in Russia: The Struggle for Emancipation,* New Haven: Yale University Press, 1967. An important new book, which I unfortunately have been unable to take proper account of because it appeared as my own work was being completed, is William Korey, *The Soviet Cage: Anti-Semitism in Russia,* New York: The Viking Press, 1973.

6. Mikhail Agursky, "Selling Anti-Semitism in Moscow," *The New York Review of Books,* Vol. 19, No. 8, November 16, 1972, p. 23.

7. Chiman Abramsky, "The Biro-Bidzhan Project, 1927-1959," in Lionel Kochan, ed., *The Jews in Soviet Russia Since 1917,* New York and London: Oxford University Press, 1972, pp. 64-65.

8. J. B. Schechtman, "The U.S.S.R., Zionism and Israel," in Kochan, *The Jews in Soviet Russia,* 1972, p. 103.

9. Bernard D. Weinryb, "Antisemitism in Soviet Russia," in Lionel Kochan, *The Jews in Soviet Russia,* 1972, p. 304.

10. Jonathan Frankel, "The Anti-Zionist Press Campaigns," *Soviet Jewish Affairs,* Vol. 2, Whole No. 3, May 1972, pp. 17-21.

11. Abraham Brumberg, *"Sovyetish Heymland* Dilemmas," *Soviet Jewish Affairs,* Vol. 2, Whole No. 3, May 1972, pp. 39-41.

6 JEWISH ELITES, ELECTORAL POLITICS
AND AMERICAN FOREIGN POLICY

1. Oded Remba, "United States Assistance to the Middle East: An Analysis of the Record," *Middle East Information Series,* No. 20, September 1972, p. 33.
2. Henry M. Jackson, *The Middle East and American Security Policy,* Washington, D.C.: Committee on Armed Services, U.S. Government Printing Office, 1970, pp. 15-17.
3. Norman Podhoretz, "The Idea of a Common Culture," *Commentary,* Vol. 53, No. 6, June 1972, pp. 4-6.
4. Irving Louis Horowitz, "Coalition for a Democratic Majority: The Operators Make Their Play," *The Nation,* Vol. 216, No. 3, January 15, 1973, pp. 72-75.
5. "The City Vote for President—Complete," *New York Post,* November 9, 1972.
6. Andrew Soltis, "Nixon Cuts into Ethnic Vote," *New York Post,* November 9, 1972.
7. Michael Curtis, "Soviet-American Relations and the Middle East Crisis," *Orbis: A Quarterly Journal of World Affairs,* Vol. 15, No. 1, Spring 1971, pp. 418-19.
8. Leslie H. Gelb, "The Coming New/Old Face in the Middle East," *Bulletin of the American Academic Association for Peace in the Middle East,* No. 2, January 1973, pp. 1-2.
9. Eugene V. Rostow, "American Foreign Policy and the Middle East," in Louis Henkin, ed., *World Politics and the Jewish Condition,* New York: Quadrangle Books, 1972, pp. 88-89.

7 JEWISH ETHNICISM AND LATIN AMERICAN NATIONALISM

1. Simon Dubnow, *Nationalism and History: Essays on Old and New Judaism,* edited with an introductory essay by Koppel S. Pinson, Cleveland and New York: The World Publishing Company/Meridian Books, 1961, pp. 76-99.

2. Werner Sombart, *The Jews and Modern Capitalism*, M. Epstein, trans., Glencoe, Ill.: The Free Press, 1951, esp. pp. 157-89.

3. Institute of Jewish Affairs in Association with the World Jewish Congress, *The Jewish Communities of the World: Demography, Political and Organizational Status, Religious Institutions, Education and the Press*, London: Andre Deutsch, 1971, pp. 39-40.

4. For a significant overview of current developments among Latin American Jewry, see *Proceedings of the Experts Conference on Latin America and the Future of Its Jewish Communities* (held in New York, June 3-4, 1972), London: Institute of Jewish Affairs, 1973.

8 THE JEWISH COMMUNITY OF ARGENTINA

1. United Nations, *Demographic Yearbook*, "Special Topic: Ethnic and Economic Characteristics," New York: United Nations, Department of Economic and Social Affairs, Statistical Office, 1956, pp. 272-74.

2. The estimates for 1960, before the new census data, was that the Argentine-Jewish population stood at 420,000. (Moisés Kostzer, "Problemas propios de la estadística relativa a los judíos en la Argentina," *Primera Conferencia de Investigadores y Estudiosos Judeo-Argentinos en el Campo de las Ciencias Sociales y la Historia*, Buenos Aires: Universidad Hebrea de Jerusalén/Comunidad Israelita de Buenos Aires, 1961; Ira Rosenswaike, "The Jewish Population of Argentina," *Jewish Social Studies*, Vol. 22, October 1960, pp. 195-214.)

3. The first concerted effort to develop a sociological account of the Jews in Argentina took place in October 1961. Called *Primera Conferencia de Investigadores y Estudiosos Judeo-Argentinos en el Campo de las Ciencias Sociales y la Historia*, the Conference, interestingly, was jointly sponsored by the Majon Leiahadut and the Comunidad de Buenos Aires (*Kehillah*), (*Boletín de la Asociación Amigos de la Universidad Hebrea de Jerusalén en la Argentina*, No. 21, May 1960, p. 15).

4. Norberto Rodríguez Bustamante, "Un esquema sociológico de la Argentina," *Revista de la Universidad de Buenos Aires*, Vol. 1, No. 3, 1958, pp. 402-10.

5. Despite the century-old battle between *espiritualismo* and *posi-*

tivismo in Argentina, the politics of nationalism, from the Argentine Constitution of 1853 which provided for the support of the Catholic Church by the government to the formation of a Christian Democratic Party a century later, has never abandoned the theme of Argentina as a nation living under a state of Christian grace. A good index of this is contained in the various census reports which give the Catholic population of Argentina as 99.1 per cent in 1895 and 93.6 per cent in 1947. In essence, anyone not explicitly declaring in favor of another religious option is listed as Catholic. (Dirección Nacional del Servicio Estadístico, *IV Censo General de la Nación: Censo de Población,* Buenos Aires: Presidencia de la Nación, Ministerio de Asuntos Técnicos, 1951.) For contrasting attitudes on the role of Catholicism in Argentine national life, see Romero and Johnson. (Jose Luis Romero, *Las ideas políticas en Argentina,* Mexico-Buenos Aires: Fondo de Cultura Económica, 1956; John J. Johnson, *Political Change in Latin America,* Stanford: Stanford University Press, 1958.) This does not imply that Catholic sentiment is uniformly hostile to the Jew. It does imply that the identification of nationalism with Catholicism often carries with it criticism of other religions. See the collection of statements from Church officials in Instituto Judío Argentino de Cultura e Información, *La Iglesia Católica se define,* Buenos Aires: 1961. Instituto Judío Argentino de Cultura e Información.

6. Gino Germani, "The Development and Present State of Sociology in Latin America," *Transactions of the Fourth World Congress of Sociology,* 1960, pp. 117-38.

7. It should be kept in mind that not until 1860 were such elementary civil liberties as marriage services extended to "those who hope for the arrival of the Messiah," i.e., those who do not subscribe to Christianity. (Boleslao Lewin, *Los judíos bajo la Inquisición en Hispanoamérica,* Buenos Aires: Editorial Dédalo 1960, pp. 99-100.

8. Carlos Néstor Maciel, *La italianización de la Argentina,* Buenos Aires, 1924.

9. Julio L. Alsogaray, *Trilogía de la trata de blancas: rufianes, policía, municipalidad,* Buenos Aires, 1933.

10. Oscar Handlin, *Race and Nationality in American Life,* Garden City, N.Y.: Doubleday, 1957.

11. Oscar Handlin, ed., "Ethnic Groups in American Life," *Daedalus* (Special Issue), Vol. 90, Spring 1961.

12. A forceful presentation of this assimilationist trend can be found in Carlos Estéban Etkin, *Abraham León y el pueblo judío*, Buenos Aires: Editorial Indoamérica, 1954, esp. pp. 71-86. Despite its basis in a *vulgarmarxismus*, there is little doubt that the views taken by Etkin represent a sizeable sector of Jewish opinion.

13. *American Jews: Their Story*, New York: Anti-Defamation League of B'nai B'rith, 1958.

14. The evidence of the Buenos Aires Jewish community does not substantiate Wirth's position that "the Jews owe their survival . . . to their social isolation." (Louis Wirth, *The Ghetto*, Chicago: University of Chicago Press, 1928.) Adaptation does not imply assimilation, nor does isolation guarantee survival.

15. Dirección General de Estadística de la Nación, *Estadística de la Municipalidad de la Capital—IV C.G.C.B.A.*, Buenos Aires, 1936.

16. Simon Weill, *Población Israelita en la República Argentina*, Buenos Aires, 1936, p. 30.

17. It has been estimated that approximately 83 per cent of foreign-born residents of Argentina are to be found in Greater Buenos Aires and the Litoral region. (Gino Germani, *Estructura social de la Argentina: análisis estadístico*, Buenos Aires: Editorial Raigal, 1955, p. 63.) Thus, Jewish figures are in no way disproportionate to general tendencies.

18. On the relative failure of Jewish agricultural colonization of the Argentine Pampas region, see Ismar Elbogen, *A Century of Jewish Life*, Philadelphia: The Jewish Publication Society of America, 1953, p. 342. On The failure of agricultural colonization to "absolve" the Jew of anti-Semitic outburst, see Nathan Reich, "The Economic Structure of Modern Jewry," in Louis Finkelstein, ed., *The Jews: Their History, Culture and Religion*, New York: Harper & Row, 1949. See also Asociación Filantrópica Israelita, *Diez años de obra constructiva en América del Sud: 1933-1943*, Buenos Aires, December 1943.

19. This is not to imply that study of the Jews outside the Buenos Aires area is without importance. Indeed the pioneering efforts of two Israeli social scientists deserve far more attention than they have thus far received. See Eijiel Harari and Itzjak Lewin, "Resultado de la encuesta sobre profesiones, idiomas y crecimiento," *Nueva Sión*, February-July, 1950.

20. Kalman H. Silvert, "The Annual Political Cycle in Argentina." *American Universities Field Staff Reports Service* [East Coast South America Series] Series 8, Number 6, 1961.

21. The differential in educational standards and illiteracy rates between the Buenos Aires region and the rest of Argentina is in itself a sufficient magnet for Jews reared to gain occupational mobility through professional education. (Germani, *Estructura social de la Argentina*, pp. 229-34.)

22. *Ashkenazim* are that portion of Diaspora Jewry formerly residing in Germany, Western Poland (which had become part of Prussia), Eastern Poland, Ukraine, and other areas of the Slavic countries and the Austro-Hungarian empire. A basic bond of the Ashkenazim was (and in certain areas remains) the Yiddish language. This ethnic-linquistic formation is usually contrasted to the *Sephardim*, that portion of Diaspora Jewry formerly residing in Spain, Portugal, and certain centers in Northern Africa and the Middle East. The basic language of the *Sephardim*, the former "aristocracy of Jewry," was Spanish.

23. A disconcerting illustration of German-Jewish alienation from the larger society is revealed by the near-total absence of news or information on the Jewish condition in Argentina or Latin America. In the weekly *Judische Wochenschau*, the only mention found of Argentina is a column on musical events in Buenos Aires—and this because the performers are generally European.

24. For this typology of Jewish immigration to Argentina I am very grateful to Boleslao Lewin the University of Buenos Aires, who placed his knowledge as well as his personal library at my disposal. For information on the earliest immigration patterns of Jews to Argentina, see Lewin, *El judio en la época colonial*, Buenos Aires, 1939.

25. Simon Dubnow, "The Doctrine of Jewish Nationalism" and "The Sociological View of Jewish History," in Koppel S. Pinson, ed., *Nationalism and History*, Cleveland and New York: Meridian Books, The World Publishing Co., 1961.

26. The Hebrew word *Kehillah* can best be defined as a total Jewish institution, integrating and organizing all civic, cultural and religious aspects of Jewish life. See *Comunidad Israelita de Buenos Aires*, Buenos Aires, 1960.

27. Rosa Perla Resnick, "Problemas relativos al bienestar social de la comunidad judía de la Argentina," *Primera Conferencia de Investigadores y Estudiosos Judeo-Argentinos en el Campo de las Ciencias Sociales y la Historia*, Buenos Aires: Universidad Hebrea de Jerusalem/Comunidad Israelita de Buenos Aires, 1961, pp. 3-11.

28. Abraham A. Roback, *The Story of Yiddish Literature*, New York: Yiddish Scientific Institute, 1940.

29. Mark Yudel, "Yiddish Literature," in Louis Finkelstein, ed., *The Jews: Their History, Culture and Religion*, vol. 2, pp. 859-94.

30. Georges Mauco, "The Assimilation of Foreigners in France," *Cultural Assimilation of Immigrants* (supplement to *Population Studies*) March 1950, p. 15.

31. David Riesman, as cited by Bernard D. Weinryb, "Jewish Immigration and Accommodation to America," in Marshall Sklare, ed., *The Jews: Social Patterns of an American Group*, Glencoe: Free Press, 1958, p. 21.

32. For a general discussion of this problem, see Gino Germani and Kalman Silvert, "Politics, Social Structure and Military Intervention in Latin America," mimeographed, Buenos Aires: Universidad de Buenos Aires, Instituto de Sociología, 1961; Irving Louis Horowitz, "Modern Argentina: The Politics of Power," *The Political Quarterly*, Vol. 30, October-December 1959, pp. 400-10.

33. An example of how severely circumscribed the upper limits of Jewish social mobility are in Argentina is shown by an analysis of the nearly 100 members of the Argentine-Israeli Chamber of Commerce. For the most part, the leading positions held by Jews are in import-export trade, subsidiary distributions for foreign commodities, and small-scale chemical and industrial production. Only two members of this group have any banking or stock-exchange operations and one of these is a manager of a "Jewish Bank." (*Revista de la Cámara de Comercio Argentino-Israelí*, No. 55, Vol. 2, April-May 1961.)

34. Iejiel Harari and Itzjak Lewin, "Resultados de la encuesta sobre profesiones, idiomas y crecimiento de la colectividad judía de Santa Fe," *Nueva Sión*, Whole No. 28, July 1950, p. 7.

35. Harari and Lewin, "Resultados de la encuesta sobre profesiones."

36. Marshall Sklare, *Conservative Judaism: An American Religious Movement*, Glencoe: Free Press, 1955.

37. Jerome E. Carlin and Saul H. Mendelovitz, "The American Rabbi: A Religious Specialist Responds to Loss of Authority," in Sklare, *The Jews: Social Patterns of an American Group*, pp. 377-414.

38. Shalom Rosenberg and Daniel B. Rubenstein-Novick, "El rol de la tradición religiosa en la comunidad judía en la Argentina," *Primera Conferencia de Investigadores y Estudiosos Judeo-Argentinos en el Campo de las Ciencias Sociales y la Historia,*

Buenos Aires: Universidad Hebrea de Jerusalén/Comunidad Israelita de Buenos Aires, 1961, esp. pp. 15-17.

39. Harari and Lewin note that the only instances found where Jewish children do not speak Spanish as their primary language are if they were born in Europe. Data for Mendoza province is from Harari and Lewin, "Resultado de la encuesta sobre profesiones," *Nueva Sión,* February 24, 1950, p. 7.

40. *Comunidad Israelita de Buenos Aires,* Buenos Aires, 1960.

41. An acute reflection of this "crisis" other than in the sphere of education, is the virtual absence of growth either in membership or in number of temples and synagogues for the past 25 years. Only five new synagogues have been established between 1939-61 —mainly for the Orthodox sector of German Jewry. This compares to 18 synagogues built in the period 1918-39. Rosenberg and Rubenstein-Novick, "El rol de la tradición religiosa en la comunidad judía en la Argentina," *Primera Conferencia de Investigadores y Estudiosos Judeo-Argentinos,* especially pp. 15-17.

42. This ghetto-less existence casts some doubt on the "universality" claimed for the ghetto as a Jewish social institution. (Wirth, *The Ghetto,* p. 121.)

43. Natan Lerner, "La vida comunitaria judía en Buenos Aires," *Primera Conferencia de Investigadores y Estudiosos Judeo-Argentinos en el Campo de las Ciencias Sociales y la Historia,* Buenos Aires: Universidad Hebrea de Jerusalén/Comunidad Israelita de Buenos Aires, 1961, pp. 10-14.

44. Oscar Handlin, "Historical Perspectives on the American Ethnic Group," *Daedalus,* Vol. 90, No. 2, Spring 1961, pp. 227-28.

45. Harari and Lewin, "Resultado de la encuesta sobre profesiones," *Nueva Sión,* July 28, 1950, p. 7.

46. This proliferating tendency is observed even in the ethnic separatism of the synagogues. In both origin and present realities the Jewish congregations divide as follows: Russian (12), Rumanian (five), Polish (14), Galician (two), German (five). (Rosenberg and Rubenstein-Novick, "El rol de la tradición religiosa," pp. 5-6.)

47. The most reliable guide and reflection of the younger elements is the newspaper *Renacimiento de Israel.* See "Resolución del Comité Central de la Organización Sionista Liberal en la Argentina," *Renacimiento de Israel,* July 1961, p. 8. Here the various strands coalesce: "liberalism" as a national posture, support for Zionism as consonant with Argentine loyalties, a forthright attitude toward anti-Semitism, stronger organizational responsibili-

ties for young Jews, a common alliance with Jews of other Latin American nations.

48. Joseph H. Fichter, "The Marginal Catholic: An Institutional Approach," *Social Forces*, Vol. 31, December 1953, pp. 167-73.

49. In this connection it might be noted that studies of Argentine Catholicism from a sociological viewpoint have yet to be undertaken, and until courses in the sociology of religion are given in the universities, prospects for such badly needed studies are grim indeed.

50. T. W. Adorno et al., *The Authoritarian Personality*, New York: Harper & Bros., 1950; Bruno Bettelheim and Morris Janowitz, "Ethnic Tolerance: A Function of Social and Personal Control," *The American Journal of Sociology*, Vol. LV, 1949, pp. 137-45; *Cuadernos del Instituto de Sociología*, "Psicología social del prejuicio," No. 23, Buenos Aires: Universidad de Buenos Aires, 1960, pp. 215-343; Bruno Bettelheim and Morris Janowitz, *Dynamics of Prejudice*, New York: Harper and Row, 1950.

51. Particularly is this the case with those Jewish *pensadores* who have tended to substitute Argentine democratic symbols for Jewish symbols of identification. There is now a fairly evident schism between the Jewish *intelligentsia* and an *intelligentsia* which is of Jewish origin.

52. Tacuara has a long record of anti-Semitic violence. It was formed in 1930 by Juan Queralta, a high school student, and took its name from the bamboo pikes that were carried more than a century ago by supporters of the tyrant Manuel Rosas. Tacuara became a branch of the Peronist youth movement, and went underground when the former leader was overthrown in 1955. Since 1960, it has been vigorously led by two students, Alberto Ezcurra Uriburu and José Baxter. Their political position is avowedly Falangist, with a strong emphasis on corporate fascism as the best form of government for Argentina. Tacuara distinguishes itself from Peronism by a strong pro-Church attitude. (Joaquín Sokolowicz, "Anti-semitismo criollo: la verdad sobre Tacuara," *Renacimiento de Israel*, July 1961, pp. 3-4, *passim*.

53. "Vandálico atentado antisemita contra la Hajshara de Ijud," *La Luz* (Buenos Aires), Vol. 31, No. 782, August 25, 1961. *La revista Israelita para toda Sud América*.

54. For an acute historical analysis of anti-Semitism, conservative and radical, see Robert F. Byrnes, *Antisemitism in Modern France: The Prologue to the Dreyfus Affair*, New Brunswick, N.J.: Rutgers

University Press, 1950, esp. Chaps. 3, 4, 5. See also Nicholas Halasz, *Captain Dreyfus: The Story of a Mass Hysteria*, New York: Simon & Schuster, 1955, esp. pp. 161-201.

55. Gino Germani, "Comparación típico-ideal entre la sociedad preindustrial rural y la sociedad industrial urbana," in Gino Germani and Jorge Graciarena, eds., *De la sociedad tradicional a la sociedad de masas*, Buenos Aires: Universidad de Buenos Aires, Facultad de Filosofía y Letras, Departamento de Sociología, 1961, pp. 349-62.

56. "El crucifijo y la libertad de cultos," *La Luz* (Buenos Aires), Vol. 31, No. 776, June 2, 1961.

57. Irving Louis Horowitz, "Storm over Argentina: Revolt Against Political Mythology," *The Nation*, Vol. 195, March 31, 1962.

58. *La Prensa* (Buenos Aires), August 16, 1961, p. 26.

10 THE JEW AS A TOTAL INSTITUTION

1. Joseph Kraft, "Letter from Israel," *New Yorker*, April 7, 1973, p. 68.

2. Raul Hilberg, *The Destruction of the European Jews*, New York: Quadrangle Books/Random House, 1961.

3. Isaiah Trunk, *Judenrat: The Jewish Councils in Eastern Europe Under Nazi Occupation*, New York: Macmillan, 1973.

4. Chaim A. Kaplan, *Scroll of Agony: The Warsaw Diary*, Abraham I. Katsh, trans., New York: Macmillan, 1965, pp. 325-26.

5. Emmanuel Ringelblum, *Notes from the Warsaw Ghetto*, New York: McGraw-Hill, 1958.

6. J. Kermish, "First Stirrings," in Gerd Korman, ed., *Hunter and Hunted Human History of the Holocaust*, New York: The Viking Press, 1973, pp. 209-30.

11 LIQUIDATION OR LIBERATION

1. Jack Nusan Porter and Peter Dreier, *Jewish Radicalism: A Selected Anthology*, New York: Grove Press, Inc., 1973.

2. Isaac Deutscher, *The Non-Jewish Jew*, Tamara Deutscher, ed., New York: Oxford University Press, 1968.

3. Albert Memmi, *The Liberation of the Jew,* Judy Hyun, trans., New York: The Orion Press, 1968.

12 POLITICAL TERRORISM AND STATE POWER

1. Maurice Merleau-Ponty, *Humanism and Terror: An Essay on the Communist Problem,* Boston: Beacon Press, 1969 (originally published in French, 1947), p. 188.
2. Irving Louis Horowitz, *The Struggle is the Message: The Organization and Ideology of the Anti-War Movement,* Berkeley: The Glendessary Press, 1970, pp. 114-20. Frank Kitson, *Low Intensity Operations: Subversion, Insurgency, Peace-Keeping,* London: Faber Publishers, 1972. Robert Jay Lifton, *History and Human Survival,* New York: Random House, 1970. Martin Oppenheimer, *The Urban Guerrilla,* Chicago: Quadrangle Books, 1969. Milton J. Rosenberg, ed., *Beyond Conflict and Containment: Critical Studies of Military and Foreign Policy,* New Brunswick: Transaction, E. P. Dutton, 1972. Jerome Skolnick, ed., *The Politics of Protest,* New York: Ballantine Books, 1969. Eugene V. Walter, *Terror and Resistance: A Study of Political Violence,* New York: Oxford University Press, 1969.
3. D. V. Segre and J. H. Adler, "The Ecology of Terrorism," *Encounter,* Vol. 40, No. 2, February 1973, p. 20.
4. Raphael Rothstein, "Undercover Terror: The Other Mid-East War," *World,* Vol. 2, No. 3, January 30, 1973, pp. 21-22.
5. For Additional Readings on Political Terror and State Power, see Hannah Arendt, *The Origins of Totalitarianism,* new ed., New York: Harcourt, Brace and World, 1966. Hannah Arendt, *On Revolution,* New York: Viking Press, 1963. James Chowning Davies, ed., *When Men Revolt and Why,* New York: The Free Press, 1971. Harry Eckstein, ed., *Internal War: Problems and Approaches,* New York: The Free Press, 1966. Ivo Feierabend, Rosalind L. Feierabend, and Ted R. Gurr, eds., *Anger, Violence and Politics: Theories and Research,* Englewood Cliffs, Prentice Hall, 1972. Ted Robert Gurr, *Why Men Rebel,* Princeton: Princeton University Press, 1970. Irving Louis Horowitz, ed., *The Anarchists,* New York: Dell, 1964.

NAME INDEX

SUBJECT INDEX

adaptation, of Argentine Jews, 135-
47, 163
affluence, of Jews and students, 180-
81
Africa, and Israel, 84
Akzia, vs. *Judenrat,* 190-91
alienation: cultural vs. economic,
170-71; and intellectual activity,
175-76; *see also* marginality
ambiguity, in Israeli victory, 4-7
anti-Semitism, 195; Argentine, 134,
137, 142-43, 156-66; and Jewish
identity, 192-93; and Jews, 182-
91; Latin American, 124-32; and
Marxism, 89; Nazi, 182-92; and
social science, 187; Soviet, 88-89,
95-101, 199
Arabs: diaspora of, 32-34; and Israel,
42-44, 59-74, 195-6, 217-21; and
Jews, 42-44, 59-74; legitimacy of,
65-66; as nation, 59-74; policies
of, 11-13; polity of, 61-74; socialism of, 65; and Soviet Union, 72-73; terrorism of, 217-21;
and United States, 104-7, 114-17
Argentina: anti-Semitism in, 134,
137, 142-43, 156-66; and Israel,
166; Jewish adaptation in, 135-
47, 163; Jewish associations in,
134, 147-64; Jewish demography in, 135-44; Jewish identity
in, 147-67; Jewish immigration
to, 135-44; Jewish leadership of,
133-34; Jewish marginality in,

142-44, 163; Jewish mobility in,
134, 140, 146-47; Jewish occupations in, 134, 145-47; Jewish political participation in, 134, 161-
65; Jewish power in, 147; Jews
of, 133-67; Roman Catholicism
in, 133-34, 155-56, 164; Sephardic vs. Ashkenazic Jews in, 140-
43, 153; and the United States,
166
associations, of Argentine Jews, 134,
147-64

Birobidjian, 92-93
black Americans: discrimination of,
188; and Jewish Americans, 84,
168, 171-78; radical, 188; and
students, 84, 168, 171-78; and
universities, 171-72, 175-76

capitalism: and Israel, 125; and
Jews, 121-32, 203
coexistence: forced, 86-101; Soviet-
Jewish, 86-101
colonialism: British, 16-18; and Israel, 7-10; and nationalism, 9-
10; *see also* neo-colonialism
communism, *see* left wing, Marxism,
and socialism
conflict: within Marxism, 194-95;
Middle East, 42-44, 59-74, 195-
97, 217-21; of survival vs. moral
works, 183-91